The
Criminal Justice System
of the USSR

THE
CRIMINAL JUSTICE SYSTEM
OF THE USSR

Edited By

M. CHERIF BASSIOUNI, LL.B., J.D., LL.M., S.J.D.

Professor of Law
DePaul University
Secretary-General
International Association of Penal Law

and

V. M. SAVITSKI, Doctor of Law

Chief, Section of Theoretical Problems
of Justice Administration
Professor of Criminal Procedure,
Institute of State and Law,
Academy of Sciences of the USSR
Deputy Secretary-General
International Association of Penal Law

CHARLES   C   THOMAS • PUBLISHER
Springfield • Illinois • U.S.A.

Published and Distributed Throughout the World by
CHARLES C THOMAS • PUBLISHER
Bannerstone House
301-327 East Lawrence Avenue, Springfield, Illinois, U.S.A.

© 1979 by CHARLES C THOMAS • PUBLISHER
ISBN 0-398-03868-6
Library of Congress Catalog Card Number: 78-22094

Library of Congress Cataloging in Publication Data

The Criminal justice system of the USSR.

   Bibliography: p.
   Includes index.
   1. Criminal justice, Administration of—Russia.
I. Bassiouni, M. Cherif, 1937-   II. Savitski,
Valerii Mikhailovich.
Law   364′.947   78-22094
ISBN 0-398-03868-6

Printed in the United States of America
C-1

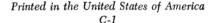

CONTRIBUTORS

S. G. Kelina, Doctor of Law
Institute of State and Law, Academy of Sciences of the USSR
All Union Institute for the Study of Causes and Development of
  Measures of Crime Prevention

V. P. Shupilov, Doctor of Law
Chief, Section of Scientific Information on Crime Combatting
  in Foreign Countries, All Union Institute for the Study of
  Causes and Development of Measures of Crime Prevention
Institute of State and Law, Academy of Sciences of the USSR
Deputy Secretary-General, International Society for Social
  Defense

A. M. Yakovlev, Doctor of Law
Chief, Section of Theory and Sociology of Penal Law,
  Institute of State and Law, Academy of Sciences of
  the USSR
All Union Institute for the Study of Causes and Development
  of Measures of Crime Prevention

With a Foreword By

John N. Hazard, LL.B., J.S.D., LL.D., LL.D.(H.C.)

Nash Professor of Law Emeritus
Columbia University

With an Introduction By

V. Kudriavtsev, Doctor of Law

Professor of Criminal Law
Correspondent Member, Academy of Sciences
of the USSR
Director, Institute of State and Law,
Academy of Sciences of the USSR

Translated by

L. A. Nejinskaya, Candidate of Law

and

L. P. Tuzina

All Union Institute for the Study of Causes
and Development of Measures of Crime Prevention

PREFACE

THIS IS THE FIRST BOOK on the Criminal Justice System of the USSR written entirely by Scholars from the USSR, in collaboration with a U.S. academician, for publication in the U.S. As such it is a landmark in the history of joint projects between jurists from these two countries. The idea for such a project was developed during this writer's visit to the USSR in 1976. The visit itself was due to cooperative relations between this writer and the All Union Institute for the Study of Causes and Development of Measures of Crime Prevention and its distinguished Director, Professor Klotchkov, who is a Vice President of the International Association of Penal Law, of which I have the honor of being Secretary-General. The Association, since its inception in 1924, has maintained cooperative relations with the USSR, and many fruitful results have been obtained. Among these was the hosting in Moscow in December 1977 by the All Union Institute of one of the Association's Colloquia in preparation of its XII International Congress (held every five years and next time in Hamburg, Federal Republic of Germany, in September 1979). The theme of that Colloquium was "Crimes of Recklessness." It was the first time since the revolution of 1917 that the USSR officially hosted an international conference on a crime-related subject with open participation to the National Reporters of the Association's sixty-eight countries membership. The All Union Institute will publish the proceedings in a special issue of the *Revue Internationale de droit Penal* in 1979.

Such instances of scientific collaboration are not new in the area of law, but these projects are the first significant ones in the field of criminal justice. They were due in large measure to many years of cooperation between penalists from the USSR and other countries in the ambit of the International Association of Penal Law.

The work on this book was carried out principally by my friend and colleague Professor Savitski, who is also Deputy Secretary-General of the Association and as such works quite closely with me on the affairs of the Association. The scheme, contents, organization, and English editorship of the book was my task. The book's approach was predicated on the assumption that the U.S. and other English-reading audiences would be interested in learning from national experts about certain aspects of the USSR's criminal justice system, which are not otherwise available in the Western world's legal literature. The topics covered and the original (translated) documents appended are a unique source of primary information.

The preparation of this book was by no means as easy as it may otherwise appear to be due to distance and language difficulties, but it was performed in a spirit of friendly cooperation and efficiency. Professor Savitski worked very diligently on this project over the last two years. To coordinate our work we met over two years in such diverse places as Varna, Bulgaria; Vienna, Austria; Paris, France; Moscow, USSR; and Chicago, USA, to go over the various drafts. Indeed several drafts had to be made, corrected, and approved and in the performance of that work I am indebted to my assistant, Daniel Derby (J.D., DePaul; Teaching Assistant, DePaul University), for his meticulous work and good spirits in coping with it.

I am also grateful to Professor Kudriavtsev, one of the USSR's foremost legal scholars, for writing the Introduction and to Professor Hazard, one of the foremost Soviet law experts in the U.S., for writing the Foreword. It is hoped that this book will provide the reader with valuable information about criminal justice of the USSR and that it will stimulate more cooperative and collaborative works between jurists from the U.S. and the USSR.

M. CHERIF BASSIOUNI

Chicago

FOREWORD

THIS VOLUME WILL INDICATE to knowledgeable Western legal scholars how strongly European traditions have influenced Soviet draftsmen and practitioners. The Soviet legal system is indubitably a Romanist-inspired legal system, although modifications deemed necessary to adapt old patterns to the new socialist-type culture are numerous. One of the much debated points among Western scholars attempting to classify the Soviet system among the "families" of law identified for generations by comparatists is whether there has been any qualitative change as a result of this adaptation of a Romanist model to a socialist-type culture.

To some Westerners, Soviet procedural forms are so similar to those in use in Western Europe, and the code structures are so conventionally Romanist, that, when taken with Soviet attitudes toward sources of law solely in what the French would call *le droit écrit*, there is no basis for a claim of originality in the Soviet system. Other Westerners are prepared to accept the argument of Soviet jurists that there is novelty, although not always for the same reasons. To the Soviet jurist the Marxist approach and the elimination of private enterprise and the "market" have introduced qualitative change. To outsiders these features are, indeed, characteristic, but there is more tendency to stress the communal humanism of Soviet law in contrast to the individual humanism of Western systems, and even to emphasize the contrast in political structures between the communist-party-led system and the traditional Jeffersonian-type democracies. One of the contributions made by this volume is the opportunity it provides Anglophonic readers to judge for themselves the merits of the pros and cons among those who attempt to determine novelty in the Soviet system.

One point emerges in reading these essays: the Soviet approach has changed markedly since the early days when law was expected

ix

soon to fade away as the handmaiden of a state that would wither as a classless society emerging from the abolition of capitalism.

There is now in place in the USSR a legal culture espousing a concept of "legality." Although there are points of difference with the Western concepts of "legality," there is evident a pressure for conformity to law. The capstone of the new legality is the 1977 Constitution; the English translation is included in this volume. It might be wise to end this observation with reference to one element of a constitutional system that will seem missing to students of constitutional law, particularly in the United States: judicial review. Without this feature, the Soviet Constitution will seem poorly and perhaps inadequately defended. There is no constitutional judicial review as in the United States or a supreme constitutional court as in the Federal Republic of Germany, Italy, or Egypt, not even a "constitutional council" such as the one provided by the 1958 French Constitution. Instead, the Procurator-General of the USSR is declared to be the constitutional defender, as he was in the 1936 Constitution of the USSR. He stands alone in that significant role.

An essay in this volume tells foreign readers what type of institution the Procurator-General represents and how he functions. Many are likely to see flaws in his position because he cannot challenge the constitutionality of legislation of the Supreme Soviet of the USSR. Further, one of his functions, while advantageous to the untutored citizen (he enters situations where administrative agencies have violated a citizen's rights), is at the same time a limitation of constitutional protection as understood in some legal systems. No citizen can proceed directly to court to defend his constitutional rights: he must proceed through the agencies of the Procurator-General. Because of this limitation, the Procurator-General is a buffer between citizen and offending state agency and could therefore be viewed as an undesirable limitation of a citizen's rights if he does not fulfill his tasks, depending upon how it is interpreted.

Soviet jurists are now active in strengthening and popularizing the USSR's 1977 Constitution's emphasis upon legality. For many of them, the 1977 Basic Law marked what they hope will be a milestone, a departure forever from the excesses of the Stalin era, a new beginning on the road hopefully to be known for practices that conform to the procedural and substantive law reforms begun in 1958.

The new Soviet "legality" minimizes the flexibility formerly characteristic of the Soviet legal system. Legal education, as described in this volume, helps to accentuate the new emphasis upon conformity to law, as does the emphasis upon conformity to codes by judges. They are no longer admonished to give priority to a socialist conscience if it seems to them to be in contrast with the codes. There are still professional critics of leadership plans and of their implementation by the administrators of the state apparatus.

It is well to remember when reading the papers in this volume that no Soviet legal specialist works without a sense of the continuing impact of the Stalin years upon the contemporary legal culture. All know that there are still individuals who are impatient with legal procedures that seem to them to hamper flexible application of the rules of law. It would be wrong, however, to conclude that there is a desire on the part of such conservatives to return to the policies of the past, most notably those of the Great Purge in the late 1930s.

While Stalin's policies have been rejected, there is still to be noted at times a streak of intolerance with nonconformists even today. The hard-liners are not prepared to keep on trying to reform recidivits, nor are they prepared to listen to those who seem to them to be professional critics of leadership plans and of their implementation by the administrators of the state apparatus. It is this streak of intolerance still remaining that has not only caught the attention of Western students of the Soviet legal system and given rise to a crescendo of protests based on humanistic grounds, but it has also colored Western thinking generally on Soviet law.

When confronted with these protests from abroad, Soviet jurists close ranks with the generalists who bridle every time they think the sovereignty of their state is impaired by Western criticism. Yet, when working quietly within the system, many of these same jurists try undramatically by persuasion to influence the intolerant to move in the direction of "legality," as advantageous to achievement of professed Soviet values. It is people with legal training who believe that fair trials can favor and not hinder acceptance of the Soviet model both within and outside Soviet borders.

This volume bears witness to the intensity of feeling and commitment of those who toil in the research institutes that provide the materials for policy-makers. Further, it indicates how legal technicians have implemented those policies once they have been established.

While books on certain aspects of the legal system of the USSR are now in most Western languages, this specialized volume should be a welcomed addition. It goes beyond anything yet prepared by Soviet authors for foreign readers to acquaint them in depth with the substantive and procedural criminal law and the system of corrections in the USSR. An additional feature of importance is that an American specialist, Professor Bassiouni, shared in editing this book with Professor Savitski from the Academy of Sciences of the USSR. Professor Bassiouni's input increases the utility of the book to Western scholars by exploring significant issues of contemporary interest.

This is the first time that editors from different systems have sought jointly to explain what Soviet jurists have in mind when they speak of "legality" and what they are trying to do to implement their legal concepts. In that co-editorship there is promise of innovative exchange of ideas that cannot but stimulate future helpful comparisons.

JOHN N. HAZARD

New York City

INTRODUCTION

A CCORDING TO THE French philosopher P. Golbach, "Justice is the foundation of all social values." This statement probably is true but somewhat exaggerated. The converse statement might be more correct: social values are the foundation of justice. However, it is clear they are closely connected. An effective system of justice is an indispensable element of a democratic society, an important means of protecting the rights and proper interests of citizens. Simultaneously, it is an effective means for teaching citizens to respect recognized social values.

It is not by chance that the task of organizing a system of justice on a truly democratic basis confronted Soviet society right after the October Revolution. It was on November 2, 1917, that the Decree on Courts No. 1 was issued, which liquidated old tsarist courts and established a new judicial system, based on the will of the working people. The Decree was signed by V. I. Lenin as Chairman of the Soviet of People's Commissars—the government of the Russian Soviet Federative Socialist Republic (RSFSR).

The need to reconstruct courts and investigative agencies (Lenin called this reconstruction a "breaking down" of the old judicial system) was due to the deep hostility of the former judicial system and of political and juridical institutions of tsarist Russia towards the people. These institutions were reactionary, bureaucratic in form, composed of tsarist officers who defended the interests of the bourgeoisie and landlords.

New People's Courts consisted of freely elected workers and peasants. "Having taken power in its hands," wrote V. I. Lenin, "the proletariate put forward a slogan: 'To elect judges from working people only by working people' and carried it out in all court organizations:"[1]

People's Courts have completely changed the nature of judicial

---

1. 38 V. I. LENIN, COMPLETE WORKS 115 (5th ed.).

policy. They have eliminated the injustice and cruelty of the tsarist system. During the first months of Soviet power in the country, there was no developed legislation; new judges often relied on their "revolutionary consciousness." This did not prevent them from finding just, humane, and correct solutions. Because these judges were original representatives of the people, they were able to protect the people's interests, which they understood very well.

However, it became necessary to make uniform and systematic the People's Courts network and to create basic norms of civil, criminal, and procedural legislation. In July, 1918, People's Commissar of Justice D. I. Kursky said at the Second All-Russia Congress of Officers of Soviet Justice,

> We . . . are already leaving the stage when we said to our local practitioners: "We have broken the old courts, do create new ones, People's Courts, let them decide cases being directed by revolutionary conscience." Now we, in the center, can see that these courts need to have norms created for them. Let them be free in the mitigation of penalties to the extent they consider proper, let them relieve from responsibility if they believe a man is innocent, let them pardon if a man is an inadvertent criminal, let all this be, but the courts need norms for operation in order to focus attention on phenomena which undermine and may kill the great deed, which has been done by the Russian proletariat.[2]

New Soviet laws creating the courts, Procurator's Office, and militia and penitentiary institutions were elaborated based on such democratic principles as a wide participation of the citizens in the administration of justice, public trials, providing all accused persons the right of defense, equality of citizens before law and court, and humanism in application of the law. It is significant that as early as 1919 the Eighth Congress of the Communist Party acknowledged great success in the implementation of such principles in the practice of the new judicial system, declaring:

> In the area of punishments, courts organized in such a manner have already brought a basic change generously applying conditional conviction, introducing social censure as a measure of punishment,

2. III MATERIALS OF THE PEOPLE'S COMMISSARIAT OF JUSTICE 10 (1918).

replacing deprivation of liberty with compulsory work at liberty, replacing prisons with educational institutions, and providing for the operation of comrade's courts.

Sixty years have now passed. The Soviet judicial system has progressively acquired more clearly outlined organizational forms, and now operates on the basis of detailed legislation. The democratic principles generated during the early revolutionary years have not faded but rather have spread and grown stronger. Now they are accurately reflected in detail in the new Constitution of the USSR, adopted on October 7, 1977.

Doubtless, the course of development of the Soviet judicial system was neither simple, nor easy. In his speech referring to the discussions on the draft of the new Constitution in May, 1977, L. I. Brezhnev said:

> We know, comrades, that certain years after the adopting of the acting Constitution (Constitution of the USSR of 1936), were obscured by unlawful repressions, violations of the principles of socialist democracy, and of Leninist norms of party and state life. This was contrary to constitutional provisions. The Party has decisively condemned such practices, and they should never be repeated.[3]

For the past fifteen to twenty years, great efforts have been made to improve Soviet law, to create strong guarantees for the protection of citizens' rights, and for the prevention of breaches of trust and bureaucratic perversions. The new Constitution of the USSR emphasizes that the Soviet State and all its bodies function on the basis of socialist law to ensure the maintenance of law and order, and to safeguard the interests of society and the rights of citizens (Art. 4). This provision is particularly relevant to the system of justice. The Constitution consolidates such principles of the organization and functioning of the judicial system as the election of members of all the courts, the collegiality of the conduct by the courts of all civil and criminal trials, the independence of judges and lay members of courts, the equality of all citizens before the law and court, the presumption of innocence, public trials, the right of the ac-

---

3. L. I. BREZHNEV, ON THE CONSTITUTION OF THE USSR 18 (1977).

cused to conduct a defense and to have his own language used in court proceedings, etc.

The present work is aimed at acquainting the American reader with both the principles governing the organization and functioning of the present Soviet system of criminal justice and the fundamentals of current legislation in the USSR aimed at combatting crime and other misconduct. The core of the system consists of the institutions of justice—the Soviet courts—and they naturally receive most attention. However, the courts do not function in isolation from other state agencies. Crimes are investigated by the militia and the Procurator's Office, advocates defend the accused, procurators exercise supervision over law observance, and penitentiary institutions execute punishment. Activities of these agencies are described as well so that readers will have a complete image of the criminal justice system as a whole.

To understand correctly the peculiarities of the organization and activities of the criminal justice institutions of the USSR, one should remember that the USSR is a federative state, consisting of fifteen union republics. The Supreme Soviet of the USSR adopts Fundamentals of the legislation of the union and union republics in different branches of law—civil law, criminal law, criminal procedure, corrective labor law, etc. These Fundamentals contain only basic provisions of the corresponding branch of legislation, in accordance with which the union republics elaborate their own civil, criminal, criminal procedure, and other codes, providing detailed regulations.

The book gives an idea of the criminal, criminal procedure, and corrective labor legislation in the USSR and union republics. The limited size of the book does not allow an opportunity to explore all legislative provisions in detail; that is why the authors refer the reader in some cases to additional literature, where particular topics are examined more substantially. For the same reason, an analysis of the legislation of all the fifteen union republics is rather difficult to accomplish. As the reader will see, the text is illustrated primarily with examples from the legislation of the largest union republic, the Russian Federation.

The new Constitution of the USSR, in Article 69, declared that it is the internationalist duty of citizens of the USSR to promote friendship and cooperation with peoples of other lands and help maintain and strengthen peace. This constitutional provision corresponds to the viewpoint of the authors, who are distinguished Soviet scholars, with knowledge of both juridical theory and practice. The main goal of the authors in writing this book is to objectively and sincerely inform the American reader about the Soviet system of criminal justice. To know each other well is an important condition for friendship and cooperation among nations. Friendship and cooperation are human values that are the foundation indispensable not only to justice but also to such equally important human values as enduring peace among peoples and states.

V. Kudriavtsev

Moscow

ABBREVIATIONS

CLC: Corrective Labor Code of the Russian Soviet Federated Socialist Republic, adopted on February 18, 1970; *see* GAZETTE OF THE SUPREME SOVIET OF THE RSFSR No. 51, Item 1220 (1970).

CL Fundamentals: Fundamentals of Criminal Legislation of the USSR, Union and Autonomous Republics, adopted on December 25, 1958; *see* GAZETTE OF THE SUPREME SOVIET OF THE USSR No. 1, Item 6 (1959).

CLL Fundamentals: Fundamentals of Corrective Labor Legislation of the USSR and the Union Republics, adopted on July 11, 1969; *see* GAZETTE OF THE SUPREME SOVIET OF THE USSR No. 29, Item 247 (1969).

CPC: Criminal Procedure Code of the Russian Soviet Federated Socialist Republic, adopted on October 26, 1960; *see* GAZETTE OF THE SUPREME SOVIET OF THE USSR No. 40, Item 582 (1960).

CP Fundamentals: Fundamentals of Criminal Procedure of the USSR and Union Republics, promulgated on December 25, 1958; *see* GAZETTE OF THE SUPREME SOVIET OF THE USSR No. 1, Item 15 (1959).

LJS Fundamentals: Fundamentals of Legislation on the Judicial System of the USSR, Union and Autonomous Republics, adopted on December 25, 1958; *see* GAZETTE OF THE SUPREME SOVIET OF THE USSR No. 1, Item 12 (1959).

PCP: Penal Code of the Russian Soviet Federated Socialist Republic, adopted on October 27, 1960; *see* GAZETTE OF THE SUPREME SOVIET OF THE RSFSR No. 40, Item 24 (1960).

CONTENTS

The
Criminal Justice System
Of The USSR

CHAPTER I

INSTITUTIONS FOR THE ADMINISTRATION OF CRIMINAL JUSTICE

V. M. Savitsky

Section 1. THE COURTS

1.1. Structure of the Judicial System

CHAPTER 20 OF THE Constitution of the USSR establishes basic principles governing legislation on functioning of the courts of all levels. These principles are further elaborated in the Fundamentals of Legislation on the Judicial System of the USSR and of the Union Republics (hereafter referred to as LJS Fundamentals), which were approved December 25, 1958,[1] and in judicial system acts later enacted by each of the Soviet union republics.

The purposes of socialist justice are to protect (a) the state and social system of the USSR, the socialist economic system, and socialist property; (b) the political, labor, housing, and other personal and property rights of Soviet citizens, guaranteed by the Constitution of the USSR and by the constitutions of the union and autonomous republics; and (c) the rights and lawful interests of state institutions, enterprises, collective farms *(kolkhozes)*, cooperatives, and other social organizations. A concomitant purpose is to ensure undeviating and strict observance of legality by all institutions, organizations, officials, and citizens of the USSR (Art. 2 of LJS Fundamentals).

PEOPLE'S COURT

The People's Court *(narodnyi sud)* is the main link of the Soviet judicial system. Such courts function in every district of big cities and in small towns that are not subdivided into districts. The structure of the People's Court is extremely simple: it is headed by a chairman, there are several judges (their num-

---

1. GAZETTE OF THE SUPREME SOVIET OF THE USSR Item 12 (1959).

3

ber depends on the volume of work in the particular district) and a corresponding number of people's or lay assessors (about 50 to 70 such persons per judge). Additionally, there are officers of the court and secretaries.

The chairman of the People's Court is appointed by the Soviet of People's Deputies of the court's district or town from among the judges elected from that district or town to the People's Court. The chairman sets basic guidelines for operation of the court, sets hours for receiving the public, supervises court activities, renders assistance to young judges, and presides at the more complicated trials.

Proximity to the population, simplicity of structure, and accessibility are the main reasons that induced the legislature to grant the People's Court general jurisdiction. Practically all criminal and civil cases (94 to 96 percent) are disposed of by such People's Courts. Such courts also handle all cases arising from administrative law violations, *i.e.*, complaints of citizens regarding actions of administrative organs, irregularities in voters' lists, charges of petty hooliganism, petty speculation, petty theft, etc.

The jurisdiction of the People's Court does not embrace certain complicated civil cases and the most serious criminal cases, such as banditry, theft of state or socialist property on a grand scale, aggravated intentional homicide, attempts on the life of a militiaman or a people's patrolman, and some other cases covered by Article 36 of the Criminal Procedure Code of the Russian Federal Republic (hereafter referred to as CPC).[2]

MIDDLE-TIER COURTS

Cases of such a character are submitted to higher courts, namely, regional courts, courts of autonomous territories, courts of autonomous regions, and supreme courts of autonomous republics. In Moscow, Leningrad, Kiev, and some other large cities there are city courts (*gorodskie sudy*) of equivalent stature and jurisdiction. Although they bear different names, all of these courts stand at the same level within the Soviet judicial system and constitute its middle tier.

---

2. The Code of Criminal Procedure of the RSFSR was approved October 27, 1960. *See* GAZETTE OF THE SUPREME SOVIET OF THE RSFSR No. 40, Item 592 (1960).

Every regional court or court of equivalent jurisdiction consists of a chairman, his deputies, members of the court, and lay or people's assessors. The work of the court is divided between judicial collegia (or panels), specializing in civil or criminal cases, and the plenum (assembly of all members) of the court.

When the court examines material evidence in a case, questions the accused, the victims, and witnesses, studies evidence or documents, and then passes judgment, it plays the role of a court of the first instance. The more important and more common function of such courts is to monitor the fairness and validity of judgments and sentences of People's Courts. These sentences are reviewed in response to appeals or protests by the accused, the alleged victim, the procurator, or other concerned parties.

In reviewing cases by way of cassation, *i.e.,* re-examining the judgment of a court of the first instance which has not yet come into legal effect,[3] the regional court plays the role of a court of cassation.

The presidium (a permanent executive committee) of a regional or other middle-tier court consists of the chairman of the court, his deputies, and several members of the court. The presidium of the court differs from the collegia for civil and criminal cases and from the People's Courts because it never exercises original jurisdiction and, therefore, never plays the role of a court of the first instance. It has other functions. They consist of reviewing judgments and sentences of People's Courts that have come into legal effect, as well as reviewing cassation decisions of various panels of the court. These review activities of the presidium of the court, which relate to judgments and sentences already having legal effect, are described as exercising judicial supervision over cases.

In contrast to the court collegia, the presidium of the court also deals with some organizational matters, hearing reports from the judicial collegia chairmen, discussing general problems of judicial practice, investigating the shortcomings of the judges

3. The sentence of the court is considered to come into force if, during the fixed time limit beginning from the day of its pronouncement (in the Russian Federal Republic the term is seven days), it was not appealed or protested by way of cassation.

of People's Courts, and if necessary imposing disciplinary measures.

Thus, regional and other middle-tier courts fulfill three main functions: examining cases as a court of the first instance, reviewing judgments and sentences of lower courts by way of cassation, and reconsidering judgments and sentences as an exercise of its power of judicial supervision.

SUPREME COURTS OF THE UNION REPUBLICS

The next link in the Soviet judicial system is the supreme court of a union republic. It is the highest judicial body of a union republic and as such supervises judicial activity of all courts of the republic. The supreme court consists of collegia on civil and criminal cases, the presidium of the supreme court, and the plenum of the supreme court. The judgments of the supreme court are not subject to protest or appeal by way of cassation, and the supreme court of a union republic has the right of legislative initiative.

There is no law providing specifically an enumeration of cases that fall within the original jurisdiction of a union republic supreme court. Article 38 of the CPC provides that "the competence of the Supreme Court of the RSFSR may cover cases of some particular seriousness or of some particular social significance. Legal action regarding them is initiated by the Supreme Court itself or by the Procurator of the Republic." Hence, the supreme court of a union republic has a right to hear any case that, in normal conditions, would fall within the competence of a lower court but which by virtue of the concrete circumstances acquires special social significance.

Judgments and sentences of the regional or other middle-tier courts may be reviewed, upon appeal or protest, by way of cassation. Decisions and sentences which have come into legal effect may be examined by way of judicial supervision.[4] By way of judicial supervision, a supreme court of a union republic may also examine protests against decisions of the presidia of middle-tier courts. The presidium of the supreme court of a

4. In those union republics that are not subdivided into districts (the Lithuanian, Latvian, Estonian, Armenian, and Moldavian Soviet Socialist Republics), the supreme court fulfills these very functions in respect of People's Courts.

union republic also examines by way of judicial supervision protests against judgments, decisions, and sentences of collegia of the supreme court itself.

Thus, all judicial functions of the supreme court of a union republic are fulfilled by its collegia and presidium. The role of the plenum of the supreme court, therefore, is supervisory in character. The plenum constitutes the highest level of judicial control within a union republic. In the majority of supreme courts of union republics, the plenum itself does not hear cases. On the basis of generalized judicial practice and statistics, and judgments of the supreme court itself, plenary sessions of the supreme court issue guidelines for judicial practice and republican legislation.[5] The plenum also brings before legislative bodies proposals for specific legislation and proposed interpretations of existing legislation. The plenum consists of the chairman, his deputies, and all the members of the supreme court of the union republic. The participation in plenary sessions by the procurator of the union republic is obligatory.

The supreme court of the republic provides uniformity and direction to activities of judicial bodies only within that union republic. To coordinate judicial activity throughout the USSR and provide needed uniformity of judicial practice on that wide scale is the task of the Supreme Court of the USSR.

SUPREME COURT OF THE USSR

The Supreme Court of the USSR consists of a chairman (the Chief Justice), his deputies, members of the Supreme Court, and people's assessors. The Supreme Court of the USSR consists of the collegium on civil cases, collegium on criminal cases, and military collegium. It also functions through plenary sessions, *i.e.*, the Plenum of the Supreme Court of the USSR.[6]

---

5. Ch. Shein, *On Leading Interpretations Given by the Plenums of the Supreme Court of the USSR*, GAZETTE OF THE SUPREME COURT OF THE USSR No. 3, Item 44 (1962). The quantitative side of this activity may be illustrated, for example, by these figures: in the period from 1961 to 1972, the Supreme Court of the RSFSR gave 65 guiding interpretations; *see* SOVIET JUSTICE No. 24, Item 5 (1972).

6. The composition, structure, and competence of the Supreme Court of the USSR are defined by the Regulations on the Supreme Court of the USSR, approved on February 12, 1957. *See* GAZETTE OF THE SUPREME SOVIET OF THE USSR No. 4, Item 85 (1957). *See also* Art. 152 of the USSR CONSTITUTION.

The collegia of the Supreme Court of the USSR function as courts of the first instance for the hearing of certain classes of extraordinary seriousness, as provided by law. Thus, for example, in 1972 the collegium on criminal cases heard charges of gross violations of rules of safety engineering at an electronics plant in Minsk, Byelorussia. As a result of an explosion in a section of that plant that turned out cases for television sets, many people were killed, much equipment was destroyed, and serious damage to buildings was caused. Those responsible were sentenced to deprivation of liberty.[7]

The collegia of the Supreme Court of the USSR also exercise the power of judicial supervision over cases when the Chief Justice of the USSR and the Procurator-General of the USSR protest judgments and sentences of the supreme courts of union republics on the grounds they contradict the legislation of the USSR or infringe upon the interests of other union republics. The Supreme Court of the USSR does not hear cases by way of cassation.

The highest judicial authority is the Plenum of the Supreme Court of the USSR, which meets four times a year. The Plenum consists of the Chief Justice of the USSR, his deputy chairmen in the Supreme Court, the members of the Supreme Court, and the chairmen of the supreme courts of the union republics *ex officio*. The Procurator-General of the USSR and the Minister of Justice participate in such plenary sessions.

The main task of the Plenum of the Supreme Court of the USSR is to consider the patterns of judicial practice and court statistics throughout the USSR and to elaborate guidelines for the courts. Some examples of guidelines in the field of criminal justice that have been issued by the Plenum during recent years follow: "On the improvement of organization of trial proceedings and strengthening of their ethical and educational impact" (Resolution of February 25, 1967); "On the practice of hearing criminal cases by way of cassation" (Resolution of December 17, 1971); "On the application by courts of legislation on combatting recidivistic crime" (June 25, 1975); "On

---

7. For the details of the case *see* SUPREME COURT OF THE USSR 417-421 (L. Smirniv, V. Kulikov, & B. Nikiforov eds. 1974; Moscow, "Juriditcheskaya Literatura" Publ. House).

further improvement of judicial activity in crime prevention" (December 3, 1976); "On judicial practice of application of legislation on juvenile delinquency cases and on inveigling of juveniles into criminal and other kinds of anti-social activity" (December 3, 1976.)[8]

In accordance with the recommendations of the Plenum, the Supreme Court of the USSR submits to the Presidium of the Supreme Soviet of the USSR proposals on the improvement of legislation currently in force and on the interpretation of laws of the USSR. It also exercises the right of legislative initiative vested in it by Article 113 of the USSR Constitution. Additionally, the Plenum of the Supreme Court considers protests of the Chief Justice of the USSR and of the Procurator-General of the USSR of decisions of the presidiums and the plenums of the supreme courts of the union republics on the grounds that they contradict USSR legislation or infringe the interests of other union republics.[9]

For deep and more comprehensive studies of matters connected with judicial practice, in 1962 the Supreme Court of the USSR organized a Scientific Advisory Council of distinguished scholars, researchers, and practitioners in the Soviet Union. This Council is a consultative agency. Virtually all complex judicial matters upon which the Supreme Court in its plenary sessions is called to express its opinion are referred for preliminary discussion in the Scientific Advisory Councils.[10]

MILITARY TRIBUNALS

Military tribunals are the remaining facet of the Soviet court system. Such tribunals are assigned the task of applying socialist justice in acting against threats to the security of the USSR, to

---

8. All the guiding interpretations given by the Plenum of the Supreme Court of the USSR, as well as the most important judgments on concrete cases, are published in the GAZETTE OF THE SUPREME COURT OF THE USSR, which is published six times a year. In addition, systematized COLLECTIONS OF THE PLENUM OF THE USSR SUPREME COURT DECISIONS are published. The last one was published in 1974.

9. In the period from 1967 to 1972, the Plenum of the Supreme Court of the USSR examined 82 civil and 500 criminal cases. See GAZETTE OF THE SUPREME COURT OF THE USSR No. 5, Item 6 (1972).

10. GAZETTE OF THE SUPREME COURT OF THE USSR No. 2, Item 11 (1971).

the fighting capacity of its armed forces, and to discipline and order in the military services (Art. 2 of the Regulations on Military Tribunals).[11]

Jurisdiction of military tribunals extends to all cases of crimes committed by persons in military service or by reservists in training camps, to crimes committed by officers, sergeants, and rank and file of the organs of State security, and to crimes committed by persons in charge of penitentiary institutions. In addition, military tribunals hear espionage cases regardless of whether those accused of such acts are military or civilian.

All cases within the jurisdiction of military tribunals are divided among them according to the military rank of the defendant and to the degree of social danger of the act committed. The highest organ of the system of military justice is the military collegium of the Supreme Court of the USSR. As a court of the first instance, it examines cases of extraordinary seriousness (including cases of crimes committed by generals or admirals) and also reviews appeals and protests by way of cassation. It also handles protests against judgments, sentences, and rulings of military tribunals of the middle tier by way of judicial supervision.

SUMMARY

This brief survey has demonstrated the unitarian principle of the Soviet judicial system, the interrelations between particular links of the integral chain, and the jurisdictional allocations of the various subsystems. It is not by chance that the Soviet judicial system is called *unitarian*. It is intentionally organized in such a way that all the links of the system, including military tribunals, form an integral and harmonious unity. All the courts are organized in strict correlation to the state structure of the USSR and to its territorial and administrative divisions. Rulings of the only supreme judicial organ of the USSR, the Supreme Court of the USSR, ensure uniformity of all the courts. All the courts have the same purposes and tasks laid down by Articles 2 and 3 of the Fundamentals of Judicial Law. All the courts fol-

11. This Act, defining the tasks, structure, and competence of military tribunals, was promulgated on December 25, 1958. See GAZETTE OF THE SUPREME COURT OF THE USSR No. 1, Item 14 (1959).

low unitarian basic rules of proceedings established by the Fundamentals of Criminal Procedure of the USSR and Union Republics (CP Fundamentals).[12] Finally, the same principles form the basis for the composition of all courts. This composition merits further consideration.

1.2. Composition of the Courts

One of the basic principles for the composition of all courts is their *elective nature*. In the USSR, all members of courts in the judicial system, beginning with People's Courts and ending with the Supreme Court, are elected either by direct suffrage or by the deputies of the corresponding unit (district, region, republic, etc.).

Members of the People's Court are elected directly by population of the district or town. People's judges are elected by universal, direct, and equal suffrage for the term of five years. People's assessors are elected at general meetings of co-workers, employees, and collective farmers *(kolkhozniks)* at the places of their work or residence, and at meetings of persons in the military at their units, for the term of two-and-one-half years, by simple voting by a show of hands. Any citizen of the USSR who has reached the age of twenty-five and enjoys his suffrage rights may be elected a judge or a people's assessor.[13]

Elections of people's judges are by electoral district, a district or town being divided into as many electoral districts as the number of judges to be elected to the given court. Each electoral district elects one people's judge. All the preparatory work is conducted by the executive committee of appropriate Soviets of People's Deputies in cooperation with local organs of the Ministry of Justice.

The right to nominate candidates to be people's judges is given to public organizations and to societies of working people as well as to the general meetings of citizens. All the candidates

12. The Fundamentals of Criminal Procedure were promulgated on December 25, 1958. *See* Gazette of the Supreme Soviet of the USSR No. 1, Item 15 (1959).

13. Regulations on the election of regional level People's Courts in the RSFSR were approved on October 28, 1960. *See* Gazette of the Supreme Soviet of the RSFSR No. 41, Item 608 (1960). *See also* Art. 152 of the USSR Constitution.

are registered by the executive committees of appropriate Soviets. After that, their names are automatically placed on the ballot. The candidate receiving a majority of the votes is elected.[14]

It should be mentioned that until 1959 people's assessors of district (town) People's Courts were elected for the term of three years. The term is now two-and-one-half years, providing an increased possibility for rotating citizens into the administration of justice.

People's judges may be removed before the expiration of their terms of office at the initiative of voters. People's assessors may be removed through a recall vote similar to that by which they are elected.[15]

An initiative to recall a judge or people's assessor may be raised by public organizations and at general meetings of working people, as well as by the local organ of the Ministry of Justice. The executive committee of the regional Soviet examines the matter and schedules voting on the recall. Recalls of judges are decided by a show of hands at meetings of electors of the district (recalls of people's assessors are decided at meetings of working people) where they were elected. If the majority of votes is for the recall, a judge or a people's assessor is considered to be recalled from the post. The executive committees of district councils are charged with surveillance over the order of recall.[16]

---

14. In 1976, in all the union republics, elections of people's judges were held. A total of 9,230 persons were elected; 95 percent had a university education (in comparison, in 1960, the figure was 71 percent; in 1965, 80.9 percent; in 1970, 87.6 percent). Three-quarters of the judges were re-elected. Among those newly elected, one-half were under forty years of age. More than one-half of people's judges are Communist Party members. One-third are women. (*See Pravda,* April 17, 1976).

15. Regulations on the manner for recall of judges and people's assessors of the courts of the RSFSR were approved on October 5, 1961. *See* GAZETTE OF THE SUPREME SOVIET OF THE RSFSR No. 40, Item 558 (1961).

16. An example is the Decree of the Presidium of the Supreme Soviet of the Azerbaijan Soviet Socialist Republic of September 5, 1975: "On scheduling voting about recall ahead of the term of the people's judge of Shemachinsky district A. Abassov." The question of his recall was raised by a meeting of workers and employees of the M. Sabir collective farm *(sovkhoz)* in connection with mean behavior of the judge. After voting, he was relieved of his post. *See* GAZETTE OF THE SUPREME SOVIET OF THE AZERBAIJAN SSR No. 17 (1975).

Higher courts are also formed on the basis of election. Elections are carried out not by the population directly but by their deputies at sessions of corresponding organs of state power. Thus, members of district and territorial courts or the courts of autonomous republics and autonomous regions, as well as people's assessors to them, are elected at sessions of regional, territorial, etc., Soviets of People's Deputies. Judges and people's assessors to supreme courts of union and autonomous republics are elected at sessions of Supreme Soviets of these republics, and judges and people's assessors to the Supreme Court of the USSR are elected at sessions of the Supreme Soviet of the USSR. The chairman, deputy chairmen, and members of military tribunals are elected by the Presidium of the Supreme Soviet of the USSR. The term of office for judges and assessors of all such courts is five years, but they can be recalled before the expiration of their term of office (Art. 152 of the Constitution of the USSR). During recent years in the country as a whole, there are about 700,000 people's assessors on the various courts.

Election to the courts of such a great number of judges and people's assessors provides for consistent translation into reality of the next principle—*collegiate examination* of cases. In the USSR, no civil or criminal case is ever decided by a single judge. Only the collegium is empowered to be the arbiter of a person's destiny.[17]

In all courts of the first instance, cases are examined by a collegium of three persons: a judge and two people's assessors (Art. 154 of the USSR Constitution). This rule is true for all courts sitting as courts of the first instance. Fairness of the decision is enhanced by the collegiate approach and further assured through reviews by way of cassation or judicial supervision. The presidium of the court conducts such review if the majority of the members are present. The plenum of the court does so if at least two-thirds of the members are present (Art. 8 of the LJS Fundamentals).

---

17. A people's judge is empowered to individually consider only certain administrative offenses (petty hooliganism, petty stealing, etc.). He may also, sitting alone, consider cases involving offenses of a noncriminal nature. Administrative penalties awarded in such cases are fines up to 50 rubles, corrective labor up to two months, and arrest up to fifteen days.

Thus all the questions that may arise during the examination of the case are discussed collegiately (collectively), with all judges participating having equal rights, and decisions are by majority vote. However, collegiality does not provide for participation of people's assessors in review by cassation or judicial supervision. The crucial role for people's assessors is at trial.

People's assessors are called upon on a rotational basis and serve not longer than two weeks per year, except when it becomes necessary to prolong the term in order to finish a trial that began with their participation. While serving on the court, people's assessors continue to receive their normal wages plus compensation for any other expenses connected with their court duties (Art. 31 and 32 of LJS Fundamentals).

People's assessors have equal rights with the judge presiding at the judicial session (Art. 154 of the USSR Constitution). They constitute the majority in the judicial bench. For that reason, even in case of disagreement with the judge, they always can pass a sentence which they consider the most appropriate. The judge in such a case must nevertheless sign the judgment, but he can state on paper his own opinion, which is not openly announced at trial but is attached to the case materials (Art. 306-307 of the CPC).

Any violation of the law of equal voting of people's assessors necessarily renders the judgment voidable. In one case, a court's judgment of conviction was found on review to have been entered despite the fact that both people's assessors were against the opinion of the judge. Because the judgment of the court did not reflect the opinion of the majority of the collegium, the Supreme Court of the USSR cancelled the judgment.[18] In another case, judgment was cancelled because the sentence was not signed by people's assessors.[19]

A necessary condition for sound and lawful administration of justice is independence of judges from any extraneous influence. The principle according to which *judges are independent and subject only to law* is established by Article 155 of the USSR

18. COLLECTED RULINGS OF THE PLENUM AND JUDGMENTS OF THE COLLEGIA OF THE SUPREME COURT OF THE USSR ON THE POINTS OF CRIMINAL PROCESS 1946-1962, at 16-17 (1964; Moscow, "Juriditcheskaya Literatura" Publ. House).

19. GAZETTE OF THE SUPREME COURT OF THE USSR No. 2, Item 25 (1973).

Constitution. Translation of this principle into reality is ensured first by the election of all court members from the bottom to the top; then by periodical reports on their activity by them—both judges and people's assessors—to the electors; and then by establishing a special process (when there is consent of the higher organs of power of the USSR or of a union republic) for criminal prosecution of judges and people's assessors and their removal or arrest. This principle also is served by the legally established rules that judges assess evidence in accordance with their inner convictions based on a comprehensive, thorough, and objective examination of all the materials of the case in their aggregate (Art. 17 of CP Fundamentals), that judicial consultations about the judgment of the court remain secret (Art. 302 of the CPC), and other rules.

Some Western critics attempt to cast doubt on the reality of the constitutional principle of the independence of Soviet judges and their subordination only to the law. Most often they refer to two circumstances: in the first place, they argue, judges who are Communist Party members are obliged to adhere to Party discipline; and, in the second place, judges can be recalled. Both arguments, however, miss their target.

Party discipline does presume the subordination of Party members to the decisions and instructions of Party organs. But these very organs are strictly forbidden to interfere in examination by courts of specific criminal and civil cases. In this connection, the Central Committee of the Communist Party of the Soviet Union (CPSU) in 1954 passed a special decision.[20] If top officials of the local Party organs try to instruct judges or to pressure them, the end is invariably the same in the long run: such officials are removed from their posts and prosecuted for abuse of power. To discourage others, these instances are reported by the press.[21] Thus, it is Party discipline that guards the independence of judges.

As for the reference to the absence in the USSR of the principle of unchangeability of judges, it should be said that this principle can hardly serve as a guarantee for their independence.

---

20. PARTY LIFE No. 6, at 16 (1954).
21. *Pravda*, Feb. 2, 1965; March 3, 1966; Aug. 10, 1975.

The appointment of judges by organs of executive power (either the government or the head of a state) makes them completely dependent on this very power because, whatever the stipulations made in appointing judges, their promotion, moves, awards, and so on, in the long run, depend on whether they are responsive to the wishes of the executive power. That is why, not only in the USSR but in many other countries too, the preferred way of staffing the court has been found to be the election of judges by the people for a certain length of time. This method provides judges with genuine independence.[22]

Section 2. THE PROCURACY

2.1. The Role of the Procurator

The Soviet Procurator's Office was established by the Decree of the All-Russian Central Executive Committee of May 28, 1922.[23] The civil war and the struggle to expel foreign troops having just ended, the young Soviet State was then beginning peaceful socialist construction, restoring its economy, and proceeding with reconstruction of former social relations. To accomplish these tasks it was necessary to ensure strict observance of the laws of the central power, overcoming strong local influences that might weaken the whole political and economic potential of the state. That was the main reason for establishing a special agency to oversee legality, the Procurator's Office.

The chief function of the Procurator's Office is to ensure strict and uniform observance of the law in all spheres of public and social life by all the ministries, state committees, and agencies; by enterprises, institutions, and organizations; by executive and administrative bodies of local Soviets of People's Deputies; by collective farms, cooperatives, and other public organizations; by officials and citizens. The Procurator-General of the USSR and subordinates in his office are entrusted with the highest supervisory responsibility (Art. 164 of the USSR Constitution).

Procurator's supervision is a specific kind of state activity. It

---

22. The principles of the organization of the courts cited here are tightly connected with the principles of their activities. *See* Section 4 of this chapter.

23. GAZETTE OF THE CENTRAL EXECUTIVE COMMITTEE OF THE RSFR No. 36, Item 424 (1922).

differs from the control over the implementation of the laws exercised by ministries and agencies, whose responsibilities include ensuring efficiency and expediency. The role of the procuracy is to assess activities only from the standpoint of observance of the law. The Procurator's Office has no right to interfere directly in the functioning of ministries, agencies, enterprises, or institutions. The only basis for involvement by the procurator is violations of laws, not the shortcomings in organization or execution of economic, administrative, educational, or other functions. For other agencies of the state authority, observance of laws is only one of the methods for solving problems, but for the Procurator's Office, assuring strict and uniform observance of laws is the only task.

When exercising such supervision, the Procurator's Office itself does not apply penalties to offenders. It has no such power. The Procurator's Office may only demand competent state agencies, officials, or public organizations to cease violations of the laws and to punish guilty persons. Moreover, it has no right to apply criminal punishments to guilty persons, because such matters are exclusively within the competence of the courts. Generally speaking, legal sanctions and restrictions are not a part of the procurator's job. The Procurator's Office has no right to supplant administrative and judicial bodies. Its role in the mechanics of legal regulation of social relations lies in exposing violations of law and in devising remedies to such illegality.

Activities of the procuracy are therefore guided by specific fundamental principles. One of these principles is the *unity* of the procurator's supervision. The concept is that every procurator acts on behalf of the State and as a representative of the integral system of the Procurator's Office and all procurators are empowered with similar authority. Thus, the procurator of the district, like any higher procurator, has the right and the duty to take measures for suppression of crimes and violations of the rights of citizens. In order to do so, the procurator has the power to initiate prosecution of guilty persons in strict accordance with the provisions of the law, to present and maintain suits before the court, to defend violated rights, to bring protests against unlawful or unfounded decisions of courts, rulings and orders of administrative bodies, etc. The principle of unity permits substitution of one procurator for another. This fact provides for continuity of procedural actions from one procurator to another. The procurator of lower instances may be entrusted with fulfilling all duties of the procurator of higher instance (with the exception of certain special provisions of the law). The procurator of a higher instance may fulfill all the duties of the procurator of lower levels.

Only certain particular powers are tied to specific procurators. Thus, only the USSR Procurator-General has the right of the legislative initiative in the USSR Supreme Soviet (Art. 113 of the USSR Constitution). The right to stop the execution of a protested court judgment, ruling, or decree does not belong to all the procurators, but only to the Procurator-General of the USSR, his deputies, the Chief Military Procurator, and the procurators of the union republics (Art. 48 of the CP Fundamentals). No one but the Procurator-General may submit to the Presidium of the Supreme Soviet of the USSR petitions to repeal unlawful rulings of the USSR Supreme Court Plenum (Art. 29 of the Regulations on Procurator's Supervision in the USSR).[24]

The principle of unity is dictated by the common task of procurators at all levels. Due to this principle, uniform interpretation of laws by all procurators is assured, as well as performance by them of all their duties of supervision of the strict observance of the laws of the USSR and of union and autonomous republics, despite any local conditions or influences (Art. 2 and 3 of the Regulations). Acting as a representative of the integral Procurator's Office, each procurator is nevertheless absolutely independent in making decisions on the basis of his inner convictions founded after analysis of facts and interpretation of the law. A higher procurator can not order a lower one to make a particular decision (to maintain an accusation in a court, to pro-

---

24. Regulations define the tasks, principles of organization, and main directions of activity of the Soviet Procurator's Office. This legislative act was approved by the Decree of the Presidium of the Supreme Soviet of the USSR of May 24, 1955. See GAZETTE OF THE SUPREME SOVIET OF THE USSR No. 9, Item 222 (1955).

test against a judgment, etc.), if such a decision would be contrary to the inner convictions of the lower rank procurator.

The Procurator's Office is organized on the principle of *strict centralization.* This means that the principle of procurators' subordination is vertical, *i.e.,* the lower procurator is subordinate to a higher one, and all the procurators to the USSR Procurator-General. Centralization of procurator's supervision is necessary to ensure uniform socialist legality in all places. Such an end cannot be accomplished without unified central guidance.

Centralization of the procurator's supervision finds expression in the manner in which procurators are appointed to and relieved of their posts: by the Procurator-General or with his confirmation only. It also finds expression in the mandatory character of orders and instructions from the Procurator-General to all the agencies of the procurancy (Art. 8 of the Regulations).

The principle of procurators' *independence* from any local legislative and administrative agencies is crucial to proper performance of the procurator's task. This principle is established by the Constitution of the USSR, Article 168, which provides: "The agencies of the Procurator's Office exercise their powers independently of any local bodies whatsoever and are subordinate solely to the Procurator-General of the USSR."

2.2. Organization of the Procurator's Office

Agencies of the Procurator's Office are organized in accordance with the framework of the USSR system, headed by the Procurator-General of the USSR. The structure of this system mainly corresponds to the administrative-territorial principle, *i.e.,* there are the Procurator's Office of the USSR and procuracies of union and autonomous republics, regions, territories, autonomous areas, towns, and districts. The Procurator-General of the USSR has the right to assign to a single Procurator's Office responsibility for several administrative regions (Art. 43 of the Regulations).

In addition to territorial Procurator's Offices, there are also some special ones, such as the military and transport (railway and water) Procurator's Offices. Transport Procurator's Offices have functions similar to those of regional Procurator's Offices and are subordinate to territorial procuracies of higher ranks.[25]

The Procurator-General of the USSR is appointed by the Supreme Soviet of the USSR and is responsible and accountable to it. Between sessions of the Supreme Soviet, he reports to the Presidium of the Supreme Soviet of the USSR. The procurators of union and autonomous republics, or territories, regions, and autonomous regions, are appointed by the procurators of union republics and subject to confirmation by the Procurator-General of the USSR. The term of office of the Procurator-General of the USSR and of all lower-ranking procurators is five years (Arts. 165-167 of the USSR Constitution).[26]

Officers of the Procurator's Office in accordance with their posts are assigned ranks established by the law.[27] When on duty, they wear special uniforms and badges of rank (Art. 57 of the Regulations). They fall under the jurisdiction of the Statute on Encouragement of Disciplinary Responsibility of the Procurators and Investigators of the USSR Procuracy, approved by the Decree of the Supreme Soviet of the USSR of Feburary 24, 1964.[28]

The structure of the Procurator's Office of the USSR includes the Main Military Procuracy, which is vested with the power to oversee legality in the military forces of the USSR. The tasks, powers, and structure of the agencies of the Military Procurator's Office are defined by the Statute of the Military Procurator's Office approved by the Decree of the Presidium of the Supreme Soviet of the USSR of December 14, 1966.[29]

2.3. Subdivisions of Procuratorial Responsibility

There are many facets to performance of the overall mission of the procuracy. Activities of the Procurator's Office are divided into four main branches: (1) supervision over observance of laws by enterprises, institutions, organizations, officials, and citi-

---

25. GAZETTE OF THE SUPREME SOVIET OF THE USSR No. 10, Item 65 (1960).
26. According to the Constitution of 1936, the term of office of the Procurator-General was seven years (Art. 114).
27. GAZETTE OF THE SUPREME SOVIET OF THE USSR No. 8, Item 100 (1964).
28. GAZETTE OF THE SUPREME SOVIET OF THE USSR No. 10, Item 123 (1964).
29. GAZETTE OF THE SUPREME SOVIET OF THE USSR No. 50, Item 1021 (1966).

zens (the so-called general supervision); (2) supervision over observance of legality by the agencies of inquiry and preliminary investigation; (3) supervision over legality in judicial agencies, *i.e.*, the observance by them of the requirement that all court pronouncements, decisions, judgments, and sentences be lawful and well founded; and (4) supervision over legality in the agencies executing court sentences of deprivation of liberty.

Each of these branches of procurator's supervision relates to a concrete sphere of social life, and each branch is characterized by certain modes and means of exposing violations of law and reaction to them inherent in its sphere. But—and this is of particular importance—all the branches of the integrated procurator's supervision and all activity of Procurator's Office agencies are closely coordinated.

This coordination of the branches and forms of supervision constantly manifests itself in practice. Thus, general supervision leads from detection of violations of the law to exposing this violation, then to instituting criminal prosecution and supervising investigation of the crime. If the investigation so warrants, the procurator presents the case to the appropriate court and prosecutes during the trial. The procurator then considers the sentence rendered by the court from the standpoint of its lawfulness and validity. If necessary, the procurator appeals the decision of the court. And finally, after the sentence comes into legal force, the procurator supervises its proper execution, particularly lawfulness of the treatment of the convicted person by the agencies executing sentences of deprivation of liberty.

Each of these main branches of Procurator's Office activities merits closer examination.

GENERAL SUPERVISION

This term is intended to mean the supervision of the procuracy over observance of laws in the field of state administration. The agencies of administration comprise, first, ministries and departments including institutions and boards subordinate to them, as well as executive-administrative bodies of local Soviets of People's Deputies, cooperatives, and other public organizations. The task of general supervision of the Procurator's Office is to secure observance of laws by such agencies, as well as by officials and citizens.

In order for the Procurator-General of the USSR and the procurators subordinate to him to expose and suppress violations of laws in the sphere of state administration, they are vested with the following powers:

1. to demand and obtain orders, instructions, decisions, rulings, and other acts issued by the ministries and departments, including institutions, enterprises, etc. subordinate to them, for the purpose of determining whether these documents are in conformity with the law;

2. to demand from the heads and from other individual officials of such agencies necessary documents and information;

3. to investigate, in response to complaints, reports and other information about violations of the law;

4. when warranted, to require that the heads and other officials of such agencies investigate and remedy any deficiencies in performance of subordinate institutions, enterprises, and organizations, as well as of subordinate officials;

5. to require officials and citizens to explain reported violations of laws (Art. 11 of the Regulations).

How does the procurator respond to the detected violations of laws? An illustration is provided by one actual case. One of the ministries of the Byelorussian Union issued an order dismissing Grigoriev, a worker in one of the research institutes subordinate to that ministry. Grigoriev was a member of a trade union, but there was no consent by the trade union to his dismissal. Following Grigoriev's complaint, the procurator brought to the minister a protest against his order, as the order was issued in violation of legislation requiring trade union consent. The protest of the procurator resulted in Grigoriev being restored to his rights and compensated for his forced absence from work.

Another example: The procurator of Chainsky district in the Tomsk area was informed that officials of the executive committee of the local Soviet violated legislation on consideration of citizens' complaints and reports. The chairman of the Soviet and the heads of the executive committee departments did not receive visitors, forwarded complaints to the very officials whose actions were objected to, delayed consideration of complaints, and so on. Upon this information, the procurator demanded that certain specific complaints be submitted to him by the executive committee. He then investigated how these complaints had been handled and demanded explanations from the officials concerning their behavior. After summarizing the results of this inquiry, the procurator presented the executive committee of Chainsky district with a demand for suppression of such violations.

Thus, the procurator's protests, objections, and proposals are the main way of responding to violations of laws in the sphere of state administration.

The procurator brings his protests directly to the agency responsible for the illegal act, or to the agency above it. The protest should be considered within ten days. The procurator who protested against the act shall be informed of the results of such consideration (Art. 13 of the Regulations).

The proposals for ending violations of laws and causes contributing to them must be considered and acted on within one month from their presentation (Art. 16 of the Regulations).

Citizens' complaints and reports are a very important source of information about violations of laws. Hence, the procurator ought to receive and to consider such reports and complaints, evaluate them properly, and take measures to restore violated rights of citizens and to protect their lawful interests (Art. 14 of the Regulations).

Exercising supervision over observance of legality, the procurator takes measures aimed not only at removal of law violations but also at prosecution of the guilty persons by way of administrative or disciplinary action, depending on the character of the violation. If the violation of the law, by virtue of its social danger, constitutes a criminal offense, the procurator initiates criminal prosecution.

SUPERVISION OVER CRIMINAL INVESTIGATIONS

The duty of investigating crimes and of finding and exposing the guilty is vested in the agencies of inquiry and preliminary investigation (*see* next section). All activities of these agencies are under constant supervision of the procurator because, should the actions of these agencies be wrong or illegal, they may bring irretrievable harm to the reputation, dignity, or freedom of a citizen. On the other hand, sluggishness or unwarranted leniency in respect of malicious criminals may result in equally grave injustice.

These factors determine the tasks of the procurator's supervision over crime investigation. The procurator is obliged:

1. to institute criminal prosecution of persons guilty of crimes, to take measures in order that not a single crime remains undetected and not a single criminal escapes responsibility;

2. to keep vigilant watch so that no citizen is illegally or without proper grounds subjected to criminal responsibility or to any other limitation of his rights;

3. to watch closely over strict observance of the rules of crime investigation by the agencies of inquiry and of preliminary investigation (Art. 17 of the Regulations).

Procurator's supervision is an important guarantee of observance of legality by the agencies of investigation. It should be emphasized that the procurator supervises investigations by guidance of the activity of the agencies of inquiry and of preliminary investigation. Unlike the supervision over the activity of the agencies of state administration (where the procurator has no administrative power and cannot remedy violations by himself), in the sphere of supervision over investigation the procurator plays the role of the organizer and director of crime combatting. That is why his competence is wider and has an administrative character. When revealing violations committed by an investigator or by an officer of the agency of inquiry, the procurator does not bring a proposal or protest, but rather removes this violation himself, using his own powers. This is the peculiar feature of the supervision of investigation.[30]

In accordance with Article 19 of the Regulations and Article 211 of the CPC the procurator has the right:

1. to give instructions to the agencies of inquiry and preliminary investigation about investigation of crimes concern-

---

30. V. M. Savitsky, An Essay on the Theory of Procurator's Supervision in Criminal Procedure 191-225 (1975; Moscow, "Nauka" Publ. House).

ing the choice, alteration, or disaffirmation of measures of preventive restriction in respect of suspected and accused persons, as well as concerning the conduct of concrete investigative actions and searches for escaped criminals;

2. to demand from the agencies of inquiry and from investigators reports on their activities;

3. to participate in the processes of inquiry and preliminary investigation and, when necessary, to take over investigation of any case;

4. to return reports on criminal cases to the agencies of inquiry and preliminary investigation together with written instructions on continuation of such investigations;

5. to cancel illegal and ungrounded rulings of the agency of inquiry and of the investigator;

6. to remove an investigator or other person carrying out an inquiry from any further investigation or inquiry activity where such persons have violated the law while investigating a case;

7. to withdraw any case from an agency of inquiry and to transfer it instead to an investigator, and also to transfer cases from one investigator to another in order to ensure a more comprehensive and objective investigation;

8. to entrust to agencies of inquiry responsibility for carrying out particular investigative actions and searches for criminals in connection with cases under investigation by the procurator's office;

9. to drop criminal cases on the grounds provided by the law.

As this enumeration shows, the powers of the procurator in the supervision over crime investigation are rather wide. His instructions on the case are binding upon the investigator, but this does not deprive the latter of his specific procedural independence (*see* Chapter II, Section 2).

Besides limits by the procurator on ongoing activities of the investigator, there are a number of investigative actions for commencement of which the investigator needs the procurator's sanction. Thus, during the investigation of a case, if there is no procurator's sanction, the agency of inquiry or the investigator cannot search a house or seize documents containing state secrets, nor impound or seize correspondence at postal and telegraph offices. In order to remove the accused from his post, the sanction of the procurator is also necessary. Only with the sanction of the procurator may the agencies of investigation drop a case and release an accused on bail, or transfer a case to a comrades' court (a non-criminal court competent to punish minor anti-social behavior), to a commission on juvenile affairs, or an administrative tribunal. Only the procurator has the right to prolong the term of inquiry and preliminary investigation. Finally, no criminal case in which inquiry or preliminary investigation has taken place can be brought to the court until the procurator has evaluated the investigation and its observance of all rules established by the law. After such evaluation, the procurator may then confirm the accusation and turn the case over to the court.

The Procurator and the Court

After confirming the accusation and presenting the case for trial, the procurator continues to carry out his function of supervision over observance of laws. Now his sphere of action embraces the sentence or other decisions of the court. But even before the sentence is passed, the procurator takes an active part in the trial. His participation starts at the preparatory stage. At this stage, the procurator gives his conclusions regarding any challenges to participants in the trial or on applications by the participants to call new witnesses, obtain new evidence, and so on. During the trials the procurator participates in interrogation of defendants, witnesses, and victims and in scrutinizing other evidence. The procurator has the right to initiate or to prosecute a civil suit initiated by a victim where this is required for the protection of state or public interests or the rights of citizens. During the trial, the procurator presents to the court his position concerning the guilt of the defendant and the measures of punishment appropriate. After sentence is passed, the procurator reviews its legality and validity.[31]

Should the procurator become convinced that the sentence is contrary to the law or that it is not adequately supported by evi-

31. V. M. Savitsky, State Accusation Before the Court (1971; Moscow, "Nauka" Publ. House).

dence at trial, it is his duty to protest this sentence to a higher court during the established period of time (in the Russian Union Republic, this term is seven days). A protest against a sentence that has not yet come into legal force is called a protest by way of cassation (or cassational protest). When the case is handled by a higher court, the procurator of the corresponding rank participates in the review process and gives his conclusion on the legality and validity of the sentence of the court of the first instance. The procurator also gives such conclusions in cases where the sentence is reviewed in response to complaints presented by way of cassation by other participants (the accused, the victim, etc.).

If illegality or invalidity of a sentence is discovered after the sentence comes into legal force, the procurator will protest it by way of supervision. The difference between the two protests lies in the fact that the protest by way of supervision may be brought not only against decisions of the court of first instance, but also against cassational rulings, sentences of the Supreme Court of the USSR and of the supreme courts of the union republics, which cannot be protested against by way of cassation. Procurators of all but the lowest rank (district or town procurators) have the right to bring protests in the areas of their competence. Decisions of any court may be protested, except rulings of the Plenum of the Supreme Court of USSR—the highest judicial authority. In a review based on a protest by way of supervision, the corresponding procurator must participate. He supports the protest he has brought or gives his conclusion if the protest has been brought by the chairman of the court.

Supervision over trial and review of criminal cases is not the only form of activity by the procurator in this sphere. Ensuring legality and validity of court decisions in civil suits is of equal importance. As with criminal procedure, the procurator must take timely measures provided by the law at every stage of civil procedure in order to eliminate violations of laws whatever their source (Art. 14 of Fundamentals of Civil Procedure of the USSR and the Union Republics).[32]

32. The Fundamentals of Civil Procedure were approved by the Supreme Soviet of the USSR on December 8, 1961; *see* GAZETTE OF THE SUPREME SOVIET OF THE USSR No. 50, Item 526 (1961).

SUPERVISION OVER EXECUTION OF JUDGMENTS

The judgment of the court takes legal effect upon the expiration of the period for cassation appeal or protest when there has been no such appeal or protest. Then comes the most important stage, its executing. In essence, only after the sentence is pronounced do the most complicated and labor-consuming activities begin, *i.e.*, the work on re-education and re-socialization of the criminal. The effectiveness of the entire program of combatting crime depends to a great extent on the way this work is done.

Again there is a major role for the procurator. "Supervision over the legality of the execution of judgment shall be exercised by the procurator," according to Article 53 of the CP Fundamentals, and this rule is translated into reality throughout the process. The procurator observes that the person sentenced to corrective labor is delivered at the appropriate time to serve the punishment, and that deductions from his earnings are made in accordance with the terms of his sentence. The procurator observes that a person upon whom a fine was imposed does not avoid paying it, etc.[33]

Particular attention is required of the procurator in his overseeing of sentences to deprivation of liberty. The greater social danger of the actions of convicts of this category makes it necessary to strictly enforce all rulings of the court, including the term of the sentence, the specified conditions for deprivation of liberty, and imposition of additional penalties (confiscation of property, for example). On the other hand, the convicts, for obvious reasons, have limited possibilities to protect their rights and lawful interests. That is why even the slightest deviation from the legally established rules for execution of sentences to deprivation of liberty (in prisons, in corrective labor colonies, in educational labor colonies for juveniles, in settlement colonies) is fraught with serious consequences.

Along with vesting the procurator with responsibility for legality observance in correctional institutions (Art. 32 of the Regulations), the legislature has conferred upon him powers for

33. G. E. BROVIN & V. T. MIKHAILOV, PROCURATOR'S SUPERVISION OVER OBSERVANCE OF LEGALITY IN EXECUTION OF JUDGMENTS (1977; Moscow, "Juriditcheskaya Literatura" Publ. House).

prevention, exposure, and removal of violations of the law. These include the right of the procurator to freely visit any time any correctional institution, to talk to convicts, to review orders and instructions of the administration, and to forbid the execution of illegal orders (Art. 35 of the Regulations).[34]

Section 3. INVESTIGATIVE AGENCIES

3.1. Initiation of Criminal Process

Before going to trial, a criminal case begins with an investigation conducted by legally empowered institutions and organizations. This is called a preliminary investigation.[35]

At this stage, necessary immediate steps, such as searches to detect the person who has committed a crime, to take evidence of it, and to prevent the escape of this person, are taken. In other words, it is the purpose of the preliminary investigation to create the conditions necessary for a speedy and sound trial of a case and a just sentence. The quality of judgments of the court and the successful functioning of the whole system of criminal justice depend to a considerable extent on the quality of the work of the preliminary investigation organs and institutions.

Preliminary investigations take two forms: the normal form of a preliminary investigation or the form of an inquiry. Correspondingly, there is some overlap in competence between the agencies of investigation.

The agencies and institutions of inquiry consist of—

1. agencies of militia;

2. the commanders of militia units, and the heads of military institutions, for crimes committed by servicemen on active duty or by reservists during their service at training camps; and for crimes committed by workers and employees in the system of the armed forces while fulfilling their official duties;

3. the agencies of state security for cases involving specified crimes;

---

34. Chapter VI, Section 1, will deal with this question in detail.

35. There are only a few categories of simple cases (such as insults, slander, slight signs of beating) that are examined by the court with no preliminary investigation. The prosecution is initiated directly in the court in such cases, upon the complaint of the victims. These cases, if necessary, may be sent for preliminary investigation on the instruction of the court or of the procurator.

4. the heads of penitentiary institutions, for cases involving crimes against the established order of the performance of duties committed by the employees of these institutions, as well as for cases involving other crimes committed within penitentiary institutions;

5. the agencies of state fire inspection for cases involving arson and violations of fire prevention rules;

6. the agencies of frontier guards for cases involving breaches of the state frontier;

7. the captains of ocean-going vessels, and heads of polar stations at periods when such stations are isolated (Art. 117 of the CPC).

The normal organ of inquiry is the militia agency.[36]

Inquiry is an activity that is secondary to the main activity of such agencies. Thus, for the agencies of militia, the inquiry is a function derived from the militia's main duty, the protection of social order. For the agencies of frontier guards, the inquiry function derives from their duty to safeguard the state frontiers. The typical and distinctive trait of inquiry is that it is always conducted in a concrete procedural form dictated by the norms of the law of the criminal process. The organs of inquiry are also charged with the duty of taking the incidental measures of search to detect the indicia of a crime and the persons who have committed it (Art. 29 of the CP Fundamentals). Such measures are procedural and are regulated by other laws and subordinate legislation. Any kind of activity of the organs of inquiry, whether procedural or not, is under the procurator's supervision.[37]

Procedural activity of the agencies of inquiry varies according to whether or not the case is one for which preliminary investigation is mandatory.[38] In the first case, the organs of inquiry ini-

---

36. Detailed description of structure, duties, and functions of the agencies of militia, including activity in the field of inquiry, is given in the monograph by the Minister of Internal Affairs of the USSR; *see* N. A. TCHELOKOV, SOVIET MILITIA (1971; Moscow, "Znanie" Publ. House).

37. *Issues on Procurator's Supervision*, COLLECTION OF SCIENTIFIC WORKS 170-180 (1972).

38. Such cases, involving crimes for which preliminary investigation is not necessary, are covered by Art. 126 of the CPC.

tiate a criminal case and carry out only urgent acts of investigation to establish and fix the traces of the crime (inspection, search, seizure, detention, etc.). That is to say, they are "hot on the scent." They then refer the case to another agency for carrying out the preliminary investigation.

Where preliminary investigation is not mandatory, the organs of inquiry carry out all the actions themselves, establishing all the facts of the crime committed and the author of it, and then submit the results of the inquiry to the procurator with whose approval the case is referred for trial (Art. 29 of the CP Fundamentals). The activity of the agencies of inquiry will be described in greater detail in Chapter II, Section 3.

3.2. The Preliminary Investigation

Preliminary investigation is conducted in the majority of criminal cases referred for trial. As a matter of fact, this includes all criminal cases except those listed in Article 126 of the CPC.

Preliminary investigation in criminal cases is conducted by (a) investigators of the Procurator's Office; (b) investigators of agencies of internal affairs; and (c) investigators of state security agencies (Art. 28 of the CP Fundamentals).

Thus, investigative machinery exists in three departments. In order to minimize duplication of effort, the competence of each department is strictly delimited by legislation (Art. 28 of the CP Fundamentals) with a view to making maximum use of the special experience and professional skills of the investigators working in each department. The different areas of competence is the only distinguishable feature among the activities of investigators of the three departments. In all other respects they are guided by common rules of investigation established by the CP Fundamentals and by the codes of criminal procedure of the union republic where they are acting, and they follow the same criminal legislation. Procedure in preliminary investigations does not depend on the type of crime involved or on which department conducts the investigation.

Section 4. THE MINISTRY OF JUSTICE

4.1. Organizational Framework

The present framework of the Ministry of Justice of the USSR is a product of gradual development. Until 1956 there existed a Ministry of Justice of the USSR plus ministries of union republics and their local subdivisions. In order to expand powers of union republics, it was recognized as expedient to abolish the Ministry of Justice of the USSR.[39] During the following seven years, the ministries of justice of union republics and their local subdivisions were abolished. Some of the functions of these organs were transferred to juridical commissions under the Council of Ministers of the USSR and councils of union republics. The function of direct guidance of judicial activity was assigned to higher courts: district and territory courts, supreme courts of union and autonomous republics, and the Supreme Court of the USSR.[40]

In order to improve the state leadership level of courts and other juridical institutions, to improve legal policy relating to the national economy, and to develop legislation for strengthening social legality, it was necessary to organize once again the Ministry of Justice of the USSR. This was done by the Decree of the Presidium of the Supreme Soviet of the USSR, August 31, 1970.[41]

Currently the system of organs of the Ministry of Justice has the following features: at the top of the system is the Ministry of Justice of the USSR, but each union and autonomous republic has its own ministry of justice which is subordinate both to the council of ministers of the given republic and to the Ministry of Justice of the USSR. There are departments of justice under executive committees of regional, territorial, and town Soviets of People's Deputies. These departments are also of double subordination: on one side they are subordinate to the executive

---

39. GAZETTE OF THE SUPREME SOVIET OF THE USSR No. 12, Item 250 (1956).
40. See V. P. BOZHJEV, T. N. DOBROVOLSKAYA, & I. D. PERLOV, ORGANIZATIONAL MANAGEMENT BY COURTS IN THE USSR (1966; Moscow, "Juriditcheskaya Literatura" Publ. House).
41. GAZETTE OF THE SUPREME SOVIET OF THE USSR No. 36, Item 361 (1970).

committee of the local Soviet, and on the other to a higher Ministry of Justice. The system of organs of the Ministry of Justice also comprises notary offices, research institutes and laboratories, educational and training institutes, and other institutions.

In accordance with the Constitution of the USSR, the Minister of Justice of the USSR is appointed by the Supreme Soviet of the USSR or, between sessions, by the Presidium of the Supreme Soviet of the USSR with the subsequent approval of the Supreme Soviet. Ministers of justice of union and autonomous republics are appointed by the Supreme Soviets of these republics. The most important problems are considered at sessions of the collegium of the ministry. The collegium consists of the minister, vice-ministers, and leading officials of the ministry.

The central machinery of the Ministry of Justice of the USSR consists of the following structural subdivisions: the department of courts; the department of military tribunals; the department of systematization of legislation and legal research; the department of law and economics; the personnel department; the department of law publicizing and legal education of the public; the bar department; the department of forensic expertise institutions; the department of notary and civil registrar's offices; the department of judicial statistics; and the department of foreign relations.

The structure of the ministries of justice of union and autonomous republics and of departments of justice under executive committees of local Soviets of People's Deputies follows the same general scheme with minor variations based on differences in the volume of their functions and their particular competences.

4.2. Responsibilities of the Ministry

The Statute of the Ministry of Justice of the USSR, approved by the Council of Ministers of the USSR on March 21, 1972,[42] prescribes the following functions of the ministry:

1. the strengthening of socialist legality, protection of rights and lawful interests of state, cooperative and public organizations, and citizens; improvement in cooperation with other state

---

42. COLLECTED DECREES OF THE USSR No. 6, at 3 (1972).

organs combatting criminal activities; and elimination of causes and conditions contributing to commission of crimes and other violations of the law.

2. maintaining and improving organizational efficiency of the courts; encouraging effective administration of justice in keeping with the principles of independence of judges and their being subject only to the law (discussed further below).

3. systematization and formulation of recommendations on codification of legislation, and providing assistance in further improvement of legislation currently in force. The Ministry of Justice of the USSR, on the instructions of the government of the USSR and on its own initiative, prepares proposals for legislative acts and decrees of the Council of Ministers of the USSR which have normative impact, and draws conclusions on the most significant normative acts submitted for consideration to the Council of Ministers of the USSR. The Ministry of Justice is also charged with compiling and issuing collections of laws of the USSR currently in force, as well as the Code of Laws of the USSR and the union republics.

4. improvement of the functioning of the notary, the offices of civil registrars, of the bar, of the agencies of forensic expertise, and of other agencies of justice. The Ministry of Justice organizes notary offices; guides their activities; makes recommendations on proper official registering of transactions, on protection of hereditary property, on certifying of copies of documents, etc. The Ministry of Justice also guides the activity of the offices of civil registrars, though these offices are departments of the executive committee of local Soviets of People's Deputies. Offices of civil registrars fulfill such important legal functions as registering births, deaths, marriages, divorces, adoptions, etc. Thus, supervision of their activity and improvement of the professional skills of personnel in these offices, with the help of training and educational institutions of the Ministry of Justice, is of paramount importance. The relationship of the Ministry to the bar is described in Section 5 of this chapter.

5. improvement of laws relating to the national economy in order to increase efficiency of public production, protect social-

ist property and strengthen state and labor discipline. In this connection, the Ministry of Justice is entrusted with implementation of the joint Decree of the Central Committee of the Communist party of the Soviet Union and of the Council of Ministers of the USSR of December 23, 1970, "On improvement of legal work in national economy."[43] For this purpose, the Ministry of Justice studies and analyzes the effectiveness of labor regulations in different ministries and agencies, at plants and enterprises, and in other organizations. It issues labor regulations that are binding on all ministries and agencies, takes measures for the improvement of professional skills of legal advisors; organizes conferences at which current needs for regulations to aid the national economy are discussed;[44] and publishes reference books and other legal literature.

6. organization of programs to publicize and explain the law to the population. The Ministry of Justice is the nationwide coordination center for this work. To publicize the law, the Ministry of Justice uses a variety of channels, including the All-Union Society on Dissemination of Political and Scientific Knowledge; legal publications and such popular scientific magazines as *The Man and the Law* (circulation of 3 million); radio; television; the activity of legal consulting centers organized on a voluntary basis directly at enterprises, construction sites, and collective farms; people's universities of knowledge of law, where people's assessors, members of comrades' courts, and people's patrolmen study; the courses on the fundamentals of Soviet law which are obligatory in the upper grades of secondary schools, and in specialized secondary and higher educational institutions. Ministry of Justice policy on publicizing the law is binding upon all ministries and agencies of the country.

7. furthering the development of legal science and its application in political, economic, and cultural progress. To perform this function, the Ministry of Justice organized various research programs on legislation development, on administration of jus-

---

43. COLLECTED DECREES OF THE USSR No. 1, at 1 (1971).

44. Information on one such conference appears in SOCIALIST LEGALITY No. 11, at 69-70 (1971).

tice, on forensic expertise, and other matters. Jointly with the Academy of Sciences of the USSR and other departments, the Ministry of Justice coordinates activity of research institutes and organizes scientific conferences,[45] symposia, and so on.

8. providing organs of the system of justice, including the courts, with highly skilled specialists and providing education and professional advanced training. For this purpose, the Ministry of Justice participates in development of state plans for education of jurists and distribution of newly graduated specialists. The Ministry also participates in developing curricula and programs on legal disciplines in institutes and universites, and in secondary schools.

4.3. Operations Related to the Courts

One of the main concerns of the Ministry of Justice and of its organs is organizational efficiency of the courts. On the whole, the orientation of this function may be described as creation of favorable conditions for proper administration of justice by the courts.

After the creation of the Ministry of Justice of the USSR, Article 38(1), "Organizational forms of courts management,"[46] was added to the Fundamentals of Legislation on the Judicial System. According to this article, the Ministry of Justice of the USSR exercises organizational management of supreme courts of union republics and lower courts, and also of military tribunals; ministries of justice of union republics exercise such management powers over supreme courts of autonomous republics, regional and territory courts, and courts of autonomous regions and areas; ministries of justice of autonomous republics and departments of justice under executive committees of re-

---

45. *See, for example,* Improvement of Organization and Strengthening of Preventive-Educational Impact of Trial Procedures (1974). Reports delivered at the All-Union Conference of Scientists and Practitioners are dealt with in this book. The conference was conducted under the auspices of the Ministry of Justice of the USSR, the Supreme Court of the USSR, and the Procurator's Office of the USSR.

46. The Decree of the Presidium of the Supreme Soviet of the USSR of August 12, 1971; *see* Gazette of the Supreme Soviet of the USSR No. 33, Item 332 (1971).

gional and territorial Soviets of People's Deputies manage regional People's Courts. Notably, the function of organizational management does not extend to the Supreme Court of the USSR.

Organizational forms of courts management relate not to the law of procedure but rather to administrative measures. Such management is carried out without application of procedural powers. It is not directly connected with the administration of justice in that it does not deal with concrete examination of concrete criminal and civil cases, but it bears a close relation to it. Article 38(1) of the Fundamentals of Judicial Legislation formulates concrete directions for exercise of the powers of organizational management of courts. The first task is to define the structure and staff of courts of all levels; then, to maintain accountability of judges and people's assessors before their electors; then, to plan and conduct elections of members of higher courts and of people's assessors to them and to military tribunals; and finally, to improve the professional skills of judges.

The organs of the Ministry of Justice also control the way the work of courts is organized. Such control usually covers planning of work, including scheduling sessions of judicial collegia, of court presidiums, and of plenums of the courts; questions of handling procedures for documents sent to lower courts; questions of reception of citizens; and questions of the timely and thorough consideration of citizens' complaints and statements. Without interfering with consideration of concrete cases, organs of the Ministry of Justice exercise control over the manner in which pretrial case materials are prepared and preparation for the trial proceedings themselves, particularly for visiting sessions of the court directly at the place of work of the defendant or the victim.

Section 5: THE BAR (COLLEGES OF ADVOCATES)

5.1. The Role of Advocates

As progress in the development of the Soviet national economy leads inevitably to more intricate economic, trade, and other relations and as efforts continue toward the strengthening of guarantees of lawful interests of citizens, enterprises, and institutions, there is a growing need for efficient legal regulation of all facets of state and social life. This need, in turn, results in the issuing of a great number of legislative and other normative acts. The more acts that are issued, the more complicated becomes the process of choosing and applying an appropriate act. Consequently, the role of that body of specialists devoted to rendering legal advice, the bar, assumes increasing importance. A direct reflection of this growing importance is the raising of the bar for the first time in Soviet legislation to the level of a constitutional agency (Art. 161 of the new Constitution of the USSR).

The Fundamentals of the USSR legislation on the judicial system lay down that

> for the purpose of administering the defense at trials as well as for the purpose of rendering legal advice to citizens, enterprises, institutions, and organizations, there exist colleges of advocates. Colleges of advocates are voluntary units of persons, engaged in lawyers' activities. They function on the basis of regulations approved by the Supreme Soviet of the Union Republic. (Art. 13)[47]

Legal representation is rendered by advocates in the following ways:

1. They give advice to citizens on different legal questions, interpreting and explaining to them different points of legislation.

2. They draw up complaints, applications, and other papers of legal character at the request of citizens, enterprises, institutions, organizations, or collective farms.

3. They represent citizens, enterprises, institutions, etc., at their request in the courts and arbitration agencies, protecting their lawful interests. This form of activity (as well as the previous one) has intensified in recent years as greater attention has been paid to legal grounds and regulations affecting the national economy. By contrast, advocates may render en-

---

47. Russian Federal Republic Regulations on the Colleges of Advocates were approved by the Supreme Soviet of the RSFSR on July 25, 1962; see GAZETTE OF THE SUPREME SOVIET OF THE RSFSR No. 29, Item 450 (1962).

terprises permanent assistance, becoming full-time legal advisers.

4. They participate in hearings of civil cases, such as labor, housing, and family dispute cases, as representatives of plaintiffs, respondents, or other persons participating in the trial.

5. They participate in criminal cases, from the stage of preliminary investigation through trial and judicial review of sentences by higher courts, as defense counsels of the accused, as representatives of victims, or for civil plaintiffs and respondents.

5.2. Colleges of Advocates

The principle of territorial subdivision is the basis of organizational structure of the bar. In the USSR there are republican (in the union and autonomous republics which have no administrative division), territorial, regional, and town (for Moscow and Leningrad) colleges of advocates which have a combined membership of about 18,000 lawyers.

Since the college of advocates is a public, self-governing organization, it manages its own activities. The highest authority of the college is the general meeting,[48] which is convened not less than once a year. The general meeting elects the presidium of the college and its revisional commission.[49] It considers and acts on reports on the presidium's activity and that of the revisional commission; passes resolutions on the work of the college; approves financial and staff proposals of the presidium; determines the numbers of personnel and estimates income and expenditures for the corresponding directory bodies; and considers other questions dealing with the activities of the college.

The presidium of the college is its executive and administrative body. The presidium and the revisional commission are elected by secret ballot (for a term of two years according to the Regulation on the RSFSR College of Advocates). The number

---

48. According to the Regulations on the College of Advocates of the RSFSR (Art. 15), conferences instead of general meetings may be held in subcolleges with more than 300 members.

49. The revisional commission controls financial and executive activities of the presidium of the colleges and of its consulting agencies.

of members of the presidium is defined by the general meeting on the basis of the number of lawyers in the collegium and the amount of work.

The presidium of the advocates college elects by open vote its president and secretary from among the members of the presidium. The members of the presidium are released from everyday duties of advocates and are paid by the college. Each member of the presidium has a specialization. Thus, for example, in the Moscow College of Advocates one of the Presidium members is responsible for work with young lawyers and probationers, another for control of legal fees, and a third for the work of different sections working under the Presidium.

The presidium convenes general meetings of the membership. The college of advocates considers applications for vacancies, organizes and supervises legal consulting agencies, appoints and removes the heads of legal consulting agencies, works to raise the ideological and political sensitivity and professional skills of advocates and monitors the quality of their work, collects and disseminates practical know-how, develops and publishes manuals, and organizes programs to publicize Soviet legislation.

The presidium also studies and compiles materials the college has at its disposal to determine the causes of criminal and other violations of the law and makes proposals to state and public organizations. It conducts conferences on practical issues, gives incentives to the most active lawyers, disposes of funds of the college according to estimates approved by the general meeting, and represents the college in state organs and in other organizations. The presidium considers failings of advocates and imposes disciplinary penalties.

All decisions of the presidium are made by majority vote. Any decisions contradictory to the legislation or regulations on the bar may be amended by the general meeting of the college. The state organ exercising guidance over the college has a right to ask the presidium to reconsider any such decision.

The main structural subdivision of the college of advocates is the legal consulting agency *(juridicheskaya konsuľtatzija)*, of which there are more than 3,500. All the members of a particular college (republican, regional, etc.) perform their professional functions (defense in the court, representation in arbitration, etc.) as members of the staff of a legal consulting agency.

Legal consulting agencies are organized by the presidium of the college of advocates in cooperation with executive committees of local Soviets of People's Deputies in districts and towns. A member of a college, however, has the full right to speak in the courts or to render other kinds of legal assistance outside the district of the legal consulting agency he works in.

Every such agency is headed by a director, appointed from among the most qualified lawyers. He organizes the whole work of the agency and distributes the duties among the lawyers in accordance with their professional skills. He exercises control over the quality of lawyers' work and over the observance of agency regulations. He also organizes and conducts meetings of lawyers and takes other measures aimed at improving their work.

The director of the consulting agency is paid for his supervisory work. If there are more than fifteen lawyers in his agency, he may be released from ordinary advocate's duties.

If necessary, the consulting agency can, with the help of its director, address inquiries to state and public organizations to obtain specific information, statistics, or documents necessary to render legal assistance.

The status of the college of advocates as that of a public self-governing organization is subject to state guidance and control over strict observance of the Regulations on the Bar. General guidance over the bar is exercised by the Ministry of Justice of the USSR, by the ministries of union and autonomous republics, by the departments of justice attached to executive committees of corresponding local Soviets of People's Deputies as provided by the legislation of the USSR and union republics (Art. 13 of the Fundamentals of Legislation of the USSR on the Judicial System).

5.3. The Law of Advocacy

The functions of an advocate may be performed only by members of a college of advocates. Any citizen of the USSR having higher legal education and who has worked in the legal profession not less than two years may become a member of a college of advocates. Persons graduating from higher juridical institutes and universities but having no work experience in the legal profession or having less than two years of such experience are admitted to a college only after having worked on probation at least six months. An exception may be made, with the permission of the council of ministers of an autonomous republic or the executive committee of a regional or territorial Soviet of People's Deputies, for persons having no higher juridical education but with practical work experience in the legal profession of not less than five years (in some republics, not less than three years). Persons having criminal records or persons whose moral or business qualities are not up to high standards cannot be admitted.

The admission of new members to the college of advocates is controlled by the presidium of the college. A member of the college has a right to leave at any time he wishes. Those lawyers who leave the college because of being elected to a post or to continue their education can be readmitted to the same college if they wish.

The advocate has a right to stand for election and vote for candidates to the directory bodies of the college, as well as to participate in discussion of all questions connected with the activities of the college. The law prohibits an advocate from being in the service of enterprises, institutions, or organizations, *i.e.*, hold two jobs simultaneously. However, this prohibition does not cover pedagogical or research activity.

An advocate must make use of all the ways and means indicated in the law for defense of the rights and lawful interests of citizens, enterprises, institutions, organizations, and collective farms taking his legal advice. However, he has no right to take the case if, in the investigation or consideration of it, an official who is a relative of the advocate is involved. The same applies where he has already been the adviser of a person whose interests are contrary to those of another client now asking for legal advice or if he has already participated in examination of the case as a judge, investigator, procurator, witness, expert, interpreter, etc.

An advocate must not reveal information confided to him by

his client. He cannot be interrogated as a witness on the circumstances of a case which he came to know by being a legal adviser or a defense counsel. Moreover, an advocate has no right to abandon the defense of an accused once he has accepted it (Art. 31-34 of the Regulations on the College of Advocates of the RSFSR).

Advocates' salaries are paid from funds the legal consulting agency obtains from citizens, enterprises, institutions, etc., for rendering legal advice. The fees for different types of advice are prescribed by the ministry of justice of the union republic.[50]

In some instances provided for by the USSR Constitution (Art. 161) legal advice to citizens is free. Examples are oral information and advice, legal advice on labor disputes and on cases of recovery of alimony, and cases involving work injuries. Advocates also draw up complaints, petitions, etc., for soldiers and invalids free of charge. Depending on the material status of the client, the presidium of the advocates college and the director of the legal consulting agency may waive fees for other kinds of legal advice.

Faultless work and untarnished conduct are among the demands made of attorneys by the law (Art. 30 of Regulations on the College of Advocates of the RSFSR). Violations of discipline and improper behavior undermine the authority of the college, so they are naturally involved in discipline. According to the Regulations on the College of Advocates of the RSFSR, disciplinary penalties include reprimands, censure, and strict censure.

Disciplinary violations of advocates are examined by the presidium of the college of advocates. After one of his colleagues, or a special commission formed for the purpose, has examined and analyzed the materials involved, the advocate involved has a right to question those judging him. He also has a right, when the work of the review commission is completed, to review for himself the materials and the findings of the commission.

Disciplinary cases proceed to an open hearing before the presidium, and the advocate whose behavior is questioned offers

---

50. In the RSFSR, for example, such an instruction of the Ministry of Justice was approved by the ruling of the Council of Ministers of the RSFSR on February 14, 1966; *see* COLLECTED DECREES OF THE RSFSR No. 3, at 22 (1966).

testimony on matter. In cases involving particularly serious violations incompatible with his further working in the college, the presidium will order expulsion.

Regulations on the College of Advocates of the RSFSR admit the possibility of expulsion from the advocates college for the following grounds:

1. demonstrated inability to perform the duties of an attorney;

2. systematic violations of the rules and regulations and careless work;

3. collecting additional fees for legal advice besides his pay from his legal office;

4. commission by the advocate of a crime.[51]

---

51. The questions of organization and functioning of colleges of advocates are treated in detail in several works; see, for example, Soviet College of Advocates (A. A. Kruglov ed. 1968; Moscow, "Juriditcheskaya Literatura" Publ. House); The Bar in the USSR (1971; Moscow, "Juriditcheskaya Literatura" Publ. House); and The Role and the Tasks of Soviet College of Advocates (A. Y. Sucharev ed. 1972; Moscow, "Juriditcheskaya Literatura" Publ. House).

CHAPTER II

CRIMINAL PROCEDURE

V. M. SAVITSKY

Section 1. GENERAL PROVISIONS

1.1. Fundamental Principles[1]

ONLY THE COURTS ADMINISTER JUSTICE

ARTICLE 151 OF THE NEW USSR Constitution states:

In the USSR justice is administered only by the courts.

In the USSR there are the following courts: the Supreme Court of the USSR, the supreme courts of union republics, the supreme courts of autonomous republics, territorial, regional and city courts, courts of autonomous regions, courts of autonomous areas, district (city) People's Courts, and military tribunals in the Armed Forces.

It should be noted that the formulation "Justice is administered only by the courts" was lacking in the Constitution of the USSR of 1936, though it did find expression in Article 7 of the CP Fundamentals. Another change is that the list of courts no longer includes any judicial agency comparable to the special courts mentioned in Article 102 of the Constitution of 1936, which could be created by special ruling of the Supreme Soviet of the USSR.

Thus, the new Constitution unconditionally secures to the courts the decisive role in the administration of Justice, and the exhaustive enumeration of kinds of courts exercising this power creates an additional guarantee of stability of the judicial system and safeguards its integrity. This serves the interests of so-

---

1. In the widest sense of the term, principles of criminal procedure embrace also principles relating to the judicial system (the election of judges and people's assessors, collegial hearing of all cases in all courts, participation of people's assessors, independence of judges and people's assessors and their subordination only to the law), as these principles produce significant effects on the functioning of the courts and the administration of justice as a whole. We shall consider here, however, only those principles which directly define the structure of criminal procedure.

45

ciety and of the individual by delineating the functions of different state agencies on the one hand and providing, on the other hand, that accusations against an individual may be handled only by the courts, in strict accordance with established democratic procedure.

EQUALITY OF ALL CITIZENS BEFORE THE LAW AND THE COURT

In the Soviet State no privileges are conferred upon any category of citizen regarding appearances in court, and there are no particular racial or ethnic courts. The social status of a citizen, his party membership, his previous service to the country, etc., do not give him any privileges before the court. An illustration of this principle is provided by a case when a member of the Communist Party had been reprimanded in accordance with penalties provided for by the Statute of the Communist Party of the Soviet Union (CPSU) for actions that were criminal in character, and this was the foundation for dropping criminal prosecution instituted against him. The Supreme Court of the Russian Federal Republic recognized such a decision to be wrong, and pointed out that imposition of party responsibility does not relieve a person of criminal responsibility.[2]

That all citizens are equal before the law and the court regardless of their social, property, or official status, nationality, race, or creed is one of the basic principles of the administration of justice in the USSR (Art. 156 of the USSR Constitution, Art. 8 of the CP Fundamentals).

THE PRINCIPLE OF PUBLIC DUTY

The court, the procurator, the investigator, and the agency of inquiry shall have the duty, within their areas of competence, to initiate a criminal case in every instance when indicia of a crime have been discovered, and to take all the measures provided for by the law to gather evidence, discover the identity of persons guilty of committing it, and punish them (Art. 3 of the CP Fun-

---

2. THE COLLECTION OF RULINGS OF THE PLENUM AND PRESIDIUM AND OF THE DECISIONS OF THE CRIMINAL COLLEGIUM OF THE SUPREME COURT OF THE RSFSR 1961-1963, at 316-318 (1964; Moscow, "Juridicheskaya Literatura" Publ. House).

damentals). This duty of state agencies to act *ex officio* is the principal moving force of criminal procedure, which provides for speedy and complete detection of crimes, conviction of guilty persons, and the assurance of correct application of the law, so that every person who has committed a crime shall be subjected to just punishment and no innocent person shall be charged with criminal responsibility or convicted (Art. 2 of the CP Fundamentals).

PRESUMPTION OF INNOCENCE

On September 18, 1973, the USSR ratified the International Convention on Civil and Political Rights approved by the United Nations General Assembly on December 16, 1966, thus binding itself to respect and observe the terms of that Convention, including the principle of presumption of innocence (Item 2, Art. 14).

Soviet criminal procedure legislation, in theory and in practice, strictly observes this principle, and its great significance for the protection of individual's rights and for establishing truth in the investigation and trial of criminal cases is apparent. The conceptual meaning of the presumption of innocence is that "the accused is considered to be innocent until his guilt is proved in the manner established by the law."[3] The reality of this position is reflected in a great number of specific legal prescriptions.

Thus, "no person may be prosecuted as an accused otherwise than on the grounds and in accordance with the procedure established by the law." (Art. 4 of the CP Fundamentals.) Prosecution as an accused is permitted only if there is sufficient evidence of guilt (Art. 143 of the CPC).

Article 14 of the CP Fundamentals is a very important element of the presumption of innocence. It says:

> The court, the procurator, the investigator, and the person conducting the inquiry shall have the duty to take all measures stipulated by the law for the comprehensive, thorough, and objective scrutiny of the circumstances of the case, and to bring to light equally the circumstances which convict and which exonerate the

---

3. I, M. S. STROGOVICH, TREATISE ON SOVIET CRIMINAL PROCEDURES 339 (1968; Moscow, "Nauka" Publ. House).

accused, and also those which aggravate and which mitigate his guilt.

The court, the procurator, the investigator, and the person conducting the inquiry shall not have the right to place the burden of proof on the accused.

It shall be prohibited to seek to obtain testimony from the accused through the use of force, threats, or any other illegal means.

Two points should be emphasized here. First, the prohibition of this procedural law is supported by a parallel substantive provision. Article 179 of the CPC provides a criminal penalty of deprivation of liberty for a term up to ten years for forcing an individual to testify. Secondly, the burden of proof of guilt is on the agencies of investigation and on the accuser. The court has no right to demand the accused to bring forth evidence of his innocence. If the accusation is not proved, the accused must be acquitted, regardless of whether he has presented evidence of his innocence. The Supreme Court of the USSR has especially called the attention of all courts to this circumstance. Cancelling one specific sentence, the Plenum of the Supreme Court of the USSR recognized as improper the statements of a court of the first instance saying that it was the duty of the accused to prove his version of the case, and agencies of investigation did not have to collect evidence supporting this version. In its ruling, the Plenum stated: "Such a statement is not based on the law. Moreover, it deeply contradicts basic principles of Soviet criminal procedure, according to which every accused person is considered to be innocent until his guilt is proved in the manner established by the law. According to the content and the spirit of Soviet law, it is not the accused who has to prove innocence, but rather the agencies of accusation must prove that the accusation is well grounded."[4] The impropriety of transferring to the accused the burden of proof *(onus probandi)* was also stressed by the Plenum of the Supreme Court of the USSR in its guiding instruction, "Strict observance of laws in judicial examination of criminal cases," issued on March 18, 1963.[5]

---

4. The Collection of Rulings of the Plenum and Decisions of the Collegiums of the Supreme Court of the USSR on Criminal Procedure Issues 1946-1962, at 46-47 (1964; Moscow, "Juriditcheskaya Literatura" Publ. House).

5. Collection of Rulings of the Plenum of the Supreme Court of the USSR, 1924-1973, at 280 (1974; Moscow, "Izvestija" Publ. House).

The laws regulating commitment of a case for trial also reflect the presumption of innocence. If the judge when examining the record of a case referred to him by the procurator comes to the conclusion that there are sufficient grounds for trying the case, he shall, without predetermining the question of guilt, issue a decree on the committal of the accused to trial (Art. 36 of the CP Fundamentals).

Article 43 of the CP Fundamentals features another important principle: "A judgment of conviction may not be founded on assumptions and shall be rendered only where, in the course of the trial, the accused's guilt has been proved." This means that the conclusion of the court may be based only on proved and proper evidence. Things which are not proved or which are doubtful are not to form the basis of a judgment of conviction, and this means nothing more than the rule of resolving doubts in favor of the accused (*in dubio pro reo*), originating from the presumption of innocence. Such a finding was formulated by the Plenum of the Supreme Court of the USSR in its guiding instruction, "On the court sentence," issued in June, 1969. It said: "The courts ought to proceed from the fact that judgments of conviction must be based on valid evidence when all the versions of the case are comprehensively examined, and all contradictions that arise are brought to light and analyzed. All doubts regarding the truth of the accusation (if it is not possible to remove them) are resolved in favor of the accused."[6]

The Plenum of the Supreme Court of the USSR has adopted a decision on "Practical Realization of the Laws Providing for the Right for Defense" (16.VI.78). The principal point affirmed by the Decision is: "The right of defense of the accused is a constitutional principle and is to be strictly observed at all stages of the criminal procedure as an important guarantee of the truth established by the pronouncement of a just and grounded judgement."

The Plenum, based on Art. 160 of the Constitution of the USSR, has established a perfectly adequate definition of the presumption of innocence. It requires all courts to: "strictly observe the constitutional principle according to which the accused is deemed

---

6. *Supra* at 582.

to be innocent until his guilt is proven in the [court] order provided for by the law and confirmed by the court's judgement which when entered has legal force [and effect]." The Decision describes all the practical consequences which derive from that definition of the presumption of innocence. It furthermore states that: "The law places the burden of proof on the accuser. So it is impossible to place the burden of proof on the accused. A conviction cannot be based on assumptions. All doubts that cannot be resolved should be interpreted in favor of the accused."*

Since the accused is deemed to be innocent he has the right to a defense, even after he is found guilty. This decision is especially important for the accused at the trial court level. (For details see ch. XVI§4)

PUBLIC CHARACTER OF THE JUDICIAL EXAMINATION

Article 157 of the USSR Constitution provides for proceedings in all courts to be open to the public. This means that at trial not only the participants but also spectators may be present. Only persons under the age of sixteen, if they are not the accused, victims, or witnesses in the case, are prohibited from attending trials (Art. 262 of the CPC).

The principle of open hearing of cases applies not only to courts of the first instance but also to judicial examination by way of cassation. As for the preliminary investigation, it is conducted under conditions of limited publicity, though the law (Art. 139 of the CPC) does not exclude the possibility of publicity for the preliminary investigation results. In some cases, public reports on the progress of an investigation are issued. Sometimes the public is informed about preliminary results such as in connection with the search for criminals or victims. Such information often aids the investigation. However, because of the presumption of innocence, it is prohibited to make statements on radio, press, or television defaming the accused.

The open character of the trial proceedings enhances the edu-

---

* BULLETIN OF THE SUPREME COURT OF THE USSR 9 (1978). *Also see* V. Savitsky, *Deemed to be Innocent* . . . , "LITERATURNAYA GAZETA" (November 1, 1978) and G. Elemissov, *Constitutional Principle of the Right for Defense of the Accused,* "SOTSIALISTICHESKAYA ZACONNOST" 15-1 (1978).

cational impact of the administration of justice and contributes to the developing of respect for laws and the feeling that it is necessary to observe them. That is why the Supreme Court of the USSR recommends conducting trials as often as possible on so-called visiting sessions of the court, directly at enterprises, in institutions, factories, etc. The ruling of the Plenum of the Supreme Court of the USSR of February 26, 1967 "On improvement of organization of trial procedures, on raising the level of culture and ethical aspects of their conduct and on intensifying the educational impact of judicial activities," says that

> the idea of visiting sessions is not simply to bring the participants to a site more convenient for gathering the most complete evidence. The effectiveness of visiting sessions arises first of all from their bringing cases of great contemporary significance and educational impact to the attention of a wide audience, for whom hearing of the case is very educational in the sense of prevention of such crimes or offenses as well as in the sense of removal of causes and conditions contributing to their occurrence.[7]

Openness of trial procedure is the general rule, but the law provides for some exceptions. For obvious reasons, the court has the right to hear a case *in camera*, that is with no public present, when it involves sex crimes, crimes committed by persons under sixteen years old, and also in some other cases for the purpose of preventing the spread of information concerning intimate aspects of the life of persons taking part in the case. Closed trials are also held in cases where an open hearing would be contrary to the interest of protecting state secrets. If matters relating to state secrets or intimate details of the lives of participants arise only during a limited portion of the trial, the public may be excluded only for that portion. It must be emphasized that in all cases judgments of the courts must be pronounced publicly (Art. 12 of the CP Fundamentals).

The USSR Constitution of 1936 provided that "Proceedings in all courts of the USSR are public, except instances stipulated by the law" (Art. 111). In the new Constitution, this principle

---

7. *Supra* note 5, at 59. During recent years, about 25 percent of all criminal cases were handled by the courts at their visiting sessions. The most important of them were broadcast by mass media.

is stated more precisely: "Proceedings in all courts shall be open to the public. Hearings *in camera* are allowed only in cases provided by law, with observance of all the rules of judicial procedure" (Art. 157). Thus, attention is focused on the necessary observance of procedural forms regardless of the character of the criminal case and the presence of the public in the courtroom.

The Language of Judicial Proceedings

The Soviet Union is a multinational state. There are more than 150 nationalities and ethnic groups living in its territory. Hence, judicial proceedings are conducted in the language of the union or autonomous republic, the autonomous region or territory, the national area, or the majority of the local population. Persons participating in the case who have no command of the language in which the proceedings are being conducted are permitted to make statements, give testimony, plead, and file petitions in their own language. The services of an interpreter are also provided to them so they can be fully acquainted with the materials in the case, participate in investigative and judicial procedures, etc. All investigative and judicial documents are provided to the accused in a translation to his mother tongue or to a language in which he is fluent (Art. 159 of the USSR Constitution, Art. 11 of the CP Fundamentals).

Conducting judicial proceedings in the language of the majority of the local population is necessary for realization of the principle of public trials. On the other hand, permitting the accused to use his own national language secures the accused's right to exercise fully his defense. The military collegium of the Supreme Court of the USSR in its judgment of September 26, 1970 held "If a preliminary investigation has been conducted in a language of which the accused is not in command, then familiarizing him with materials of the case with no assistance by an interpreter is cause for returning the case for additional investigation."[8]

Public Participation

The public and its representatives play a role of no small im-

---

8. Gazette of the Supreme Court of the USSR No. 1, Item 40 (1971).

portance in criminal procedure. Under the term "public" we mean mass public organizations (trade unions, the Young Communist League, sports unions, organizations of artists, writers, etc.), working peoples collectives at enterprises, in institutions, collective farms, territorial organizations of citizens at places of residence, etc.

1.2. The Use of Evidence

In the processes of investigation and trial of criminal cases, the investigator, the procurator, and the court must determine the existence or nonexistence of facts or circumstances on which the decision as to the accused's guilt or the measure of his punishment depend. Since all these facts refer to the past, neither the investigator, the procurator, nor the court may watch or perceive them directly, in their material shape. In criminal procedure these facts are established with the help of evidence theory.

Epistemologically, evidence theory is one of the variants of cognizability only by its specific object, and specific means, conditions, and limits. The aim of evidence theory is the objective truth, *i.e.*, such a content of conclusions on crime circumstances which adequately reflects objective reality existing beyond our consciousness. Until knowledge of judges, investigators, or procurators of the circumstances in the case is adequate to determine the truth, the object of evidence theory has not been accomplished.

The Soviet theory of criminal procedure rests upon the materialist doctrine of Marxism-Leninism and, with respect to evidence, that has important bearing on whether absolute or relative truth is its object. According to Marxist-Leninist doctrine, the content of the truth in criminal procedure does not depend on certainty as to a particular fact. Many complex circumstances with endless traits, relationships, and degrees are examined in every case. For dialectical materialism, there is no clear line between absolute and relative truth. Human thinking by its nature can bring and does bring us to absolute truth, which consists of the sum of relative truths. The truth in criminal procedure is relative, in the sense that its content is framed by the subject and by the limits of evidence, and does not exhaust the range of possible evaluation of all facts in all their details and relationships. At the same time, this truth contains the elements of absolute truth, as all the facts having significance for the case are cognizable in all the essential traits and in the most comprehensive way.

Under all conditions, the truth in criminal procedure is the objective one, which adequately though incompletely reflects reality. It is inadmissible to substitute for this truth approximate or probable opinions on the circumstances of the case. Only positive knowledge of the facts, knowledge that excludes any possibility of different interpretation, may serve as a basis for the verdict of guilty.[9]

Such certainty is reached with the help of evidence.

> Evidence in criminal cases shall be any facts on the strength of which the organs of inquiry, the investigator and the court may, in accordance with the procedure established by the law, determine the existence or nonexistence of a socially dangerous act, the guilt of the person who has committed the act, and any other circumstances of importance for the correct decision of the case.
>
> These facts shall be established: by the testimony of witnesses, the testimony of victims, the testimony of the suspected person, the testimony of the accused, the findings of an expert, material evidence, the records of investigative and judicial action, and other documents. (Art. 16 of the CP Fundamentals.)

Thus, the notion of evidence has two meanings. First, evidence means the facts on the strength of which the existence of crime and of guilt of specific persons are established. Second, evidence means the sources provided for by the law, from which the investigator and the court obtain information relating to the facts of importance to the case, and through which they establish these facts.

Both the investigator and the court must examine and assess evidence in accordance with these two meanings: First, is the source reliable? Second, if the source is reliable, is it possible to

---

9. *See* EVIDENCE THEORY IN SOVIET CRIMINAL PROCEDURE (1972; Moscow, "Juridicheskays Literatura" Publ. House) and M. S. STROGOVICH, *supra* note 3, at 308-332.

conclude on the strength of this fact that the accused is guilty?

These two meanings of evidence allow us to formulate rules of their relativity and admissibility. By *relativity of evidence* is meant the inherent quality of having an essential objective connection with any of the important facts in the case. Evidence is considered to be relative to the case if it bears on a factor essential to proving the case in question. In general outline, relevance is defined by the elements of the *corpus delicti* in respect of which criminal procedure has been initiated. The law establishes circumstances subject to proof in criminal cases as follows:

> In the conduct of the preliminary investigation and the trial of a criminal case in court the following shall be subject to proof:
>
> 1. the event of the crime (time, place, *modus operandi,* and other circumstances attending the commission of the crime);
>
> 2. the guilt of the accused in the commission of the crime;
>
> 3. circumstances affecting the degree and nature of the responsibility of the accused;
>
> 4. the nature and extent of the damage caused by the crime.
> (Art. 15 of the CP Fundamentals.)[10]

Admissibility of evidence relates to its meaning as the source of information about facts. The source of information depends on both its ultimate origin and its procedural form of derivation. These sources are exhaustively established by Article 16 of the CP Fundamentals and may not be narrowed or widened. Thus, only evidence obtained from these sources is admissible for use in criminal proceedings.

The rules of admissibility of evidence are mainly negative in character. They point out the sources which are inadmissible or inapplicable to establishing facts in the case.[11] Sometimes these rules have a positive character, prescribing the necessity for

---

10. Article 68 of the CPC adds one more point to the four enumerated above: "Circumstances contributing to the commission of a crime shall also be subject to proof."

11. For example, Article 72 of the CPC lists those persons who cannot give testimony as a witness: (1) legal adviser of the accused; (2) person with mental or physical defects due to which they are unable to perceive correctly circumstances having importance in the case and to give adequate testimony on them. In accordance with Article 94 of the CPC, facts testified to by a witness who cannot explain the source of his information may not be treated as evidence.

using only certain circumstances or only certain sources. Thus, according to Article 49 of the CPC, it is obligatory to obtain an expert's conclusion in order: (1) to establish the cause of death and nature of bodily injuries; (2) to define the state of mind of the accused or a suspect in instances where their culpability or their present capacity are an issue; (3) to define the physical or mental state of a witness or of a victim in instances when there are doubts regarding their ability to adequately perceive circumstances of importance to the case and to testify to them; and (4) to establish the age of the accused, a suspect, or the victim in instances when it is of importance for the case and the appropriate documents are missing. Hence, these circumstances cannot be proved by any means other than an expert's conclusion.

The classification of evidence is based on different distinctions. Based on the character of the source of information, types of evidences are divided into *personal and material evidence*. Personal evidence has as its source specific persons and the information they give in oral or written form. Material evidence is derived from material objects, and the information itself is not reproduced in linguistic form.

Evidence may also be classified as *primary or secondary* according to the correlation between the source of information about the fact and proof of the fact itself. This subdivision is of great significance because of the rule that the investigator and the court must base their conclusion on primary evidence.

As a rule, the persuasiveness of proof decreases the further it lies from the primary source of information about the facts of a crime. Secondary evidence, however, may be of significance as a means of obtaining primary evidence, as a means of verifying primary evidence, or as a substitute for primary evidence where primary evidence is irretrievably lost or inaccessible to the investigator and the court.

Evidence may also be classified, according to whether it establishes a main fact or is a fact tending to prove a main fact, as *direct or circumstantial*. Direct evidence establishes the main fact, commission by the accused of the crime he is prosecuted for, or his innocence. Circumstantial evidence establishes a fact which may make a main fact more or less likely to be true.

Thus, direct evidence immediately connects the accused with the crime. Circumstantial evidence connects the accused not with the crime itself, but with some other accessory fact which makes it possible to conclude that the crime was committed by the accused.

Direct evidence has no advantage over circumstantial evidence. The value of any evidence depends on specific situations and on the correlation of this evidence with other evidence. In order to find a person guilty, the totality of evidence must be considered. No single item of evidence, whether direct or circumstantial, can serve as a foundation for a verdict of guilt. This is a firm position of Soviet criminal procedure from which there are no exceptions.

Theory and practice of criminal procedure have evolved the following rules on the use of circumstantial evidence:

1. Every circumstantial fact must be proved with absolute certainty.

2. There must be an overall pattern of circumstantial evidence; isolated items of circumstantial evidence cannot be used for making conclusions in the case.

3. All circumstantial evidence must be consistent. It should represent a chain of circumstances, the links of which are tightly connected.

4. All the circumstantial evidence must bear a causal relationship to the main fact.

5. All the circumstantial evidence collected in the case must support in its totality only one possible conclusion: guilt or innocence of the accused. It must make impossible any other conclusions.

Only by observance of all these rules is circumstantial evidence allowed to establish the reality of the fact of a crime.[12]

Depending on the relation of evidence to the accusation, it may be classified as *accusatory or justifying*. Accusatory evi-

12. A. E. VINBERG, G. M. MINKOVSKY, & R. D. RACHUNOV, CIRCUMSTANTIAL EVIDENCE IN SOVIET CRIMINAL PROCEDURE (1956; Moscow, "Gosyurizadt" Publ. House).

dence is that which establishes facts of the *corpus delicti* or those aggravating the responsibility of the accused. Justifying evidence is that which, on the contrary, fully or partially disproves elements of the *corpus delicti* or point out the circumstances mitigating responsibility of the accused.

Although it is not always easy, especially at early stages, to determine the character of an item of evidence as accusatory or justifying, the practical significance of this classification is great. The law demands establishing, in every case, circumstances "both of accusatory and of justifying character," and to describe them in detail in corresponding procedural documents (Arts. 20, 205, and 314 of the CPC). The necessity of distinguishing between accusatory and justifying evidence in the court sentence has been stressed in a number of guiding instructions of the Plenum of the Supreme Court of the USSR.[13] This requirement makes it the duty of the investigator and of the court to analyze evidence comprehensively, which becomes a necessary condition for making preliminary investigation and trial thorough, valid, and objective.

THE STAGES OF THE PROCESS OF PROOF

This process of establishing and examining of facts with the help of evidence consists of specific activity relating to evidence.

The initial stage of proof is *detection of evidence*, the search for persons who knew about the crime committed, detection of traces of the crime, etc.

The next stage is *examination and procedural registration of evidence*. Every known witness should be interrogated and material evidence should be examined. Registration of evidence is carried out in the procedural form established by the law. All evidence should be critically examined. That is, the investigator and the court must be convinced of the correctness (or incorrectness) of the evidence. This is done by way of examination of the evidence itself, such as cross-examination of witnesses; by way of detection of new evidence strengthening or disproving this evidence; and finally, by way of comparison of this evidence with other evidence in the case.

---

13. THE COLLECTION OF RULINGS OF THE PLENUM OF THE SUPREME COURT OF THE USSR, 1924-1973, Item 582-583 (1974).

Assessment of evidence is the result of such critical examination and consists of recognition of the existence (or nonexistence) of a given fact. In other words, assessment means the conclusion as to whether the evidence is reliable.[14]

> The court, the procurator, the investigator, and the person conducting the inquiry shall assess the evidence in accordance with their inner convictions based on a comprehensive, thorough, and objective examination of all the circumstances of the case in the aggregate, being guided by the law and the socialist concept of justice.
>
> No evidence shall have predetermined value for the court, the procurator, the investigator, and the person conducting the inquiry. (Art. 17 of the CP Fundamentals.)

The proposition that judges must assess the evidence in accordance with their inner convictions means that judges recognize a particular item of evidence as reliable only to the extent that such evidence convinces them. No one, including the law, can compel judges, before they have assessed the evidence comprehensively, to give preference to one item over another.

Inner conviction, as the result of cognitive activity in criminal procedure, is the state of the mind of the investigator, the procurator, or the judge, when he is convinced of the existence or nonexistence of the facts of a crime or in the reliability or unreliability of a given conclusion. This state of the mind differs in principle from intuition, from guesses, and from other unaccountable feelings, because it is formed in the course of objective cognition of actual reality.

Inner convictions of judges are tightly connected with socialist legal consciousness under which is understood the totality of common views and attitudes of Soviet law, its aims and ends, and its principles. Though inner convictions are formed as a result of the examination of a specific case, they necessarily are formed in the light of legal consciousness, in the light of ideas on justice, legality, humanism, and so on.

---

14. The assessment of evidence should not be mechanically separated from testing its validity and is dependent on it. On the other hand, testing validity itself depends on the degree of conclusiveness of the evidence, *i.e.*, on the assessment. Hence, when distinguishing stages of proof we should remember that these stages are relative, that there is no clear border line between them.

Evidence is assessed by judges in its aggregate, though preliminary evaluation evidence occurs as each item is examined. However, when the conclusion is being formed, no single item of evidence may be considered by itself, separately from others. The Supreme Court of the USSR constantly emphasizes that all the materials of the case without exception must be assessed, that validity of specific evidence is determined by total assessment of all the circumstances of the case.[15]

1.3. Pretrial Disposition

After the investigator or official conducting the inquiry has officially presented an accusation against a person and has interrogated him, he has the right to apply to him one of several measures of preventive restriction.[16] In exceptional cases, a measure of preventive restriction may be applied to a person suspected of a crime even before the accusation is presented to him.

Measures of preventive restriction are the following: a written undertaking not to leave the place, personal surety or the surety of social organizations, bail, detention in custody, and other measures determined by the legislation of union republics. Juveniles may be placed under the supervision of their parents or other persons *in loco parentis.* For persons in active military service, supervision by the commanders of military units may be applied as a measure of preventive restriction (Art. 33 of the CP Fundamentals, Arts. 89 and 394 of the CPC).

Measures of preventive restriction are applied where there is reason to believe that the accused may go into hiding from investigation, destroy evidence, or engage in criminal activity. If there is no reason to so believe, then measures of preventive restriction may not be applied. In such a case, the accused pledges to come when summoned and to report any change in his place of residence. Such a pledge neither limits his freedom of movement nor infringes on his rights. If the accused violates his

---

15. GAZETTE OF THE SUPREME COURT OF THE USSR No. 2, Item 15, Item 29 (1968); GAZETTE OF THE SUPREME COURT OF THE USSR No. 6, Item 14 (1969); and GAZETTE OF THE SUPREME COURT OF THE USSR No. 2, Item 36 (1970).

16. The concept "measures of preventative restriction" used in legislation, theory, and practice represents "measures preventing the suspected person from avoiding investigation and trial."

pledge, a measure of preventive restriction is then applied to him.

The right to apply measures of preventive restriction is vested in the officials conducting the inquiry, the investigator, the procurator, and the court. The law establishes that, when there is a question as to which measure of preventive restriction to apply or whether to apply any restriction, account should be taken not only of fears of the risk of the accused's disappearing, etc., but also of the seriousness of the accusation against him, his personality, his profession, the state of his health, family status, and other circumstances (Art. 91 of the CPC). Only one measure of preventive restriction can be applied at one time. The choice of the measure is formally arranged by special resolution.

In practice, *a written undertaking not to leave the area* is the restraint used most often. It consists of an undertaking by the accused not to go away from the place of his residence without permission of the investigator, the procurator, or the court. The accused is warned that if he violates his written undertaking, a more strict measure of preventive restriction will be applied (Art. 93 of the CPC).

Personal surety requires that trustworthy persons vouch in written form for proper behavior of the accused and for his coming to the investigator or to the court when summoned. There must be at least two such guarantors. A guarantor must be informed about the character of the case and be warned that in the event of improper behavior of the accused or his not coming to the investigator or to the court when summoned, a fine up to one hundred rubles may be assessed against each of the guarantors or a measure of social censure may be applied to them (Art. 94 of the CPC).

The surety of social organizations are obligations of such organizations to secure proper behavior of the accused and his coming to the investigator or to the court when he is summoned. This obligation must be approved by the general meeting of the members of the social organization or working collective (Art. 95 of the CPC).

Bail consists of depositing a sum of money at the state bank by the accused or another person or organization in order to secure the coming of the accused to the investigator or to the court when summoned. Bail may be applied as a measure of preventive restriction only if it is sanctioned by the procurator or by the court. The amount of bail is defined by the agency that chose this measure after considering the circumstances of the case. If the accused violates the restriction and does not come to the investigator or to the court, the bail is forfeited (Art. 99 of the CPC).

For juveniles, besides the measures mentioned above, placing them *under the supervision* of parents, of guardians, or of trustees may be applied. Juveniles who are living in special educational institutions may be put under the supervision of the administration of these institutions. Such a measure consists of a written undertaking to secure proper behavior and the attendance of the juvenile when he is summoned. Persons undertaking such an obligation are warned about the character of the crime the juvenile is accused of and about their responsibility in case the obligation is violated. The character of responsibility in this case will be the same as in case of personal surety (Art. 394 of the CPC).

The most strict measure of preventive restriction is *detention in custody*. It is applied when other measures cannot secure observance by the accused of his duties (1) to come when summoned to the investigator or to the court, (2) not to create obstacles to the investigation, or (3) not to continue criminal activities. For persons accused of the most serious crimes, enumerated by Article 96 of the CPC, detention in custody may be applied on the sole basis of social danger of the crime. On the other hand, detention of juveniles is permitted only in exceptional cases (Art. 393 of the CPC).

Conditions of preventive detention are governed by the Decree of the Presidium of the Supreme Soviet of the USSR of February 8, 1977.[17] Before this decree, preventive detention was permitted for persons accused of any crime for which the law provides a punishment of deprivation of liberty, but now detention is permitted only where the crime involved has a potential

---

17. Gazette of the Supreme Soviet of the USSR No. 7, Item 120 (1977).

sentence of deprivation of liberty of more than one year. Also, preventive detention was previously specifically authorized for persons accused of committing hooliganistic acts of even comparatively small social danger. This special provision is now abolished.

A person may be subjected to arrest only pursuant to a decree of the court or a warrant issued by the official conducing the inquiry or by the investigator, sanctioned by the procurator (Art. 54 of the USSR Constitution, Art. 6 of the CP Fundamentals). Neither the investigator, the official conducting the inquiry, nor the judge have the right independently to apply this measure of preventive restriction.

Section 2. PARTICIPANTS AT THE TRIAL

2.1. The Court

The central figure in criminal procedure is the court, which controls the result of a trial of a criminal case. Justice in criminal cases may be administered only by the court, and no person may be deemed guilty of a crime or be subjected to punishment except by a judgment of the court in conformity with the law (Art. 160, Constitution of the USSR). Other participants in the trial have the right to file various petitions to the court, express their opinions, present evidence and so on, but only the court can make any judgment on the case.

The court is under a duty to develop a complete, unbiased, and objective record of the circumstances of the case in order to establish the truth. The court is not limited to the information received from agencies of investigation of criminal cases, nor to the evidence presented by the procurator, accused, civil defendant, victim, or other participants of the case. If necessary, the court itself may and must request and consider further evidence. Judges and people's assessors are never bound by an opinion of the participants in the trial. They directly examine and assess all evidence and pronounce a judgment based on the law and in conformity with their own inner convictions. The court may not prefer one of the parties before hearing and considering all the evidence.

The composition of the court in a criminal case is one judge and two people's assessors. The hearing of criminal cases in all courts is collegial. That is, in the administration of justice, people's assessors have all the rights of a judge, and decisions are by majority vote (Art. 168 of the Constitution of the USSR). The judge presides at hearings, directing them so as to bring in evidence necessary to the establishment of the truth and to eliminate irrelevancies, and he maintains order in the courtroom, thus providing the court hearing with an informative character (Art. 23 of the CPC).

Only the legal members of the court may make judgments, meaning that (1) each judge and people's assessor may participate in the activities of that court to which they have been elected, and no other; and (2) only disinterested judges and people's assessors may try a case.

To provide for an objective examination of the case, the law forbids a person to sit as a judge or a people's assessor on a court if, in the case to be tried, any of them is a victim, a civil plaintiff, a civil respondent or their representative, or has ever taken part in the case as a witness, expert, specialist, interpreter, person who conducted inquiry, investigator, accuser, or legal counsel, or is related to any such person.

If there are circumstances that create doubt whether a judge or a people's assessor is disinterested, he may be challenged. This explains why a judge who takes part in trial of the court of the first instance does not participate in the hearing of the case by way of cassation, or as a judicial supervisor. He may not participate in a new hearing of the case in a court of the first instance where the prior judgment has been vacated or reversed. The same rules apply to judges who examine cases in a court of the second instance or as a judicial supervisor. They may not participate in a new hearing of the case in any other court (Art. 60 of the CPC).[18]

2.2. The Procurator

It shall be the duty of the procurator, at every stage of the

18. *See, e.g.,* Rudenko (Plenum Sup. Ct. U.S.S.R. 1967), in BULLETIN OF THE SUPREME COURT OF THE USSR No. 2, Items 34-36 (1973).

criminal proceedings, promptly to take all measures provided for by the law to eliminate any breaches of the law, regardless of their source (Art. 20 of the CP Fundamentals). This general function is fulfilled by different methods depending on the stage of the procedure. At the stage of investigation of a crime, the procurator initiates a criminal case, then directs and coordinates activities of the agencies of inquiry and preliminary investigation. He is entitled to give directions to these agencies concerning particular investigations or particular investigatory activities, to overrule illegal and ungrounded decisions, or to remove the investigator or person conducting inquiry from the case. Only with the procurator's sanction may a person be arrested or dismissed from his job. Only a procurator may authorize searches of homes or interception of mail and telegrams. Thus, the procurator possesses considerable authority over investigation agencies, which allows him to correct errors in their activities immediately.

When a case goes to trial, the procurator's responsibilities change. He may no longer give instructions to anyone, being, like all other participants, subject to the court proceedings. The procurator continues to supervise law observance, acting as the state prosecutor. He supports the accusation based on his conviction that the accused has committed a crime. Where, as a result of the trial, the procurator becomes convinced that the record does not support the accusation, it is his duty to withdraw the accusation and to explain to the court his reason for so doing (Art. 40 of the CP Fundamentals).

The procurator's legal duty extends to ensuring that the other participants at trial observe the law, regardless of who failed to observe the law or whose rights were infringed. If, for example, counsel puts suggestive questions to the accused, the procurator should draw the court's attention to the counsel's improper behaviour and ask the court to stop such violations of the law. If the court itself allows such violations, the procurator includes his objections in the minutes of the hearing, and upon completion of the trial submits a protest to the higher court.

It should be emphasized that the procurator's position as a supervisor of legality does not give him any advantage in proving his case, or refuting his opponents' arguments. All participants in the trial, including the procurator, enjoy equal rights in presenting evidence, participating in scrutiny of the evidence, and in filing petitions (Art. 38 of CP Fundamentals).

2.3. The Investigator

Preliminary investigations of criminal cases are conducted by investigators of the Procurator's Office and of agencies of the Ministry of the Interior and state security agencies, operating within their spheres of competence. All investigators, regardless of their department, work under the procurator's supervision.

However, the procurator's supervision does not deprive the investigator of independence and initiative. All decisions concerning conduct of an investigation are made by the investigator independently, except when a procurator's approval is required. Investigators' decisions on a criminal case must be respected by all institutions, enterprises, organizations, officials, and citizens.

The investigator is independent in making the most important decisions in an investigation: who is responsible; what crime has been committed, and whether or not the case should be referred to a court. All questions connected with assessment of evidence are decided by the investigator according to his inner convictions. In the event the investigator disagrees with instructions from the procurator on such matters, he has the right to take the dispute to the higher procurator, with a written statement of his objections (Art. 30 of CP Fundamentals). The procurator shall then either countermand the instructions of the lower procurator or assign a new investigator to the case.

The investigator has the right to give assignments and instructions to the agencies of inquiry concerning the conduct of searches and other investigatory acts. Such assignments and instructions of the investigator are binding upon agencies of inquiry (Art. 30 of CP Fundamentals).

If causes and conditions contributing to the commission of the crime are established during a preliminary investigation, the investigator proposes to the enterprises, institutions, and organizations involved steps to be taken to eliminate such causes and conditions. The proposal must be examined within a month and the investigator should be advised about the measures taken (Art. 140 of the CPC).

An investigator may be removed for the same grounds as a judge except that his participation in the preliminary investigation of the case is not a ground for such a discharge (Art. 64 of the CPC).

A person conducting an inquiry is an administrative worker, most frequently for the militia, who by virtue of Article 118 of the CPC has responsibility for primary search and investigation activities in the case. For most crimes, subsequent functions are then transferred to an investigator, but some categories of simple cases may be completed without such transfer. A person conducting an inquiry is subject to a procurator's supervision, and unlike an investigator, he is obliged to follow all of the procurator's instructions without exception. Should the person conducting the inquiry disagree with the procurator's instructions, he may submit a statement to the procurator's superior but must in the meantime obey them (Art. 120 of the CPC).

2.4. The Accused

The accused is that person in reference to whom evidence is collected which gives a foundation to accuse him of committing a crime and against whom a formal accusation has been filed, constituting a decision to prosecute him in court.

An accused person is presumed innocent until his guilt is established by a court sentence that has come into legal force. Soviet legislation not only provides that an accused has a right to legal assistance (Art. 158 of the USSR Constitution) but also provides for a whole system of measures through which the accused may practice this right.

First, the investigator, procurator, and the court are required to assure the accused an opportunity to defend himself by means and methods established by the law (Art. 13 of CP Fundamentals). This duty of the officials serves as a substantial guarantee to the accused of all of his subsidiary rights, which together constitute the constitutional right of defense.

The accused has the right to know the charges against him and to respond to them. This right is ensured by requiring the investigator to present a statement to the accused upon prosecution of him containing all the established circumstances of the crime as well as the accusation itself (Art. 144-149 of the CPC).

If an investigator fails to fulfill his duty, there may be serious consequences. For instance, in one case, Karekashiants and two other persons were convicted for an assault with intention to commit murder and robbery. The Supreme Court of the USSR examined the case and established that, in the statement of the prosecution of the accused, the participation of each person had not been clearly defined; it found that this had hampered the right of the accused to defense and cancelled the sentence.[19]

After the accused becomes acquainted with the accusation, he may present evidence. It should be stressed that the accused has the right to present evidence but is not obliged to do so. Any attempt to coerce an accused to present evidence by means of force, threat, or other such measures is prohibited (Art. 20 of CPC) and violators face strict penalties (in especially grave cases, up to ten years of deprivation of liberty; Art. 179 of CPC).

The accused also has the right to enter petitions on such matters as interrogation of witnesses or designation of an expert witness. The accused may file a complaint in response to refusal of any petition, or regarding any other actions or decisions of the investigator, procurator, or court, with a higher court or higher ranking procurator (Art. 22 of the CPC).

If the accused thinks that the investigator, procurator, or one of the judges is not objective or has a personal interest in the case, he may challenge him.

Upon completion of the preliminary investigation, the accused may have access to all the materials of the case and participate personally at the court hearing. He has the right to the last word in the trial (Art. 21 of CP Fundamentals and Art. 46 of CPC).

If the accused believes that the court has convicted him wrongly, he may appeal the judgment by way of cassation to a

---

19. GAZETTE OF THE SUPREME COURT OF THE USSR No. 2, Items 34-36 (1973).

superior court. The law guarantees that, in examining a case by way of cassation, the court may mitigate the punishment assigned by the court of first instance or reduce the charge but shall not have the right to increase the punishment or increase the charge. The same is true when a court of first instance examines the case after the original judgment has been vacated pursuant to a complaint by counsel for the accused. Increased punishment is possible only in cases when, during the new trial, evidence is introduced that shows the accused has committed a graver crime (Arts. 43 and 53 of CP Fundamentals).

Procedurally, the position of an accused is similar to that of a suspect, that is, the person is suspected of committing a crime and consequently is either detained or subject to some other measure of preventive restriction (Art. 52 of the CPC). However, the suspect differs from the accused in that the evidence collected so far cannot serve as a ground for an accusation but does establish that he is socially dangerous and justifies immediate application to him of preventive restriction.

The agency of inquiry or the investigator has the right to detain a person suspected of committing a crime for which the punishment includes deprivation of liberty, provided one of the following grounds also exists:

1. such a person has been caught committing the crime or immediately after its commission;

2. eye-witnesses, including the victims, have directly identified the person as having committed the crime;

3. clear traces of the crime have been discovered on the suspected person, on his clothing, in his possession, or in his dwelling;

4. the suspect has attempted to escape, he has no permanent place of residence, or his identity has not been established.

The agency of inquiry or the investigator must make a record of every instance of detention of a suspect, stating the grounds on which he has been detained and must notify the procurator within twenty-four hours. It is the duty of the procurator to approve the detention or to order release of the detained person within forty-eight hours of receiving notification of his detention (Art. 32 of CP Fundamentals, Arts. 2-4 of the Provision for Short Term Detention of Persons Suspected of Committing Crime).[20] Thus, the suspect may be kept in custody without a procurator's approval for up to three days.

As a rule, measures of preventive restriction are applied only to an accused, but in exceptional cases, they may be applied before an accusation has been made. In such instances, the accusation must be presented within ten days from the moment the measure of preventive restriction is applied. If the accusation has not been presented within this period, the measures of preventive restriction are revoked (Art. 33 of CP Fundamentals).

A suspect has the right to know of what he is suspected and to give his own explanations, to present evidence, to enter petitions and make challenges, and to file complaints regarding the actions and decisions of the person conducting inquiry (investigator or procurator). A suspect must be interrogated instantly or at least within twenty-four hours of the start of his detention or being subjected to a measure of preventive restriction (Arts. 52 and 123 of CPC).

2.5. The Defense Counsel

The right of the accused to conduct a defense includes his right to assistance of a defense counsel. The law defines the defense counsel's role in criminal procedure in the following way: "It shall be the duty of the defense counsel to make use of all legal means to bring to light circumstances exonerating the accused or mitigating his responsibility, and to render to the accused all necessary legal aid" (Art. 23 of CP Fundamentals).

Advocates and representatives of trade unions and other mass organizations may act as defense counsels. With the permission of the court or of a judge, close relatives and their legal representatives, as well as other persons, may be allowed to act as defense counsels (Art. 47 of CPC). In practice, the great majority of defense counsels are advocates. A defense counsel may not be interrogated as a witness of those circumstances of the case

---

20. This provision was adopted by Decree of the Supreme Soviet of the USSR of July 13, 1976. See GAZETTE OF THE SUPREME COURT OF THE USSR No. 20, Item 426 (1976).

which he learned while fulfilling his functions as a defense counsel (Art. 72 of CPC).

A defense counsel is chosen and invited by the accused himself or other people *per procurationem*. If the accused has expressed a wish to have a defense counsel but could not for some reason contact one himself, the participation of a defense counsel is accomplished by the investigator or the court contacting the collegium of advocates (Art. 48 of CPC). The request of the accused to have a defense counsel assigned to him must be honored, since otherwise the judgment would be vacated because of an infringement of the accused's right of defense.

The participation of a defense counsel is also mandatory—

1. if a state or social accuser takes part in the case;
2. if the accused, due to physical or mental deficiencies, cannot exercise his right of defense himself;
3. if the accused is a minor;
4. if the accused does not know the language in which the proceedings are conducted;
5. if the accused has committed a crime for which the death penalty may be imposed;
6. if the accused persons have contradicting interests and one of them already has a defense counsel.

In all these cases the defense counsel must participate in the trial, and in the last four instances, in the preliminary investigation as well.

The role of the defense counsel was limited to participation at trial until December 25, 1958, when the CP Fundamentals were adopted based on the necessity of a further democratization of Soviet criminal procedure, widening considerably the right of the accused for a defense, granting him the right to have a defense counsel in the preliminary investigation as well as in the court. The defense counsel now is allowed to participate in the case from the moment the accused has been informed of the completion of the preliminary investigation and has been handed a record of the proceedings in the case.

Further alterations of the CP Fundamentals[21] have brought a further expansion of the right of the accused to defense so

---

21. GAZETTE OF THE SUPREME SOVIET OF THE USSR No. 36, Item 425 (1970).

that now the defense counsel may participate in any criminal case from the moment an accusation is presented if the procurator consents.

The defense counsel has the right to meet with the accused in private as often and for as long as necessary, to have access to all the materials of the case and to make copies as necessary, to present evidence, to enter petitions, to make challenges, to participate at trial, and to file complaints against the actions and decisions of the investigator, the procurator, and the court. Moreover, with the permission of the investigator, the defense counsel may be present when the accused is questioned and when investigative actions in response to petitions of the accused or his defense counsel are undertaken. In cases where the defense counsel has the right to participate in the case from the moment of the accusation, he may be present at the presentation of the accusation and the questioning of the accused as well as at the conduct of other acts of investigation, and with the investigator's permission put questions to the accused, witnesses, the victim, and experts. The investigator, however, has the right to revoke the defense counsel's questions (Art. 2(e) of CP Fundamentals, Art. 12 of Provision for Preliminary Taking into Custody, Art. 51 of CPC).

Any infringement of the right to defense of the accused constitutes grounds to vacate a judgment against him. For example, one Zhitnov, who was accused of rape, stated at trial that he refused legal assistance from the attorney Ganushchak because she was unfamiliar with the facts of the case and did not agree with him, yet the court continued the trial and convicted him; upon review of the case by the protest of the Deputy Chairman of the Supreme Court of the USSR, it was noted that the court of first instance had failed to explore the causes of his refusal of defense counsel and had not specified whether Zhitnov had persisted in his wish to change counsel or chosen to defend himself. The Supreme Court of the USSR found that this constituted an infringement of the right to defense of the accused and vacated the judgment.[22]

---

22. BULLETIN OF THE SUPREME COURT OF THE USSR No. 4, at 23-24 (1974).

Although an advocate has no right to abandon the defense of an accused once he has accepted it, the accused on his own initiative has the right to challenge his legal counsel at any state of the procedure. This is true in all cases, including those where the defense counsel's participation is mandatory. The only exception is in cases involving minors and others incapable of conducting their own defense, including those who do not know the language in which the proceedings are conducted. A refusal of defense counsel by the accused in such cases is not binding upon the investigator, procurator, or court (Art. 50 of CPC).[23]

2.6. The Social Accuser and Social Defender

At the end of the 1950s when the Communist Party of the USSR took decisive measures aimed at ending violations of the law which had taken place previously, renewing legislation and democratizing social and state life, the influence of mass organizations of working people and collectives of workers and employees and their representatives increased considerably. In the sphere of the administration of justice, this trend is manifested in the existence and growing importance of the institution of social accusers and social defenders.[24] This institution is provided for by Article 15 of LJS Fundamentals and Article 41 of the CP Fundamentals, as well as in the new Constitution of the USSR: "Representatives of public organizations and of work collectives may take part in civil and criminal proceedings" (Art. 162).

Depending on its attitude towards the crime involved and the accused's personality, a social organization selects a social accuser or a social defender to participate in the trial. The question of whether an accuser or a defender is to be named is decided by the general assembly of the organization or by its elected execu-

---

23. For details on the procedural role and activities of the defense counsel, *see* G. P. SARKISSIANTS, THE DEFENSE COUNSEL IN CRIMINAL PROCEDURE (1971; Tashkent); A. D. BOIKOV, DEFENSE COUNSEL'S ROLE IN CRIME PREVENTION (1971; Moscow, "Juriditcheskaya Literatura" Publ. House); and Y. I. STETSOVSKI, ADVOCATE IN CRIMINAL PROCEDURE (1972; Moscow, "Juriditcheskaya Literatura" Publ. House).

24. P. P. JAKIMOV, JUSTICE AND THE PUBLIC (1977; Sverdlovsk).

tive body on the basis of information supplied by the investigator or procurator who conducted the investigation of the case. Leaders of labor collectives or representatives of social organizations have the right to preliminary information regarding accusations. The procedure for nomination of social accusers and social defenders, as well as their responsibilities, should be explained to such leaders or representatives.[25]

Social representatives often speak to the courts. Lately, social accusers have taken part in the trial of about 9 percent of all criminal cases and social defenders in about 5 percent. Data of selected studies have shown that in a majority of criminal cases (51 percent of the cases tried with the participation of social accusers and 73.2 percent of those with social defenders) their viewpoint on the question of culpability of the accused and the proper measure of punishment, as expressed in the court record, has been adopted by the court in its judgment.[26] It is clear, therefore, that social representatives render a substantial assistance to the court in its administration of justice.

2.7. The Victim of the Crime

A person to whom moral, physical, or material injury has been inflicted in the commission of a crime is a victim. Protection of rights and lawful interests of the victim is one of the most important functions of the procurator and of the court, dictated by the necessity to take prompt measures directed to redressing the legal rights of the victim, since "Respect for the individual and protection of the rights and freedoms of citizens are the duty of all state bodies, public organizations and officials" (Art. 57 of the Constitution of the USSR).

The victim had very limited rights before the CP Fundamentals were adopted in 1958, and his procedural position did not differ substantially from that of a witness during the investigation and trial. The law now makes the victim an active partici-

---

25. Decision of the Plenum of the Supreme Court of the USSR of December 3, 1976 on "Further Improvements of Judicial Activities in Crime Prevention," in BULLETIN OF THE SUPREME COURT OF THE USSR No. 1, at 14-15 (1977).

26. E. N. LEVAKOVA, SOCIAL ACCUSATION AND DEFENSE 7-8 (1976; Moscow, "Juridicheskaya Literatura" Publ. House).

pant in the criminal procedure, with opportunities to protect his rights and interests which were infringed by the crime. Evolution of the procedural position of the victim is a natural result of the development and improvement of the democratic fundamentals of justice in the USSR.

A victim has the right to give testimony on the case, to present evidence, to enter petitions, to make challenges, to have access to the material of the case from the moment of completion of the preliminary investigation, and to file complaints against actions of the person conducting the inquiry, the investigator, the procurator, and the court, as well as against the judgment or rulings of the court and decrees of the people's judge, to maintain the accusation at trials of certain cases, and to have his representative at the inquiry, preliminary investigation, and trial.

The victim enjoys equal rights with other participants in the trial, in presenting evidence, participating in the scrutiny of the evidence, and filing petitions. A person who has suffered material loss from a crime has the right to bring a civil suit against the accused. In cases of crimes which result in the death of the victim, the above-mentioned rights are acquired by the close relatives of the deceased (Arts. 24 and 38 of CP Fundamentals, Art. 53 of CPC).

Legislation of some union republics provides for the right of the victim to participate, with permission of the investigator, in the conduct of some investigative actions. Thus the victim may participate in an investigative experiment (Art. 183 CPC), survey (Art. 191 of Criminal Procedure Code of the Ukraine), or search (Art. 194 Criminal Procedure Code of Azerbaidjan).

A wide scope of rights granted to the victim allows the latter to fulfill successfully a procedural function, which by its juridical nature is an accusation and thus to defend his lawful interests.[27]

---

27. The following works are dedicated to the victim: V. M. SAVITSKY & I. I. POTERUJA, THE VICTIM IN SOVIET CRIMINAL PROCEDURE (1963; Moscow, "Gosyurizdat" Publ. House); L. D. KOKOREV, THE VICTIM OF CRIME (1964; Voronezh); and V. A. DUVIRVNI, THE VICTIM AT PRELIMINARY INVESTIGATION (1966; Saratov).

2.8. The Civil Party Plaintiff and the Civil Party Defendant

According to Article 25 of the CP Fundamentals, a person who has suffered material loss from a crime shall have the right, in the proceedings in a criminal case, to bring against the accused or persons bearing material responsibility for the acts of the accused a civil suit which shall be tried by the court jointly with the criminal case. In such a case the victim becomes a *plaintiff*. A civil suit can be brought at the time of the preliminary investigation, or referral of the case to trial, but before the trial begins (Art. 29 of CPC). The investigator or person conducting the inquiry should explain to the victim his right to bring a civil suit and, if the suit is brought, declare the victim a plaintiff (Arts. 54 and 137 of CPC).

The civil plaintiff or his representative has the right to present evidence, enter petitions, participate at trial, request the agency of inquiry (the investigator and the court) to take measures to secure the claim entered by them,[28] maintain the civil suit, have access to material of the case from the moment of completion of the preliminary investigation, make challenges, file complaints against the actions of the person conducting the inquiry, the investigator, the procurator, and the court, and also enter complaints against those portions of the judgment or the rulings of the court which relate to the civil suit.

If a civil suit has not been brought, the court has the right to decide the question of material compensation for damage caused by the crime on its own initiative, if such actions are required for the protection of state and social interests and when the damage is caused to a person who for some reason cannot defend his own interests. (Art. 29 Criminal Procedure Code of the

---

28. Such measures may include those directed to the search for stolen valuables, etc. If the court establishes at the moment of the committal for trial that, during the preliminary investigation, measures have not been taken to provide for a civil suit, the court may take such measures itself, or oblige the corresponding investigating agencies to take them (Art. 223, CPC). If the victim's right to compensation for material damage has been left without provision, in practice such a situation is deemed to be a violation of the law; *see, e.g.,* BULLETIN OF THE SUPREME COURT OF THE USSR No. 1, at 13-14 (1973).

Ukranian SSR, and Art. 24 of Criminal Procedure Code of the Uzbek SSR).[29]

Parents, guardians, trustees, and other persons, or institutions, enterprises, and organizations which by law are responsible for the acts of the accused, may be brought to trial as *civil defendants*. In all other cases a civil suit is brought against the accused directly.

The civil defendant or his representative has the right to make objections to the civil suit, to present evidence, to enter petitions, to have access to the material of the case within the limits established by law, to participate in the trial, to make challenges, to file complaints against the acts of the person conducting the inquiry, the investigator, the procurator, and the court, and also to file complaints against those portions of the judgment and the rulings of the court which relate to the civil suit (Art. 26 of the CP Fundamentals, Art. 55 of CPC).[30]

Section 3. STAGES OF THE CRIMINAL PROCESS

3.1. Initiation of Action

Criminal procedure comprises a number of stages, beginning with the initiation of proceedings. After that, the agencies of inquiry and of preliminary investigation investigate the matter. If sufficient proof of the guilt of a specific person is collected, the case moves to the next stage, committal for trial. The case is then tried and a judgment is rendered. If the judgment of the court is appealed, the case then moves to a higher court for re-

---

29. The question of the necessity to compensate the damage to the victim from a special state fund, when it is impossible to compensate it at the expense of the criminal, is being discussed in literature. A. G. Mazalov & V. M. Savitsky, *The Unsolved Problem of Damage Compensation to the Crime Victim*, "PRAVOVEDENIE" No. 3, at 47-54 (1977).

30. For a detailed description of the problem see V. G. DAEV, CURRENT PROBLEMS OF CIVIL SUITS IN CRIMINAL PROCEDURE (1972; Leningrad U. Publ. House); L. L. LINATULLIN, DAMAGE COMPENSATION IN CRIMINAL PROCEDURE (1974; Kazan); S. A. ALEXANDROV, LEGAL GUARANTEES OF DAMAGE COMPENSATION IN CRIMINAL PROCEDURE (1976; Gorki); V. YA. PONARIN, EXAMINATION OF CIVIL SUITS AT INVESTIGATION OF CRIMINAL CASES (1978; Voronezh); and A. G. MAZALOV, CIVIL SUIT IN CRIMINAL PROCEDURE (1977; Moscow, "Juridicheskaya Literatura" Publ. House).

view. If there is no appeal or the appeal is unsuccessful, the sentence comes into legal force and is executed. This is the usual pattern for criminal proceedings. In some instances, however, the case may be re-examined by way of judicial supervision or it may be reopened because of newly discovered evidence.

Upon receiving a report that a crime has occurred, the agency receiving it must decide whether to formally institute criminal proceedings. If the decision is to proceed, then the agency of inquiry, the investigator, the procurator, or the judge renders a decree (and the court renders a judgment) on the initiating of a criminal case. Likewise, if there is to be no further action, then a decree or a judgment of refusal to initiate a criminal case is rendered.

The significance of a decree to initiate a criminal case is that it puts in motion complex judicial machinery; without such a decree, no investigatory action, including those dealing directly with the limitation of rights of citizens (arrest, search, inspection, etc.) may be carried out.[31]

The following circumstances give rise to the initiation of a criminal case: (1) reports, statements, or letters of citizens; (2) information received from trade-unions, Young Communist League *(Komsomol)* organizations, voluntary people's brigades protecting public order, comrades' courts, and other public organizations; (3) information received from enterprises; factories, institutions, and officials; (4) articles, notes, letters, etc., published in the press; (5) a confession; and (6) discovery of the indicia of a crime by the agency of inquiry, by the investigator, by the procurator, or by the court (Art. 108 of the CPC).

If a report indicates on its face that a crime has been committed, then it is immediately followed by the initiation of a criminal case. When there are no indicia of a crime, the initiation of a criminal case is rejected. Sometimes, however, it becomes necessary to demand additional material in order to establish the indicia of the crime. Such verification of a report must

---

31. The only exception to this rule is the possibility of examining the scene of the crime in emergency cases. If there are grounds for it, the criminal prosecution should be instituted immediately after this examination (Art. 178 of the CPC).

be accomplished without the help of investigatory actions and should be done within three days from the moment the first information was received. Within the same period, the decree on the initiation of a criminal case or on the rejection of it should be rendered (Art. 109 of the CPC).

The law makes it mandatory for the agency conducting inquiry, the investigator, the procurator, and the court to initiate a criminal case in every instance where the indicia of a crime have been discovered (Art. 3 of the CP Fundamentals). There are some exceptions to this rule based on the principle of the public interest in the criminal procedure, covering such instances as the so-called private accusation involving minimal bodily injuries, such as simple battery, defamation, and insults, and the so-called private-public accusation, such as rape with no aggravating circumstances, which may be criminally prosecuted only upon the victim's complaint. The absence of such a complaint requires immediate termination of the case regardless of the stage of criminal procedure (Item 7, Article 5 of the CP Fundamentals).[32]

There is no inquiry or preliminary investigation in cases of private accusation because of their relative simplicity and small social danger. The complaint of the victim is made directly to the judge, who has the duty to take measures for reconciliation of the victim with the accused. If the judge does not succeed, and if there are sufficient grounds, he initiates a criminal case and commits the accused for trial (Art. 109 of the CPC).

There remain several exceptional instances in which criminal cases may be initiated in the absence of a complaint from the victim even for private accusation matters. The legislation of the union republics gives the procurator the right to initiate a case if it is of particular social significance, or if the victim cannot protect his rights and personal interests because of his helplessness, his dependence on the accused, or for some other reason (Item 3, Art. 27 of the CPC).

---

32. In practice, this norm of the law is strictly observed. *See, for example,* COLLECTED RULINGS OF THE PLENUM AND DECISIONS OF THE COLLEGIA OF THE SUPREME COURT OF THE USSR ON THE CRIMINAL PROCEDURE PROBLEMS 1946-1962 at 13 (1964; Moscow, "Juriditcheskaya Literatura" Publ. House) and GAZETTE OF THE SUPREME COURT OF THE RSFSR No. 4, at 10-11 (1968).

As for such instances of private-public accusation as rape, the legislation of the union republics, except the Latvian, Kazakh, and Kurghiz Republics, does not permit initiation of a case in the absence of a clearly manifested wish of the victim.

In instances when there are no grounds to initiate a case, the investigator, the procurator, the judge, or the agency of inquiry rejects it by rendering a decree. This rejection may be appealed to the corresponding procurator or to a court of a higher instance (Art. 113 of the CPC).

3.2. Pretrial Investigation

When a criminal case is initiated, investigation begins. The character of the investigation depends on a number of conditions provided for by the law and may take either the form of an inquiry or of a preliminary investigation. Sometimes it may take the form of both.

The activity of the agencies of inquiry differs according to whether or not they are carrying out cases for which preliminary investigation is necessary. In the first situation, the agency of inquiry, having initiated a criminal case, carries out urgent acts of investigation to establish and fix the traces of the crime: inspection, search, seizure, taking of evidence, detention and interrogation of suspects, and questioning victims and witnesses. Such actions by the agency of inquiry must be completed within ten days from the moment of initiation of the case, for after that the case is transferred to an investigator (Art. 119 of the CPC).

If the agency of inquiry initiates a case and it does not require a preliminary investigation, or if the case was moved to the agency by the procurator who initiated it, the agency takes all necessary measures to detect the indicia of a crime and the persons who have committed it. The term for carrying out this duty is limited to one month. The materials of inquiry are then submitted to the procurator, with whose approval the case may be brought to trial.[33] In such instances, inquiry takes the

---

33. Such cases comprise about 17 to 18 percent of all the investigated cases; see V. M. SAVITZKY, AN ESSAY ON THE THEORY OF THE PROCURATOR'S SUPERVISION IN CRIMINAL PROCEDURE 148 (1975; Moscow, "Nauka" Publ. House).

same procedural form as a preliminary investigation, with the following exceptions: (1) the defense counsel does not participate in the process of inquiry; (2) the victim, the civil plaintiffs, and civil defendants are not given access to the material of the case until the process of inquiry is completed; (3) unlike a preliminary investigation, the official conducting an inquiry must follow all the instructions of the procurator, even if he disagrees with them (Art. 120 of the CPC).[34]

In the overwhelming majority of criminal cases that lead to trials, a *preliminary investigation* is conducted. In Soviet criminal procedure, as in Continental criminal procedure, the preliminary investigation is carried out by a special official, here the investigator who acts under the guidance and supervision of the procurator (*see* Chapter III, Section 2). All three procedural functions—accusation, defense, and decision making—are in the hands of the investigator. Thus, at this stage, there is no contest of parties or oral hearing.

Preliminary investigation is carried out in full accordance with the system established by the law, which provides the sequence and priority of distinct procedural steps. Preliminary investigations may be subdivided generally into the following relatively distinct parts.

ACTIONS PRIOR TO INSTITUTION OF CRIMINAL PROSECUTION

If the criminal case was initiated by the investigator and taken for execution by him, then a single decree is rendered, but if the investigator receives the case from a procurator or a court, he renders a separate decree on his institution of criminal proceedings (Art. 129 of the CPC).

After that, the investigator proceeds to search and otherwise

---

34. In special literature some authors support the view that such exceptions entail a limitation of the rights of the participants and do not correspond to the principle of the free assessment of evidence, so they should be cancelled. See, for example, II M. S. STROGOVITCH, TREATISE ON THE SOVIET CRIMINAL PROCEDURE 37-38 (1970; Moscow, "Nauka" Publ. House); E. F. KUTZOVA, GUARANTEES OF PERSONAL RIGHTS IN SOVIET CRIMINAL PROCEDURE 37 (1972; Moscow U. Publ. House); P. A. LUPINSKAYA, DECISIONS IN CRIMINAL PROCEDURE 36-37 (1976; Moscow, "Juriditcheskaya Literatura" Publ. House).

gather evidence. Evidence is taken by interrogation of witnesses, victims, and accused persons, by getting experts' conclusions, by inspections, searches, and seizures, by confrontations, and by investigatory experiments. Every step is regulated by the law in detail. The law not only provides for the manner of carrying out of an action but also measures safeguarding the observance of the rights of all persons interested in the case.

By way of illustration, citizens of the USSR, according to the Constitution (Art. 55), are guaranteed inviolability of the home. That is why a search of a home may be executed only on the basis of a decree of an investigator or of the agency of inquiry, sanctioned by the procurator. In some exceptional instances, when it is not possible to get the procurator's sanction immediately and the slightest delay might result in serious harm to the investigation, a search may be undertaken with no prior sanction of the procurator, but the procurator must be informed within twenty-four hours of the search and its results.

A search may be conducted only in the daytime, except in cases of emergency. Upon starting the search, the investigator should produce the necessary decree. During the search, the presence of not less than two persons specially invited to witness the legality of attendant procedural actions is required. The person in whose home the search is carried out or the adult members of his family should also be present. If this is not possible, representatives of the local Soviet of People's Deputies are invited. The right of such persons to witness the legality of procedural actions attendant to the search and to make statements and have them recorded must be explained to them. The investigator also has the duty to protect the privacy of persons residing in the home. A copy of the record of the search is given to the person whose home was searched or to the adult members of his family or to the representatives of the local Soviet (Art. 35 of the CP Fundamentals, Art. 168-77 of the CPC).

INSTITUTION OF CRIMINAL PROSECUTION AGAINST A PERSON

This step includes bringing the accusation against him, his interrogation, and the application of measures of preventive restriction to him.

FURTHER INVESTIGATION

Focusing at this point on the case against the accused, there may be further acts for verification of the witnesses' evidence, establishing the exact circumstances of the crime, and revealing the character or personality of the accused.

THE INVESTIGATOR'S DECISION

Next, the investigator must decide whether to terminate the preliminary investigation or refer the case to trial, with approval of the procurator. The investigator informs the accused, his legal adviser, the victim, and the civil defendant or the civil plaintiff of his decision and lets them examine the case material. These persons are then entitled to petition for additional investigation. If these petitions are of importance for the case, the investigator must then carry out additional investigation. If the petitions are groundless, the investigator rejects them and explains to the petitioners their right to appeal his decision to the procurator (Arts. 200-204 of the CPC).

One way an investigation may be terminated is by the formulation of an indictment, a procedural act in which the investigator assembles all the evidence collected, states his assessment of it, and formulates his conclusion as to the guilt of accused. This document and the record of the case are then submitted to the procurator (Arts. 205-207 of the CPC). A preliminary investigation may also end by termination of criminal proceedings, where the investigator establishes that no crime has occurred or that the evidence is insufficient to establish the guilt of the accused. In addition, a criminal prosecution is to be terminated upon the expiration of the period of limitation, or if there has been an amnesty (Art. 208 of the CPC).

The whole procedure of preliminary investigation, from the moment of institution of proceedings up to the moment of submitting the case and the indictment to the procurator or termination of proceedings, may not exceed two months period. This term is sufficient for accomplishing the investigation of 90 percent of all criminal cases. If a need to prolong the term of investigation arises, the procurator of the region has the right, in response to a demand of the investigator, to extend it for no

longer than two months. A further extension of the term of a preliminary investigation may be permitted only in exceptional instances by the procurator of the union republic or by the Procurator-General of the USSR (Art. 133 of the CPC).[35]
If the accused requires extra time to study the case material, the term of investigation must be prolonged. If the accused expresses the wish to have his defense counsel study the material of his case, presentation of the case to a court should be postponed until the arrival of defense counsel, but not longer than five days. If the defense counsel chosen by the accused cannot come during this period of time, the investigator can take measures to appoint a different defense counsel (Art. 201 of the CPC). Attempts to expedite procedure at the expense of the accused's right to defense are not permitted.[36]

ACTION ON THE INDICTMENT

The procurator verifies the extent of objectivity, validity, and comprehensiveness of the investigation, whether the indictment is based on sufficient evidence of the guilt of the accused, whether the rights of persons participating in the process have been respected, etc. The verification should be accomplished within five days. On the basis of the verification, the case may be transferred by the procurator to the court for trial, if the procurator is convinced that the accused person is guilty, or it may be returned to the investigator or to the agency of inquiry for additional investigation or for the termination of the case (Arts. 213-217 of the CPC).[37]

3.3. Assignment to Trial

The case next goes through the stage of committal for trial. During this stage, the court controls the quality of the investiga-

---

35. The law establishes exact time limits for accomplishing every stage of the criminal procedure. That is why under ordinary conditions the procedure lasts (beginning with the moment of instituting the prosecution up to the review of the sentence by way of cassation and its coming into legal force) four or five months on the average.

36. A. P. GULIAJEV, PROCEDURAL TERMS IN THE STAGES OF INSTITUTION OF CRIMINAL PROCEDURE AND PRELIMINARY INVESTIGATION (1976; Moscow, "Juriditcheskaya Literatura" Publ. House).

37. N. V. ZHOGIN & F. N. FATKULLIN, PRELIMINARY INVESTIGATION IN SOVIET CRIMINAL PROCEDURE (1965; Moscow, "Juriditcheskaya Literatura" Publ. House).

tion conducted. Committal for trial serves as a filter which rejects cases which lack essential elements of a crime, acting as an additional guarantee against unfounded trials.

The peculiarity of this stage is that the question of guilt is not a factor. The court considers the narrower preliminary questions of whether there is sufficient evidence for taking the case to the next stage of the procedure (trial), whether the conclusions of the bill of indictment are properly grounded, and whether there has been a violation of the law. Thus, making a decision on the committal of the accused for trial does not mean at all recognition of his guilt.[38]

Committal for trial is usually conducted by the judge sitting alone. In some cases, however, the case must be examined in an administrative session of the court, in which two people's assessors and the procurator participate in addition to the judge. This collegiate approach to committal for trial is required where (1) the judge disagrees with the conclusions of the bill of indictment; (2) there is a need to change the measure of preventive restriction that was applied to the accused during the preliminary investigation stage; (3) the accused is a minor and (4) the crime is one for which the death penalty may be assigned (Art. 36 of the CP Fundamentals).

The administrative session of the court begins with the report of the judge. Then, the procurator expresses his opinion. If the court has received any petitions from the accused, his defense counsel, or other participants in the process, the petitioners may be summoned. Witnesses and experts may not be summoned. After the procurator states his conclusions regarding any petitions

---

38. Nonobservance of this rule is considered to be a serious violation of the law. An example is the case of Saparov where, at the stage of committal for trial, a decision was made to try the case without calling witnesses, as "their testimony does not contradict the testimony of the accused, and moreover, the accused does not deny the facts referred to him." Having made such a decision the court assessed the validity of the testimony of the witnesses and of the accused. Since there was no other evidence in the case, the question of guilt of the accused was actually predetermined at the stage of committal for trial. That was the reason for which the Supreme Court of the USSR amended the court's decision on Saparov's case and returned the case for re-examination. *See* COLLECTED DECREES OF THE PLENUM AND DECISIONS OF THE COLLEGIA OF THE USSR SUPREME COURT ON THE PROBLEMS OF CRIMINAL PROCEDURE, 1946-1962 (1964, at 190).

before the court, the judge and the people's assessors withdraw and render a ruling.

The court may render a ruling returning the case to the procurator for additional investigation; a ruling committing the accused for trial; a ruling suspending the prosecution; or a ruling terminating the case. Where there is no obstacle to further action on the case, the court renders a ruling on the committal of the accused for trial. At that point, the accused becomes a defendant.

Several other matters are disposed of at this stage: the participation of the procurator or of the social accusers and social defenders; which persons will be called at trial, including the prisoners, victims, witnesses, and experts; presentation to the prisoner of a copy of the bill of indictment; setting of the place and time of trial, and other matters (Arts. 226-228 of the CPC).[39]

3.4. Trial

Democratic in character, Soviet criminal procedure at the decisive stage, which is the trial, is founded on the principle of a contest among the parties:

1. The accuser supports the accusation in court, but he does not decide the case by himself. The main question, the question of the defendant's guilt, as well as subsidiary questions is decided only by the court, which is neither accusing nor defending the person, but acting purely as an agency of justice (Arts. 7 and 40 of the CP Fundamentals).

2. The accuser and the defendant participate in the procedure as parties, having concrete procedural interests and equal rights in presenting evidence, in participating in the scrutiny of the evidence, and in questioning each other's statements and assertions (Art. 38 of the CP Fundamentals).

3. The court is not bound by the arguments of the parties and does not limit itself in its decision to evidence submitted. The court is absolutely independent in the choice of procedural

---

39. This series of questions is dealt in detail in the monograph by J. M. GAPLERIN & V. Z. LUKASHEVITCH, COMMITTAL FOR TRIAL IN SOVIET CRIMINAL PROCEDURE (1965; Moscow, "Juriditcheskaya Literatura" Publ. House).

means to bring forth additional evidence. The judicial session in each case shall proceed without interruption, with the exception of time allotted for rest (Art. 37 of the CP Fundamentals).

The trial consists of several consecutive stages. The *preparatory stage* begins with opening of the session at the appointed time by the chairman, who announces what case is to be heard and takes attendance of the participants.

In order to secure the right of the defendant for defense at trial, a copy of the indictment is presented to him at least three days in advance of the opening of the session. Compliance with this requirement is checked by the chairman at the preparatory stage of the trial.

Then the composition of the bench to hear the case as well as the names of the accuser, defense counsel, secretary, expert witnesses, and the interpreter are announced. The defendant and other participants in the proceedings are then asked if they have challenges to participation in the proceedings of the announced persons.

After the question of challenges is settled, the chairman explains to the defendant, the victim, the civil plaintiff, and the civil defendant their rights in the proceedings. Then he asks the parties whether they have requests to present to the court for calling new witnesses or obtaining other evidence. He next asks their opinion on hearing the case without those persons whose absence was noted in taking the roll. At this point, the preparatory stage terminates (Arts. 267-77 of the CPC).

Judicial inquiry is the next stage of the proceedings. It begins with the reading of the bill of indictment.

After that, the chairman asks the defendant whether the bill of indictment is clear to him and whether he acknowledges his guilt. After hearing the answer of the defendant, the chairman asks the parties to propose the order of judicial inquiry. After that, the bench proceeds to direct examination of evidence.

Judicial inquiry goes beyond the scope of the findings of the preliminary investigation. Judicial inquiry is itself an independent examination of all the evidence, often including new, previously undiscovered evidence. The judge and the people's assessors comprehensively examine and thoroughly assess all of the evidence in open sessions, then form their inner convictions on the principal points of the case (Arts. 278-294 of the CPC).

When judicial inquiry is completed, *judicial pleadings* begin. The essence of this stage of the proceedings lies in the fact that the participants in the proceedings, in their speeches, analyze the main evidence presented, point out the social meaning of the case, and formulate legal conclusions.

Pleadings consist of the speeches of the state and social accusers, of the civil plaintiff and civil defendant or their representatives, of the defense counsels or the defendant if he has no defense counsel. The victim does not participate in pleadings.[40]

After the pleadings, the chairman gives the defendant his *last word*. The right to the last word is one of the most important guarantees for the defendant. As the court sentence will determine his fate, it is for the defendant to speak last, immediately before the moment the bench retires to deliberate. If the defendant is deprived of the last word or if, after his word, some other participants speak out, this constitutes a serious violation of the law which requires automatic reversal.

There is no time limit on the last word of the defendant, but the chairman can stop him if he digresses to circumstances that have nothing to do with the case. Asking the defendant questions during his last word is prohibited. Having listened to the last word of the defendant, the bench leaves the trial hall to discuss and render its judgment (Arts. 297 and 299 of the CPC).

Rendering of judgment is the conclusive, final stage of the trial. The judgmént of the court must be legal and valid (Art. 43 of the CP Fundamentals), that is, it must be rendered in

---

40. This question is solved differently by the legislation of the various union republics. Thus, the Criminal Procedure Codes of the Uzbek and Lithuanian Republics give the victim the right to participate in pleadings if the procurator does not participate in it. The Codes of the Ukrainian and the Kazakh Republics provide for participation of the victim in pleadings independently from the accuser's participation, but only in certain kinds of cases. In the author's opinion, the most expedient is the participation of the victim in pleadings in all the cases where the victim so desires. For the arguments, *see* V. M. SAVITSKY, STATE ACCUSATION IN THE COURT 292-297 (1971; Moscow; "Nauka" Publ. House).

strict compliance with the law and must be founded on the facts of the case which were produced at trial.

The judgment may be conviction or acquittal. A conviction may not be founded on assumptions and shall be rendered only where in the course of the trial the defendant's guilt has been proved. If guilt is not proved, or if the occurrence of a crime has not been established, or if the defendant's act did not contain the elements of a crime, he is to be acquitted. The judgment of conviction or acquittal must contain the evidence that served as the ground for the judgment and the court's reasoning (Arts. 301 and 309 of the CPC).

Deliberations are in private. A series of questions are voted on in strict sequence: the first is whether the act of which the defendant is accused occurred; the second is whether this act contains the elements of a crime; the third is whether the defendant was the person who committed the crime. None of the judges may abstain from voting, but the chairman votes last. All the questions are decided by simple majority vote. The judge or people's assessor who is outvoted has the right to express his particular opinion in written form. This opinion is not read when the judgment is pronounced, but it is attached to the case material. A copy of the judgment is presented to the convicted or acquitted person within three days (Arts. 300-320 of the CPC).

Along with rendering a judgment, the court may, if there are sufficient grounds, render a so-called particular decision (*tchasnoe opredelenie*). By means of this decision, the court attracts the attention of the administration of enterprises, institutions, organizations, etc., and of other persons to the reasons and conditions contributing to the crime and demands that remedial measures be taken. Persons to whom such particular decisions are addressed must inform the court within a month of the measures they have taken (Art. 321 of the CPC).

3.5. Appeal

The defendant, his defense counsel and legal representatives, and also the victim, the civil plaintiff, the civil defendant and their representatives in case of disagreement with the court's judgment may appeal it to a higher court. It is the procurator's duty to appeal every illegal or invalid judgment. In the RSFSR the time limit for filing an appeal is seven days from the time a judgment is rendered or a copy of it is presented to the defendant.

The standard form of appeal is by way of cassation, which means that the higher court is not bound by the arguments of the appellants and reconsiders the case in full, even those aspects not related to the appeal, such as positions of defendants who have not themselves appealed. The review is done on the basis of the record of the case, plus additional materials.

In reviews by way of cassation, the procurator states his opinion concerning the legality and validity of the judgment. The defense counsel may also participate. The accused is not always required to participate, but if the accused desires to participate, he will be allowed to do so.

The review by way of cassation starts with a roll-taking, then dealing with challenges, statements, and petitions. Then, one of the members of the court summarizes the case and appeals filed. After that, pleadings begin. The bench listens to the procurator's conclusion, to additional testimony of the accused and his defense counsel, and then retires to render a judgment.

As a result of the examination of the case by way of cassation, the court shall take one of the following decisions: (1) to leave the judgment unchanged and the appeal unsatisfied; (2) to vacate the judgment and refer the case for a new investigation or a new trial; (3) to vacate the judgment and terminate the case; or (4) to change the judgment but only to the benefit of the defendant.

The decision of the higher court takes effect immediately. A judgment that has taken legal effect is binding on all state and public institutions, enterprises, and organizations, officials and citizens and is to be executed throughout the territory of the USSR (Arts. 44-47 of the CP Fundamentals and 325-355 of the CPC).

3.6. Execution of the Sentence

Translation into reality of the court's prescription for treatment of the offender in a corrective labor colony or deduction from his salary of restitution money is beyond the scope of criminal procedure itself, but in the course of the execution of the judgment, there often occur problems of a procedural character. Examples are those connected with the suspension of the execution, with the substitution of one type of penalty for another, or with conditional release on medical or other grounds. All these questions fall under the competence of the court that rendered the judgment or of the court at the place where the offender is held.

The convict, as a rule, is summoned to the court. Depending on the character of the question considered, the civil plaintiff, a medical official, and a representative of the administration of a corrective labor institution or of the commission on juvenile affairs may also be summoned to the court. The participation of the procurator is always necessary.

Hearing of the case starts with the report of the chairman, after which those summoned to the session make statements and the procurator offers his opinion. The court then retires to deliberate (Arts. 356-369 of CPC).[41]

3.7. Extraordinary Review

The above sequence of stages in criminal procedure is the usual course, but in exceptional cases this sequence may be interrupted. One such unusual intervention is review by way of judicial supervision.

Such a review may occur only with respect to a court judgment that has taken legal effect. Hence, it is extraordinary, and this circumstance predetermines the peculiarities of referring a case for supervisory re-examination.

Review by judicial supervision occurs only upon the protest of the chairman of a court of a higher level than that which rendered the judgment or on the protests of a procurator of a higher rank than the procurator who participated in the last hearing on the judgment.

Such officials may, in response to a complaint or on their own initiative, bring a supervisory protest against a judgment.

41. I. D. PERLOV, EXECUTION OF THE JUDGMENT IN SOVIET CRIMINAL PROCEDURE (1963; Moscow, "Juriditcheskaya Literatura" Publ. House).

The procedure for re-examination of a case by way of judicial supervision is similar to that for cassation. The list of the courts whose jurisdiction allows them to re-examine cases by way of supervision is provided in Article 374 of the CPC. It is important to emphasize that a judge who participated in the previous examination of the case cannot take part in re-examination of that case by way of judicial supervision (Art. 48 of the CP Fundamentals, Arts. 371-383 of the CPC).[42]

3.8. New Evidence and New Trials

Another unusual occurrence in criminal procedure is the reopening of cases because of newly discovered evidence. Such a step may take place with respect to judgments having taken legal effect where the evidence was not known to the court that rendered the judgment.

A case may be reopened because of newly discovered evidence if it is established that the judgment was based on false testimony of witnesses or on an invalid conclusion of an expert, or any other invalid evidence. A case may also be reopened where there were criminal abuses by officials who conducted the trial.

In order for a case to be reopened, the procurator conducts an investigation, and then, if the facts are proved, he refers the case to the court, which either vacates as invalid and unjust the prior judgment or rejects the argument of the procurator. Where the judgment is vacated, a new preliminary investigation and trial are instituted. (Art. 50 of the CP Fundamentals, Arts. 384-390 of the CPC).

---

42. I. D. Perlov, Examination of Cases by Way of Judicial Supervision in Criminal Procedure (1974; Moscow, "Juriditcheskaya Literatura" Publ. House).

CHAPTER III

LEGAL EDUCATION AND TRAINING

S. G. KELINA and A. M. YAKOVLEV

Section 1. JURIDICAL SCIENCE

1.1. The Impact of Theory on Practice

THE SOVIET UNION possesses a wide network of institutions engaged in research on issues of juridical science. Such work is conducted at law schools, juridical institutes, at the Institute of State and Law of the Academy of Sciences of the USSR and at the institutes of state and law and academies of sciences of the union republics, and at some departmental institutes, such as the All-Union Scientific-Research Institute on Soviet Legislation of the USSR Ministry of Justice, the All-Union Institute for Study of Causes and Development of Measures for Crime Prevention of the USSR Procuracy, the All-Union Scientific-Research Institute of the USSR Ministry of the Interior, the All-Union Scientific Research Institute of Judicial Expertise of the Ministry of Justice of the USSR, and others.

Applying modern methods of sociology, psychology, and computer-assisted statistical methods to analyze in depth trends in crime as a whole and of separate categories of crimes, these institutions develop courses and write monographs dedicated to various aspects of the juridical sciences.[1] They also prepare reports to state directive bodies and participate in the drafting of legislation. Such work features specific recommendations aimed at increasing the effectiveness of criminal procedure and penitentiary law, and improving the organization and operation of

---

1. Three fundamental works on the subject were published in the 1970s: COURSE ON SOVIET CRIMINAL LAW (2 volumes; 1970, 1971; Moscow, "Nauka" Publ. House); COURSE ON SOVIET CRIMINAL LAW (3 volumes; 1968, 1973, in press; Leningrad U. Publ. House); and M. S. STROGOVICH, COURSE ON SOVIET CRIMINAL PROCEDURES (2 volumes; 1968, 1970; Moscow, "Nauka" Publ. House).

agencies charged with combatting crime and strengthening the legal order.

The most important aspect of the influence of juridical science on practice is the participation of legal scholars in drafting legislation and their rendering practical assistance to the organs of investigation, the courts, and the procuracy.

The active influence of scholars on the framing of legislation is a characteristic feature of juridical science in the Soviet Union. For example, the draft of the CP Fundamentals was formulated by practitioners of the highest courts and Procurator's Office, members of the Juridical Commission of the Council of Ministers of the USSR, and by a large group of scholars. The draft was distributed for discussion among scientific and practical institutions, and on the basis of their comments was revised considerably and published in newspapers and magazines in June, 1958, for public consideration.

Another role of scholars in juridical science is to act as advisors. All drafts of directives of the Plenum of the Supreme Court of the USSR or of the union republics are submitted for consideration to scientific and educational institutions in Moscow and other cities. On some occasions, drafts of solutions to complicated problems arising in practice are also sent to the same institutions. For example, in 1976 the Supreme Court of the USSR directed a letter, asking whether voluntary construction and voluntary appropriation of land (Crimes provided for in Art. 199, the RSFSR Criminal Code) constitute lasting crimes, to scientific institutions including the Institute of State and Law of the Academy of Science of the USSR. This question arose in connection with the examination of a protest of a specific criminal case.

A permanent Scientific-Advisory Council at the Supreme Court of the USSR was created in 1962 as an agency working on a social basis. Since 1968, it has become a structural part of the Supreme Court of the USSR. The provision of the Plenum of the Supreme Court of the USSR of December 3, 1962, "Establishment of a Scientific-Consultative Council of the Supreme Court of the USSR," provides "that this council is aimed at improvement of the quality of examination of questions connected with the study of judicial practice, drafting of clarifying directives, and strengthening of contacts of judicial bodies with legal scientific institutions.[2]

The council is headed by a vice-chairman of the Supreme Court of the USSR. It consists of more than forty members, including outstanding scholars, scientists, and leading administrators of various juridical institutions. The composition of the Council is approved by the Plenum of the Supreme Court. The Council has two sections, civil and criminal, and may form *ad hoc* groups to discuss specific items. Items of a general character are discussed at plenary sessions.

The Scientific-Advisory Council examines all drafts of directive documents of the Plenum of the Supreme Court of the USSR, drafts of letters of instruction, surveys of judicial practice, and complicated and difficult problems in the practical work of the agencies of justice. Members of the Council attend the sessions of the Plenum of the Supreme Court of the USSR and participate in debates.

The Scientific-Advisory Council organizes conferences of scholars and practitioners where they discuss the most urgent problems of combatting crime. The conference resolutions often result in concrete measures. Thus, a discussion that took place at such a conference in 1968 dedicated to problems of improving legislation and judicial practice regarding juvenile delinquents played an important role in the development of the document of the Plenum of the Supreme Court of the USSR of September 12, 1969, "Judicial practice in cases of minors involved in criminal and other antisocial activities."[3]

During the conference held by the Council in 1967 dedicated to the contacts of judicial bodies with juridical scientific and educational institutions, an opinion was expressed in favor of creation of a system of institutions charged with advanced training of judicial workers. A federal institute for advanced training of personnel of the agencies of justice was founded July 30, 1970, on the basis of a decision by the Central Committee of the

---

2. COLLECTED DECISIONS OF PROBLEMS OF THE SUPREME COURT OF THE USSR 1924-1963, at 62 (1947).

3. *Supra* at 559.

Communist Party of the Soviet Union and the Council of Ministers of the USSR, "Measures directed to improvement of work of the agencies of the courts and procuracy."

Section 2. PREPARATION FOR PRACTICE

Education of lawyers is done at the law faculties of universities and law schools, or institutes. The term of education is five years at the university or four years at law institutes. University teaching includes a wider theoretical basis while law institutes stress practical aspects.

Law faculties exist in thirty-nine universities in the USSR,[4] including the universities of all union republics. Law institutes are located in Sverdlovsk and Saratov in the Russian Federation and Kharkov in the Ukraine. There also exists a system of studies by correspondence, managed by the All-Union Law Correspondent Institute in Moscow, which has branches and consulting offices all over the country.

Higher legal education is also provided in schools under the Ministry of Interior of the USSR, which train specialists for the Ministry of Interior system (militia, investigation, corrective-labor institutions, departments and divisions of the interior at executive councils of the local Soviets, etc.). Senior courses are provided at the Academy of the USSR Ministry of Interior.

Growth of the number of research workers and scholars reflects the rate of development of juridical science and education. For the last two decades, the number of scholars and researchers has increased more than four times. At present, there are about five thousand scholars and researchers in the field of law throughout the country. Over 360 persons hold Doctorate degrees and 2500 are candidates of law. Seven of the scholars are correspondent members of the USSR Academy of Sciences and 17 are members and correspondent members of the academies of sciences of the union republics.

Recent years have shown a considerable growth in the number of students of law. In 1974, over 90,000 students were studying

---

4. S. S. ALEXEEV, INTRODUCTION TO THE LEGAL PROFESSION 705 (1976; Moscow, "Juridicheskaya Literatura" Publ. House).

law at the universities and institutes, one-and-one-half times as many as in 1964.

During the period from 1965 to 1975 (after the Decree of the Central Committee of the Communist Party of the Soviet Union "Measures for further development of juridical science and improvement of juridical training in the country,"[5] was adopted in 1964) law faculties were established at eleven universities in the Russian Federation alone. The enrollment of students in law schools has grown overall by 11 percent during these five years, and by 21 percent counting full time students only.[6]

Teaching is accomplished by persons holding higher degrees: over 90 are doctors of law and over 500 are candidates of law. In 1977 there were about 200 postgraduate students teaching.

In spite of the growth of the number of lawyers, the demand for them grows even faster. The need for lawyers in law enforcement agencies, courts, the procuracy, the Ministry of Interior, associations and notary offices is only 60 to 65 percent satisfied. The agencies of state administration and the administration of certain branches of the people's economy want to employ 66 percent more lawyers. During the period 1975-80, the growth of this need is expected to continue. The structure of the need may be defined in the following way: 70 percent by law enforcement agencies, 20 percent by various economic establishments, 10 percent by state administration. By 1985, the agencies of justice will require approximately 1,500 more specialists with university level training and about the same number of specialists at the technical level. This demand is the basis for further expansion of the network of law schools.

A similar process of expansion and improvement is taking place in the teaching disciplines in law schools. Along with strictly legal disciplines, such disciplines as pedagogy, psychology, professional ethics, legal aspects of automation, and economics, management, and planning of the people's economy are taught.

Specialization in the training of some groups of lawyers is

---

5. *Isvestia,* August 4, 1964.

6. L. K. Suvorov, *Legal Education in Higher Educational Institutions of the RSFSR: Problems and Perspectives,* "Pravovedenie" No. 1, at 7-19 (1977).

achieved by adding special subjects to the main courses. Besides the theoretical studies, students get practice in criminalistic technique. Periods of practical work are provided for by all the curricula, including work in the courts, the procuracy, the militia, etc.

Law schools provide graduates with jobs at agencies of the system of justice, Procurator's Offices, agencies of the Ministry of the Interior, in courts and bar associations, at economic establishments and offices of legal consultants, and with legal departments of ministries and administrative offices. Institute graduates may be nominated for election as a judge.

The most capable graduates are recommended for postgraduate study, where they earn the scientific degree of candidate of law upon completing and defending a thesis. The next highest degree is the doctor of law, which requires a doctoral dissertation.

Lawyer-practitioners have an opportunity to advance their knowledge through the All-Union Institute for Advanced Training of Workers in Justice of the Ministry of Justice of the USSR.

The procuracy of the USSR has an Institute for Advanced Studies of Senior Material in Moscow with a branch in Kharkov and an institute for advanced training of investigators under the Procurator's Office of the USSR and organs of the Ministry of Interior of the USSR at Leningrad.

A new institute was established by the USSR Ministry of Justice on May 4, 1977, to advance theoretical knowledge and practical qualifications of senior staff of the Ministry of Justice, including judges, legal advisers, attorneys, notaries, and state arbitrators. The students learn about developments in Marxist philosophy, economics, and sociology; study new legislation and solve problems arising in its application; and learn the practice of management in agencies of the system of justice.

The principal functions of this institute follow:

a. advanced qualification of the senior staff of the agencies of the system of justice and courts based on a deeper theoretical knowledge, professional skills, knowledge of the latest developments in legal thought and practice, modern forms and methods of scientific labor and management organization, and advanced practice;

b. providing methodological assistance to the ministries of justice of the union republics and organizing permanent courses of advanced training of functionaries in the system of justice in the republics;

c. participating in the formation and implementation of proposals concerning improvement of advanced training of the staff of agencies of the system of justice and examination and promotion.

Teaching is in the form of lectures delivered by leading officers of the USSR *Gosplan* (State Planning Committee), the Ministry of Justice of the USSR, the Office of the Procurator-General of the USSR, the Supreme Court of the USSR, the Ministry of the Interior of the USSR and other agencies, as well as by leading legal scholars.

Besides the lectures, the students have practical work and seminars, which constitute a considerable part of the curriculum. Seminars consist of discussions of important issues in activities of the system of justice with the help of specialists. The institute also organizes and conducts scientific practical conferences.

The term of study is up to three months for full-time students and up to ten months for part-time students.

The study is completed by writing and defending a paper containing a theoretical analysis of a chosen problem, and a generalized practical examination. The students receive a certificate upon graduation.

The same forms are used for advanced training of investigators and procurators of the Institute of Advanced Training of the Procuracy of the USSR. The main purpose of this training is to teach modern methods and new ideas in the theory and practice of combatting crime. This institute also provides for advanced training of the senior staff of the procuracy. The teaching is based on the latest developments in legal thought, criminalistic technique, and modern forms and methods of management and administration. Considerable attention is focused on the procurator's supervision, and on improvement of the organization of work of a procurator. The teaching process is concluded with a scientific and practical conference.

The institute has the chairs of general supervision and of procurator's supervision of preliminary inquiry and investigation and trial of civil and criminal cases. The full-time course lasts up to three months.

Since 1966, 9,500 student-investigators have finished the course of the Institute for Advanced Training of Investigators of the Procuracy of the USSR and Ministry of the Interior of the USSR, located in Leningrad. The most characteristic feature of this program is individualization of the study. The student chooses the subject most useful for his work. The emphasis of the curriculum is on problems of investigatory technique and methods of investigation of certain types of crime. The terms of study vary: district investigators study for three to four months; senior investigators, investigators of especially important cases, and investigators specializing in certain kinds of cases study from one to one-and-one-half months. Nine hundred investigators finish the program each year.

Studies at the institute have a positive impact on the careers of investigators. For example, 160 of the investigators who graduated from the institute from 1973 to 1976 received promotions.

CHAPTER IV

CRIMINOLOGICAL FOUNDATION
OF THE CRIMINAL PROCESS

A. M. YAKOVLEV

Section 1. CRIMINOLOGY AS A SCIENCE

1.1. Organization of Research

IN THE USSR, the development of criminology as a branch of science dates back to the 1920s. As early as 1918 a special part of statistical records (moral statistics) served as the foundation for the criminological examination of criminality. In the large cities all over the country, scientific centers dealing with studies of criminality and criminals were established. In 1925, the State Institute for Studies of Criminality and Criminals was organized.

In this Institute studies were conducted in the following directions:

1. study of socioeconomic factors of criminality;

2. biopsychological examination of the personality of the criminal from the positions of psychology and psychiatry and elaboration of the problems of nonimputability;

3. research in the field of criminal investigation technique;

4. penitentiary studies aimed at developing rational methods for re-socialization of offenders.

The Institute also conducted work on assembling and analyzing statistical data on criminality.

Research was interrupted in the middle of the 1930s but was renewed in the early 1960s. At present, the main center for criminological research is the All-Union Institute for the Study of the Causes of Crime and Elaboration of Preventive Measures[1] in Moscow. Research in the field of criminology is also conducted by faculties of law at universities in Moscow, Leningrad, Voronej, Riga, and other places.

---

1. The Institute is a member of the International Society of Criminology.

Criminology is one of the rapidly developing branches of science with a considerable number of works published, including candidate and doctoral papers. Criminological concepts are exerting increasing influence on penal legislation and the practice of law enforcement.

At present, the state of criminality may be characterized by the following data: Comparable indices show that the number of persons committing crimes in 1967 was less than half the number for 1946 (per 100,000 persons).[2]

Within the limits of this general tendency, however, there are some variations. In 1958, 1962, and at the end of the 1960s, there was a marked increase in crime. Deceleration of the rate of decrease in crimes and the growth of crime rates was most pronounced in regions with the most rapid economic growth. The increase is heaviest among crimes committed by negligence, such as traffic offenses. The increase is as high as 9 percent in some localities.

Offenses against socialist property account for 14 to 19 percent of all crimes. There is a marked increase in the proportion of petty larceny offenses. Crimes against private property are also increasing. The proportion of these crimes varies between 14 and 16 percent.

Violent crimes make up about 15 percent of the total. In spite of a decrease in intentional homicides and rapes at the beginning of the 1970s, the rate of such crimes remains rather high.

The largest category of crimes is that consisting of infringements of public order—hooliganism (about 30 percent). Convictions for offenses by officers of the Soviet state machinery and for economic crimes constitute 7 to 8 percent of all criminal convictions.

The proportion of persons convicted for crimes involving group criminality varies between 11 and 12 percent. In criminological research, crimes are subdivided into two main groups: mercenary and violent crimes. The first group comprises the stealing of state and personal property and other offenses detri-

---

2. S. Ostroumov, Criminal Statistics and Crime Combatting 24 (1974; Moscow, "Znanie" Publ. House).

mental to such property, including speculation, bribery, and other offenses characterized by mercenary motives. The second group comprises criminal infringements on the life and health of individuals, including those arising from hooliganism. The proportion of all crimes represented by the first group is 55 percent. The second represents 25 to 30 percent. The male : female ratio among criminals 6 : 1 in 1965 and 8 : 1 in 1967.

A great influence on the state of criminality is exerted by alcoholism. Thus, about two-thirds of all intentional homicides; three-fourths of all serious bodily injuries, assaults, and robberies; more than one-half of all thefts of personal property; and more than two-fifths of all traffic violations are committed under the influence of alcohol.[3] There exists a direct correlation between alcoholism and intentional homicides, as the chart below demonstrates:

Motives	Homicide committed in the state of alcoholic intoxication
Jealousy	62.9 percent
Family relations	66.7
Mercenary motives	39.5
Vengeance	64.4
Hooliganistic motives	96.6
Quarrels and scuffles	85.3
Concealing other crimes	73.3
Other motives	29.0

There is also a correlation between the state of criminality and mobility of population. Studies show that a considerable proportion of persons committing crimes are persons who had changed their place of residence to another territory. Thus, among the districts characterized by the highest level of newcomers, nine-tenths are districts of the highest crime rates. On the other hand, seven-tenths of the districts characterized by the lowest level of newcomers are marked by the lowest crime rates.[4]

Studies of samples of offenders serving sentences in the Lith-

3. CRIMINOLOGY 119-122, 211-314 (1976; Moscow, "Juriditcheskaya Literatura" Publ. House).

4. ALCOHOLISM—THE WAY TO CRIMINALITY 8 (1966; Moscow, "Juriditcheskaya Literatura" Publ. House).

uanian Soviet Socialist Republic showed that the rate of convictions for robberies and assaults with intent to commit robbery among rural residents was only one-third as great as that among dwellers of small towns (with population under 10,000) and one-fifth as great as among dwellers of medium-size and large towns.[5] Town dwellers among juvenile delinquents constitute 75 to 78 percent, while rural dwellers constituted 22 to 25 percent.[6]

Family instability, including weakening or break-up of family relations, is considered to be a significant criminogenic factor. In the USSR (per every 1,000 of population) in 1966 there were registered 9 marriages and 2.8 divorces; in 1967, 9.1 marriages and 2.8 divorces; in 1968, 9.1 and 2.7; in 1969, 8.9 and 2.7.[7]

Divorce, desertion of the family, and family disorganization adversely affect juveniles. Among the families of juvenile delinquents covered by one criminological survey, in 25 to 30 percent of them, parents were systematically abusing alcohol, in 50 percent of families of delinquents, there were constant scandals and brawls; and in 7 to 10 percent of the families, the parents' conduct was immoral.[8]

The proportion of all crimes that are committed by juvenile delinquents (that is by persons between the ages of 14 and 18) does not exceed 10 percent. The main juvenile offenses are crimes of theft and hooliganism (80 percent). Serious violent crimes (murders, serious bodily injuries, rapes) comprise a relatively small proportion (6 to 8 percent). About 76 percent of delinquent acts are committed in towns (the proportion of juveniles in the town population is about 50 percent).[9] Socially dangerous acts by juveniles under fourteen (the age of legal maturity for the commitment of serious crimes) or juveniles under sixteen (the age of legal maturity for all types of crime)

---

5. PERSONALITY OF THE OFFENDER 128 (1975; Moscow, "Juriditcheskaya Literatura" Publ. House).

6. *Supra* at 136.

7. NATIONAL ECONOMY OF THE USSR IN 1968, at 40 (1969; Moscow, "Statizdat" Publ. House).

8. G. Minkovsky, *Some of the Causes of Juvenile Delinquency in the USSR and the Measures of Its Prevention,* SOVIET STATE AND LAW No. 5, at 88 (1966).

9. CRIMINOLOGY 286 (1976; Moscow, "Juriditcheskaya Literatura" Publ. House).

are not recorded under current law and are not considered to be crimes.

There is also a marked dependence of the etiology of urban criminality on the density of population. One study showed that in the regions of the city with a density of residents of 60 persons per hectare (using samples with populations of 10,000 residents) there is a stable level of crime. When the density of population is 50 residents per hectare, the crime level declines.[10]

General statistical characteristics of criminality show that (1) the urban crime rate is higher than the rural; (2) the bigger the town, the less favorable the crime indices; (3) there exists a direct correlation between the scale of migration and criminality; and (4) in the newly constructed towns, some concrete indices of criminality (for example juvenile delinquency) are higher than in the older towns.

1.2. Scope and Methods

The leading tendency in the development of Soviet criminology is its formation as an independent branch of science. The prerequisite for this movement was further refinement of the methods of criminological research and of its basic theoretical premises. At present, the problem of detecting illegal behavior has acquired special significance for criminological research.

The initial premise that both criminal law and criminology deal with phenomena designated by the same concepts of crime, criminality, and the personality of the offender is characteristic of criminology. Criminological literature emphasizes that nowhere but in criminal law are there definitions of what constitutes a crime and who is a criminal. Hence, it is precisely the act itself and its author as defined in detail by penal legislation that serve as the initial subjects for criminological research.

From this common point, however, the methods of criminal law and criminology inevitably diverge. Awareness of the divergence of methods of these two sciences at the present state of development of Soviet criminology is necessary to understand the nature of criminological examination of criminality and

10. V. Orechov, Social Planning and Problems of Crime Combatting 97 (1972; Leningrad U. Publ. House).

criminals. The divergence of these sciences' methods springs from their different objective functions. Combatting crime is a general social task served by both of two related yet distinct activities. The first is determining responsibility for crimes committed, and the second is prevention of crime by focusing on its causes.

In order to accomplish these obviously different tasks, criminal law and criminology are inevitably guided by different basic principles and accordingly use different methods of scientific analysis.

The problem of crime prevention by elaboration of recommendations for the law enforcement agencies, organs for the administration of justice, and organs of state administration and public organizations also falls within the realm of criminology.

Thus Soviet criminology is the science of criminality, its state, structure, dynamics, and causes, of the personality of the offender, and of the ways and means of crime prevention in socialist society.

During recent years the development of Soviet criminological concepts increasingly demonstrates the evolution of Soviet criminology from a branch of criminal law into an independent science.

The fundamental philosophical premise that all kinds of human activity and forms of behavior (legal or illegal) are socially determined forms is the basis for this natural evolution.

A. Sakharov noted[11] that there are more than a few difficulties and contradictions of both subjective and objective character under socialism. In particular, there is the contradiction between the growing needs of members of socialist society and a level of production not yet sufficient to satisfy them; inequality of shares from the distribution of public production; the difference between mental work and manual labor, skilled and unskilled types of labor, and hard and easy jobs.

A. Hertzenson[12] also pursued sociological reasoning to find the

11. A. B. Sakharov, On the Personality of the Offender and the Causes of Criminality in the USSR (1961; Moscow, "Juriditcheskaya Literatura" Publ. House).

12. A. A. Hertzenson, Introduction to Soviet Criminology (1965; Moscow, "Juriditcheskaya Literatura" Publ. House).

causes of crime. He noted that such phenomena as alcoholism, housing problems for part of the population, insufficient material well-being for some categories of working people, drawbacks in family environment and academic education of the growing young population, and inadequacies of some other educational institutions contribute to juvenile delinquency.

In a monograph by V. Kudriavtzev,[13] the problem of socially determined criminal behavior was considered in detail for its ability to reveal the causal relationships of individual criminal behavior. That work signaled the division between the criminal law approach to deviant conduct as a product of will or intent and the sociological "cause and effect" explanation approach. Certainly, Kudriavtzev observed, it may be possible to consider the voluntariness of a particular form of behavior as the immediate cause of the succeeding act. This, however, adds nothing to either the theory of criminology or its practice. From the scientific standpoint, this approach does not go beyond the narrow view which equally fits idealistic and simplistic stereotypes. From a practical point of view, however, reducing the causes of criminality to the "evil will" of criminals offers only repression as a method for combatting crime and provides no basis for considering more basic preventive measures of a social character.

Kudriavtzev argues that recognition of the decisive role of social milieux in explaining all kinds of behavior including deviant behavior forms the foundation of the scientific approach of Soviet criminology.

In a book by A. Yakovlev,[14] the problems of crime causation and the personality of the offender were considered for the first time in Soviet criminology with the use of principles and propositions of social psychology. Yakovlev begins his analysis with a clarification of psychophysiological foundations of the process of socialization of the individual; then, he traces the interactions of individuals in the frameworks of social groups and communities, and analyzes special elements of the process of social adjustment. In so doing, he sheds some light on the defects

---

13. V. N. KUDRIAVTZEV, CAUSATION IN CRIMINOLOGY (1968; Moscow, "Juriditcheskaya Literatura" Publ. House).
14. A. M. YAKOVLEV, CRIMINALITY AND SOCIAL PSYCHOLOGY (1974; Moscow).

of sociopsychological order which form the foundation of the criminal behavior.

Contemporaneously, there was an improvement of the methodological grounds of Soviet criminology. In a book published in 1974, J. Bluvshtein[15] examined theoretical presumptions of mathematical methods used in analyzing criminality and made proposals for concrete methods of criminological measurements.

Comprehensive characteristics of social factors influencing criminality were suggested by G. Avanesov in a book on criminology that formulated principles and methods for crime forecasting as well.[16] To a number of sociodemographical factors, the author includes factors connected with urbanization, migration of population, and changes in the age and sex structure of the population. To a number of economic factors he included factors affecting the level of material well-being of different groups of the population, the pricing and availability of goods, and the scale and the speed of housing construction. He also advocated measuring factors of sociopsychological order, such as the weakening of traditional forms of social control, changing of the role of the family in the upbringing of children caused by women's involvement in the sphere of public production, and the growth of psychophysiological burdens caused by more complicated conditions of life.

During the middle of the 1970s the development of Soviet criminology was characterized by the fact that problems of combatting crime were treated by criminologists in a broader sociological context. Thus, I. Karpetz considers the problems of crime prevention in connection with the acceleration of scientific and technological progress and complication of social structures of Soviet society.[17] In V. Kudriavtzev's book,[18] criminological problems are considered in connection with the general problem of

---

15. J. D. BLUVSHTEIN, CRIMINOLOGY AND MATHEMATICS (1974; Moscow, "Juriditcheskaya Literatura" Publ. House).

16. G. A. AVANESOV, CRIMINOLOGY, FORECASTING AND MANAGEMENT (1975; Moscow).

17. I. I. KARPETZ, CONTEMPORARY PROBLEMS OF CRIMINAL LAW AND CRIMINOLOGY (1976; Moscow, "Juriditcheskaya Literatura" Publ. House).

18. V. N. KUDRIAVTZEV, THE CAUSES OF OFFENSES (1976; Moscow, "Nauka" Pub. House).

prevention of offenses of all kinds, and the author's idea is that the causes of offenses take the form of discord among elements within such social systems as society as a whole, its classes, social groups, and individuals.

Section 2. THE SOCIOLOGY OF CRIME

2.1. Social Processes and Institutions

The key feature of social life is its dynamic character. There are no static forms of social life, only processes moving at various rates.

It is for this reason that studying the complex interrelations of positive and negative social processes and forecasting the changes which will be caused by further social, scientific, and technological development are so necessary.[19]

The progress of social processes and acceleration of the rates of social changes affect normative order in society. The character of the impact of social processes on the normative order depends on interaction of these processes with social institutions and social communities.

As a social process, sociology concerns itself with relatively homogeneous series of phenomena, connected both by cause-and-effect and functional relationships. Social processes alter relations among people and the character of social interactions.

Social processes lead to social changes, to disappearance of former elements of particular social systems and appearance of new elements, or to changes in the character of interaction among the elements of the system. The fundamental tenet of the Marxist theory is that there is a continuous process of development in any concrete, historically preconditioned system of production of its most important and dynamic factor: productive forces. Forces which precondition changes of the character of relations of production then lead to a change of the whole social structure of society.

Development of public forces of production is accompanied by subordinate processes, such as migration of population, growth of towns, and industrial process.

These and some other social processes result in a change of the

19. V. N. Kudriavtzev, *Sociological Problems of the Study of Antisocial Behavior*, SOCIOLOGICAL STUDIES No. 1, at 5-59 (1974).

character of social institutions and social communities. In order to reveal the mechanism of the impact of social changes on criminality, it is necessary to define the concept and functions of social institutions and social communities and to define their role in behavior regulation. "To provide for stability of social relations, on which . . . the existence of groups or of the society depends, they (the group or society) create a peculiar system of institutions, controlling the behavior of their members. In these systems of social control the most important role is played by institutions."[20]

The most significant social institution is the system of upbringing, education, and training of the new generation. The family is also a social institution, the function of which is also determined by the system of legal and other social norms.

Social institutions, therefore, are not merely "the system of institutions in which particular persons, elected by group members, have the authority to fulfill concrete social and impersonal functions for the sake of satisfying the existing individual and public needs and for the sake of regulating the behavior of other group members."[21] It is important as well that a social institution is always an intercoordinated system of norms, the origin and grouping of which are preconditioned by the contents of the particular social task the social institution performs.

Social institutions ensure the possibility for the members of society or appropriate social groups to accomplish their goals. They regulate behavior, stabilize social relations, secure coordination and integrity in the actions of society members, and strive to attain higher levels of social conformity. According to Layman's definition "by a social institution we mean the unity of people fulfilling specific functions in the framework of social integrity and community-oriented functions, as well as traditions, norms, and values; the unity that has its own internal structure and hierarchy and is notable for the specific stable character of ties and relations, both internal and external."[22]

20. Jan Shchepan'sky, Elementary Notions of Sociology 95 (1962; Moscow, "Progress" Publ. House).

21. *Supra* at 97.

22. D. I. Layman, Science as a Social Institution 20 (1971; Moscow, "Nauka" Publ. House).

Under the conditions of intensified progress of social processes and the acceleration of the rate of social change, there may appear a situation in which changed social requirements are not adequately reflected in the structure and functions of corresponding social institutions. As a result of such a discrepancy, there may spring up phenomena of dysfunction. The social processes and changes may manifest themselves in the functioning of social institutions, both in the external sphere and in the character of the contents of their activity.

Outwardly, the phenomena of dysfunction of social institutions may find expression in the shortage of trained professionals, material means, or organizational imperfection. More importantly, from the point of view of their contents, dysfunctioning of a social institution finds expression in vagueness of its aims and functions and in the loss of its social prestige and authority. Disparity between the institution's activity and the character of social requirements leads to decreasing significance of the role of that particular social institution and results in degeneracy of its separate functions into symbolic, ritual activity with no rational aim (bureaucratism).

Dysfunctioning in a social institution's activity is evident when it loses its essential quality of depersonalized activity. Depersonalization of any social institution's activity is a decisive premise for its normal functioning. The principle of depersonalization means that fulfillment of all the functions of the institutions does not mainly and exclusively depend on personal peculiarities of those who must perform the essential tasks ensured by this institution; it does not depend on their inclinations, preferences, and other subjective factors. This principle is assured by accurate definition of social roles and by an objectively functioning mechanism for their due implementation. A loss of depersonalization means that the institution to this degree ceases to function in correspondence with objective needs and objective aims, that it alters its functions according to the interests of particular persons, their personal traits and features. As a result, such a social institution is less capable of attaining its objective social goal. "The typical trait of the institution is a socially significant function, i.e., providing for concrete social goals and correspondingly developing concrete (material and spiritual) values."[23]

In their totality, dysfunctions of social institutions can lead to such consequences as abuse of power, protectionalism, bribery, and other breaches of legality connected with performance of official functions.

Most important, however, is that failure to satisfy the social goal may give birth to a spontaneous rise of normatively outstanding kinds of activity tending to accomplish the goal abandoned by the dysfunction of legal institutions at the expense of infringements of existing norms and rules, including legal norms.

Such an activity, in its extreme manifestations, can result in illegal activity. Thus, dysfunctioning of some economic institutions may affect the rise of some types of property and economic crimes, such as speculation, theft, or stealing of socialist property.

Prevention of such infringements may be ensured if (a) the corresponding social goal is adequately served by the functioning of existing and newly created social institutions, (b) a change or transformation of the social goal itself is taking place, or (c) changes of attitudes towards this goal are taking place in the social consciousness.

It is important to distinguish a social goal as derived from an existing condition, i.e., as real absence or lack of material social wealth, and as a subjectively derived phenomenon, i.e., the way this category is realized and reflected in social consciousness, the degree of acuteness with which this requirement is perceived and accepted by the consciousness of social classes, strata, groups, and individuals. Consequently, it is not the goal itself that is of importance but the sociopsychological perception of it, because it is this perception that directly conditions socially significant behavior of people.

Sociological literature often speaks about the widespread sociopsychological phenomenon of ascribing tremendous social significance and value to obtaining higher education. It was also

23. *Supra* at 19.

noticed that the orientation toward getting higher education "by all means" does not represent by itself some socially neutral or indifferent sociopsychological phenomenon. The point is that, to every stage of society's development, there corresponds a particular optimal level of education. Accordingly, "premature transition to such forms of education that are not stipulated by real needs of national economy gives birth to requirements (in the character of labor levels of culture, standards of life, etc.) which cannot be satisfied by society at the present level of productivity of labor."[24]

The most important system of social institutions comprises the totality of institutions regulating the processes of social mobility, whether "vertical" (transition from one class, strata, professional group to another) or "horizontal" (migration from the country to towns, to new developments).

All these processes of social mobility characterize important changes in social position of the person that demand from him perception, mastery, and adequate performance of new social functions. Social mobility alters the social groups to which the person belongs and this demands from him following new social norms and rules. A significant condition of social mobility is also getting an adequate education.

Sociological studies show that an inadequate, inflexible general system of basic education, professional training, or university education leads to such social expenses as school dropouts, disadvantages in employment, and psychological difficulties. The totality of such factors may have a negative effect on the level of youth offenses.

Criminological literature also contains data analysis on the problem of migration (horizontal mobility) on criminality. The direct correlation between the intensity of migration processes and the increase in the number of offenses in particular regions is marked, as well as the higher rate of criminality in towns (especially newly constructed or still under construction). The explanation of these and similar phenomena may be extended

---

24. V. P. Shiebkin, *Some Questions on the Adjustment of Youth to Labor,* SOCIAL STUDIES 118 (1965; Moscow, "Nauka" Publ. House).

if the impact produced by social processes of this kind on social institutions is taken into consideration.

2.2. The Role of the Community

By social communities is meant the whole variety of stable and relatively stable forms and ways that people live together, including formal and informal social groups. Social communities are characterized by inner organization (group norms, means of control, etc.), by existence of group values (i.e., a system of priorities), by a special common feeling, and by a feeling among members that they are set apart from others.

Social groups or communities may be, like social institutions, defined both from the point of view of their external structure and from the standpoint of their internal functions. Thus, the description of the objective data on groups includes the data on demographic structure of the group, its professional composition, educational level of its members, etc.

From the functional point of view, groups are characterized by the direction of the group members' actions toward achieving group aims. The group ensures the coordination of these actions and this leads to strengthening of group conformity. Conformity is provided by certain patterns of behavior, norms defining relations within the group, and sociopsychological mechanisms directing group members' behavior.

Among the many types of groups of particular importance from the point of view of their impact on behavior are such social units as the family, workers' collectives, groups of people spending leisure time together, and all types of territorial communities (villages, settlements, small towns, etc.).

Among the major social functions of the family, one should particularly note the function of providing for succession of the elements of culture by their transmission from one generation to another. The family provides for socialization of youth in the course of learning by children of norms of social intercourse; inspires a feeling of security among family members; satisfies emotional needs through common feelings, in exchanges of emotional experience and moods; and protects against psychological imbalances and feelings of being isolated. The result of successful functioning of the family as a social group lies in the effective prevention of deviations from social norms in the overwhelming majority of spheres of social life.

The territorial community also has an impact on the character of its members' behavior, especially in the sphere of informal contacts and of spending leisure time together. Professional groups, when they function successfully, not only solve purely professional needs but also inspire their members with the feeling of labor solidarity, provide for professional prestige and authority, and control the behavior of group members through professional morality and ethics.

Dynamic social processes may produce as byproducts undesirable results with a destructive impact on such social groups and communities and lead to their partial disorganization. As has already been noted in criminological literature, rapid technological development, urbanization and consequent increases of urban population, the complication of social relationships, changes of social structure, and other such processes may create definite additional problems for combatting antisocial phenomena.[25]

Disorganization affects both the external structure of social communities and their internal functional character. Thus, if from the external perspective such social processes as migration, urbanization, and industrialization lead to disintegration of the extended family, fluctuation of manpower availability, influxes of migrants among natives in territorial communities, and alterations of the natural sex-age structure, then disorganization of functions of such communities finds its expression in the shattering of values, in discrepancies in standards and patterns of behavior, and in weakening of the normative structure of the group. This in turn leads to increased deviations in behavior of the members of such communities and social groups.

Phenomena of this kind are connected with weakening of the sociopsychological impact of a community, which served as a means of in-group conformity, solidarity, cohesion, and mutual

25. V. N. Kudriavtzev, *Sociological Problems of the Study of Antisocial Behavior*, Social Studies (1965; Moscow, "Nauka" Publ. House).

understanding, directed against centrifugal tendencies. The result is destruction of the community.[26]

Deviations of this kind, in their extreme forms, give birth to criminality of an aggressive, violent character. Family disorganization may give birth to juvenile delinquency; disorganization of professional groups may lead to deterioration of work ethics. Under these conditions, normal social communities are not always able to continue to perform all of their vital functions, such as to inspire the individual with an integrated system of norms of behavior and with feelings of solidarity and conformity, and to place the regulated system of levels of social prestige and approval at his disposal.

Unsatisfied needs of this type may sometimes manifest themselves in the commission of illegal acts of a violent character as self-assertion and in spontaneous formation of smaller groups that can inspire their members with feelings of conformity, solidarity, and prestige; however, this is at the expense of pressing on them norms and patterns of behavior deviating from the demands of law and morality.

Prevention of criminality of this type should be connected with stabilization of threatened normal social communities, with raising the level of social cohesion, and with strengthening the mechanisms of formal and informal social control. By measures of informal social control is meant the totality of means of social impact and influence produced by social groups (by groups of co-workers, by communities, by families, etc.) on behavior of the members of these groups. These measures of social control are subdivided into measures of a positive character (approval, incentives, raising of prestige or of social status in the group) and into measures of negative character (censure, moral disapproval, ostracism, etc.).

To take into account both the details of interaction among social processes on one hand and interaction and institutions and social communities on the other, the socioeconomic, political, and class structure of the society within which such interaction takes place are of primary significance.

---

26. B. D. PARYGIN, THE FOUNDATIONS OF SOCIO-PSYCHOLOGICAL THEORY 183 (1971; Moscow, "Mysl" Publ. House).

While the decisive social process leading to radical changes in social structures is the process of development of productive forces of society, the precise mode of production and the nature of prevailing relations of production predetermine the character of such interaction.

For antagonistic social formations—and for contemporary capitalist society an antagonistic character for such interactions is inevitable—criminality is the typical manifestation. F. Engels wrote that ". . . history, up to now, proceeds like a natural process and is as a matter of fact subject to the same laws of development."[27] Such a situation is typified by antagonistic social formations.

For the socialist type of society, where for the first time in history on a statewide basis it became possible to forecast and regulate scientifically the development of the most significant social processes, the antagonistic mode of interaction of social processes with social structures of the society is largely blunted. The removal of the contradictory character of the interaction is in principle possible only at the highest level of socialist development. Under modern conditions, criminality is still combined with the existence of particular contradictions of a nonantagonistic character, which are being removed in the course of social development. "The general character of the course that social processes are taking in our society creates in principle the necessary base for prevention or neutralization with the help of a system of purpose-oriented undertakings (including measures of social prevention), of the impact of incidental negative phenomena connected with concentration of masses of population in large settlements, with rapid growth of towns, with moves of population, etc."[28]

Section 3. CRIME PREVENTION

3.1. Significance of the Overall Social Order

The system of crime prevention comprises, from the standpoint of the contents of preventive measures, measures of a general social and a special criminological character.

---

27. K. MARX & F. ENGELS, 37 WORKS 396.

28. N. A. GORSHENEVA & G. M. MINKOVSKY, COMBATTING JUVENILE DELINQUENCY IN LARGE TOWNS 9 (1975; Moscow).

General social measures of prevention include the activities of state organs and public organizations in the field of socio-economic and cultural development, both of the country on the whole and of particular regions, towns, districts, enterprises, etc. This activity includes the problems of leveling incomes of different groups of the population; increasing the level of wages; enlarging the funds for public consumption; the transition to obligatory secondary education and efforts to reduce school drop-outs; measures directed at strengthening the family; cutting down the proportion of less-mechanized, less-skilled types of labor; and development of democratic forms of social control over the activity of officials. All these measures are aimed at general perfection of the economic and social structure of society, and at the same time, they perform functions of general crime prevention.

The principle of planned development of the economy creates a real base for effective translation into reality of such measures. During the last ten years in the USSR, *plans of social development* have been widespread. These plans play the role of supplements, and in a number of cases the role of significant amendments to the plans of national economy, the rapid development of which may, if social consequences of such development are not taken into consideration, have a negative influence on the level and dynamics of crime.

An important part of the local social development plans are the plans of social prevention, which include planning and forecasting of social effects of economic development, migration processes, and urbanization, and which serve as the basis for advanced development of complex sociopreventive measures.

At present, most plans of social development focus on the following concerns: (1) general characteristics of the subject of the plan; (2) economic, production, scientific, and technological projections; (3) changes in the character of activity, labor, the professional skills structure, and cultural-technical level; (4) raising standards of life; (5) development of social activity; and (6) moral and ethical upbringing and education.

An overview of the directions in planning social development on the national scale may be gained by considering the tasks solved during the ninth five-year period of development (1970-1975). By the end of this period, the level of average monthly wages of workers and employees reached 146-149 rubles and that of collective farmers *(kolkhozniki)* reached 98 rubles. The volume of public funds for consumption reached 90 billion rubles by 1975. During that period, new houses were built with a dwelling space of 567 to 575 million square meters. Almost 60 million people experienced improved housing conditions.

The plan of social development for one of the regions of Leningrad for 1971 to 1975, for example, envisaged an increase of wages of working people by 5.8 percent and a reduction in the proportion of workers receiving low wages (less than 80 rubles per month) from 8.8 percent to 6.4. Eighty percent of the families in the region moved to new apartments.

The plan of social development of another region of the same town envisaged bringing the number of workers with higher education and partial or complete secondary education to 85 percent and reducing the proportion of unskilled industrial workers from 53 percent to 48 percent.[29]

Planning of this type opens real possibilities for intensive positive impact on the totality of socioeconomic conditions conducive to commission of crimes.

Such important social groups as the family, schools, and working collectives are also objects of general social prevention. The direct correlation between juvenile delinquency and conditions of family upbringing is recognized by all Soviet criminologists. "Unhealthy" families or families with problems include families marked by alcoholism of parents, by conflicts, by lack of supervision over children, etc.

Measures of social prevention in this field comprise intervention against abuses of parental rights as provided by law; counseling to ameliorate friction, counseling parents on the problems of family pedagogy, and similar measures aimed at regulating interpersonal relations within the family.[30]

---

29. V. P. ORECHOV, SOCIAL PLANNING AND PROBLEMS OF CRIME COMBATTING 78 (1972; Leningrad U. Publ. House).

30. A. G. Chartchev, *On the Ways of Further Strengthening the Family in the USSR*, SOCIAL STUDIES (1965; Moscow, "Nauka" Publ. House).

According to Article 19 of the Fundamentals of Legislation of the USSR and the Union Republics "On marriage and the family" of June 27, 1968, a court may, upon an appropriate action by government or nongovernment organizations or on an action brought by a procurator, deprive either or both parents of their parental rights and place children in the care of trusteeship and guardianship bodies. The law enumerates the following bases for removal of parental rights: either or both parents may be deprived of parental rights where it is established that they have neglected their duties in bringing up their children or abused their parental rights, maltreated children, exerted a harmful influence on them by their immoral antisocial behavior, and where the parents are chronic alcoholics or drug addicts.[31]

School, as a social collective, is a major object of social prevention. Social alienation, rooted in family disturbances, may lead to breaking of normal social ties of a juvenile with his schoolmates and teachers.

Pupils remaining for the second year in the same class and "drop-outs" from schools are considered to be serious symptoms of the predelinquent state. The main direction of social prevention in relation to school is extending the process of education to overlap with the function of upbringing. The task of the schools is not simply to pass on information to pupils but also to involve them in a system of real interpersonal relations based on moral-ethical principles.

The system of interpersonal relations in the collectives of co-workers is also an object of social prevention. Thus, the plan of social development of one enterprise envisaged the following points: (a) organizing, through the sociological service at the enterprise, a lecture bureau for the study of fundamentals of social psychology as a basis for improving work of the whole enterprise; (b) conducting a sociopsychological study of the factors affecting young workers' adjustment to labor and to the work situation; (c) regulating relations to primary groups on the horizontal level (worker-worker) and the vertical level (supervisor-employee); (d) revealing sociopsychological aspects of

---

31. GAZETTE OF THE SUPREME SOVIET OF THE USSR No. 27, at 241 (1968).

manpower fluctuation; and (e) constant surveys of public opinion, at the enterprise, on problems of business and social life.[32]

The territorial community is also an object of social prevention. The aims of preventive measures in this context are mobilization of social activity for the resolution of problems that are of concern for all members of the given community, such as organization of public services and amenities, organization of places where young people can spend their leisure time, the work of voluntary organizations, etc. The sociopsychological problem that is to be solved consists of overcoming alienation and anonymity of interpersonal relations in the urban mode of life; working out of common interests and purposes through the norms of socially positive behavior oriented at conformity of the members of the territorial community; and organization of means of constructive cooperation.

3.2. Specific Areas of Concern

Special criminological measures of prevention are aimed at situations and persons showing symptoms of being conducive to commission of crimes.

Specific measures of criminological prevention are directed at juveniles who show potential for becoming delinquents,[33] socially dangerous alcoholics, and persons who have served a criminal sentence but do not show any signs of resocialization. Preventive measures in relation to such persons correspond to measures of general social prevention aimed at prevention of juvenile delinquency, criminality caused by alcoholism, and criminal recidivism.

JUVENILES

Commissions and inspectorates on juvenile affairs are among the agencies conducting special prevention of juvenile delinquency.

Commissions on juvenile affairs function under the executive committees of the local town, district, or regional Soviets of People's Deputies and under councils of ministers of autonomous

32. V. P. ORCHOV, *supra* note 29, at 96.
33. GAZETTE OF THE SUPREME SOVIET OF THE RSFSR No. 23, at 536 (1967).

and union republics. Their activity is regulated by statutes approved by decrees of the Supreme Soviets of autonomous or union republics. In the RSFSR, for example, it is the Decree of the Supreme Soviet of the RSFSR of June 3, 1967.[34]

Commissions are at the head of a whole system of early prevention. They integrate and direct the efforts of various institutions and organizations, both state and public, in the field. This purpose shapes both the mode of formation and composition of the commissions.

The following are among the activities of commissions:

a. "detection" of inadequate supervision of children; protection of rights and interests of juveniles; and social adjustment of children and adolescents;

b. control over the activities of educational and cultural institutions for children and adolescents;

c. curtailing specific sources of negative influence upon juveniles;

d. implementing measures to positively influence juvenile offenders and persons responsible for their upbringing;

e. control over activities of special educational institutions and educational-labor colonies;

f. prevention of recidive crimes.

There are special legal provisions (Art. 7 of the statute) saying that the decisions of the commission on questions within its competence are binding on all institutions and enterprises, and their administration, officials, and citizens. A two-week period is established to inform the commission on measures taken in response to its decisions. Violation of its decisions may result in public censure, administrative responsibility, and even, in some malicious cases or cases leading to harmful consequences, to criminal responsibility.

Local commissions on juvenile affairs integrate and coordinate the efforts of local organs and institutions in the fields of people's education, public health, social maintenance, culture and internal affairs, as well as efforts of teachers.

---

34. According to Soviet legislation, a person can be subjected to criminal responsibility only if at the time of the crime he is at least fourteen or sixteen years of age, depending on the seriousness of the crime.

Commissions on juvenile affairs develop and implement, both by themselves and with the help of corresponding state organs and public organizations, general measures of a preventive character.

Commissions (by joint efforts with organs of people's education, of vocational training, of social maintenance and of militia, as well as public participation) detect, register, monitor, and take measures for care of orphans, juveniles whose parents do not provide for them, school "drop-outs," youngsters who neither work nor study, and other juveniles in need of assistance (Art. 9 of the Statute).

In particular, commissions charge organs of people's education with placing children in schools and other educational institutions, with establishing trusteeships and guardianships; organs of social maintenance with placing children in special institutions for mentally retarded or handicapped children; organs of vocational training with placing them in vocational schools; and administrations of enterprises, factories, etc., with employing juveniles. If necessary, commissions organize financial assistance to needy families and place children from such families in boarding schools or prolonged day programs in ordinary schools.

Commissions also consider cases of petty violations committed by juveniles. Another group of cases considered by commissions are cases of socially dangerous acts committed by adolescents under the age of criminal responsibility.[35]

The Decree of the Supreme Soviet of the USSR of February 15, 1977, became a very important prophylactic measure for juvenile delinquency. This Decree defined basic duties and rights of inspectorates on juvenile affairs, of special reception and diagnostic centers for juveniles, and of special vocational-educational institutions for prevention of delinquency by unsupervised juveniles.[36]

---

35. The Decree of the Supreme Soviet of the USSR of February 15, 1977; *see* GAZETTE OF THE SUPREME SOVIET OF THE USSR No. 8, at 138 (1977).

36. The Decree of the Presidium of the Supreme Soviet of the USSR of February 15, 1977, "On amendments to the fundamentals of criminal legislation of the USSR and the union republics by Article 39"; *see* GAZETTE OF THE SUPREME SOVIET OF THE USSR No. 8, at 137 (1977).

Inspectorates focus mainly on upbringing and preventive work in the areas where they are situated. For this purpose, they detect minors who lack proper supervision. If the reason lies in the parents' inability to provide for upbringing of children, such families are rendered assistance.

Inspectorates on juvenile affairs have wide powers. They function under the guidance of the organs of the Ministry of Internal Affairs, of people's education, and of the local Soviets of Peoples' Deputies. They conduct their work among youngsters who have served their sentences or were sentenced to conditional punishment or to a type of punishment not involving placement in an educational institution, and with youngsters who were paroled or amnestied.

Detection and registration of such juveniles is aimed at putting their behavior under constant supervision and influencing it to prevent deviations from accepted norms.

If a juvenile commits a minor offense which is not a crime, he is taken not to the general department of a police station (the so-called *dejurnaya tchast*) but to a special "children's room" of the police station to avoid contact by the juvenile with adult offenders.

He may be kept in the "children's room" not longer than three hours. After that, he must be taken to his parents or he must be placed in a children's institution.

Prevention of recidivism among juveniles is another branch of the inspectorate's activities. Educational labor colonies send information about the coming release of a juvenile offender to the place of his residence. Inspectors register such juveniles and, together with public organizations, render them assistance and guidance. The length of the after-care period is one or two years.

Rather important functions in the field of combatting juvenile delinquency are performed by a special type of institution for juveniles, reception-diagnostic centers (*priemniki-raspredeliteli*), where cases of juveniles under the age of eighteen are examined. These centers place juveniles in children's institutions, boarding schools, or special educational institutions.

One of the most important reflections of the influence of

criminology on criminal law is the prerogative given to the court, in considering the cases of first-time juvenile offenders, to suspend sentences of deprivation of liberty for terms of up to three years. The period of suspension varies from six months to two years. As a basis for such a decision, the court makes its own assessment of the character and social danger of the crime committed, the personality of the juvenile, and all other circumstances of the case, as well as of the likelihood of the juvenile's re-education and reintegration into society.

ALCOHOLICS

In the system of social prevention measures, an important place is occupied by mandatory medical treatment of socially dangerous alcoholics.

According to current legislation, there are three general types of mandatory medical treatment.

The first is assigned to persons, including alcoholics, who have committed socially dangerous criminal acts but have been recognized as not culpable. Hence, they are subjected not to criminal responsibility but to mandatory medical treatment.

In accordance with criminal legislation (Art. 11 and 58 of the CPC and parallel provisions in the codes of union republics), mandatory measures of a medical character such as placing offenders in mental institutions of general or special types may be assigned by the court.

The second type of mandatory medical treatment is envisaged by Article 62 of the CPC. In conformity with this norm, for crimes committed by drug or alcohol abusers, the court (upon petitions by social organizations or collectives of workers, a comrade's court, or health organizations) may, along with the penalty for the crime committed, assign mandatory medical treatment to such persons. Such persons, if sentenced to penalties not involving deprivation of liberty, are liable to mandatory treatment in the medical institutions with special medical and labor regimes. If such persons are sentenced to deprivation of liberty, they are liable to medical treatment while serving that sentence and after release, if necessary. Termination of mandatory medical treatment is decided by the court upon the recommendation of the institution where he was placed.

A special type of treatment for alcoholism is the mandatory program of medical treatment and labor re-education of chronic alcoholics and, in the majority of the union republics, of drug abusers in special treatment labor institutions *(letchebnotrudovoj profilaktorij)* (hereafter referred to as TLI).

The main differences between this type of treatment and the first two follow:

1. TLIs contain drunkards who have committed no crime but who have avoided voluntary medical treatment and have continued drinking. They violate labor discipline, public order, and the rules of the socialist mode of life in spite of measures of social pressure and administrative penalties.

2. TLIs contain only able-bodied drunkards.

3. Subordinate legislation envisages minimal and maximum terms of this course of treatment, within the limits of which the court sets a definite term.[37]

4. This type of mandatory treatment is an institution of Soviet administrative law, while the first two are regulated by the criminal law and the law of criminal procedure.

5. The registration of materials on persons placed in TLI differs greatly from the order for investigation and registration of cases of persons who are subjected to mandatory treatment in accordance with Articles 58 and 62 of the Penal Code of RSFSR.

6. Trials of cases on placing persons in TLIs are conducted by means of simplified procedure.

7. The legal status of persons under TLI treatment differs

---

37. In seven republics (the Moldavian, Latvian, Lithuanian, Azerbaijan, Tadjik, Turkmen, and Uzbek) the established term is from six months to one year, in two republics (Russian and Kazakh) from one to two years, in three republics (Estonian, Byelorussian, and Kirghiz) from six months to two years, in the Ukranian republic from six months to one year for drunkards and from one to two years for drug abusers.

In case of successful treatment and exemplary conduct of a person placed in a TLI, the term of treatment may be reduced by the court on the recommendation of the administrative and medical conclusions of the TLI. Reduction of terms of treatment cannot be applied to persons who have been placed in TLI repeatedly.

considerably from the legal status of those undergoing mandatory treatment in conformity with Articles 58 and 62 of the
Penal Code of RSFSR.[38]

CRIMINAL RECIDIVES

Measures on prevention of recidivism comprise the measures
of after-care assistance to all persons released from prison and
the establishment of administrative supervision over some categories of persons released.[39]

By law, persons released from penal institutions are provided
with free travel to their place of work or residence along with
food and money for the trip. If such persons do not have suitable clothing or footwear or the money to buy them, they shall
be provided with clothing and footwear free of charge.

Persons released from prison shall be provided with work by
the executive committees of local Soviets of Peoples' Deputies,
taking into account, if possible, their profession, within fifteen
days after applying for help in obtaining employment. In cases
of need, released persons shall be given living accommodations.

Instructions of the executive committees of local Soviets of
People's Deputies to provide employment to persons released
from prison shall be binding on the heads of enterprises, institutions, and organizations.

Invalids and aged persons shall be placed, at their request, in
homes for invalids and the aged. Minor orphans, if necessary,
shall be sent to boarding schools or placed under guardianship
by commissions of juvenile affairs.

Administrative supervision shall be established over especially
dangerous recidivists and over persons who have served sentences
for grave crimes if their behavior while serving the sentence

38. The Penal Code of the Russian Soviet Federated Socialist Republic, adopted
on October 27, 1960, in legal force since January 1, 1961 (hereafter referred to
as the PC); *see* GAZETTE OF THE SUPREME SOVIET OF THE RSFSR No. 40, Item
24 (1960).

39. COMMENTARIES OF THE FOUNDATIONS OF CORRECTIVE LABOR LEGISLATION
OF THE USSR AND THE UNION REPUBLICS (1972; Moscow, "Juriditcheskaya
Literatura" Publ. House).

showed obstinate unwillingness to take the path of reform and join in an honest life of work.[40]

Administrative supervision is a compulsory measure. It is not aimed at abasement or compromising the supervised person at his place of residence or work, but rather at preventing them from committing new crimes, as well as producing a re-educational influence upon them.

Administrative supervision shall be established in the following cases: (a) with regard to especially dangerous recidivists recognized as such by the court sentence; (b) with regard to those who had sentences to deprivation of liberty for grave crimes or who were sentenced more than twice for any intentional crimes, if their behavior while serving the sentence reflected an obstinate unwillingness to take the path of re-education and join in an honest life of work; (c) with regard to persons sentenced to deprivation of liberty for committing a grave crime or for any intentional crime, who, after having served the sentence or being paroled, systematically violate public order and rules of the socialist mode of life.

Administrative supervision over the persons released from places of confinement is established at the place of permanent residence of the offender. First, the local organ of militia issues a reasoned decision on whether administrative supervision should be established. The decision should state the grounds for establishing administrative supervision, the term of its duration, and restrictions to be applied. It is then confirmed by the chief of the town or local police department.

In establishing administrative supervision, the organs of militia explain to the supervised person his rights and duties and also warn him about his responsibility for violation of the rules of administrative supervision.

Supervised persons have to provide notice of any changes in their place of work or residence and about business trips outside the region or town. If private trips are permitted, the super-

---

40. "Regulations on administrative supervision by militia organs over the persons released from places of confinement" were approved by the Decree of the Presidium of the Supreme Soviet of the USSR of June 26, 1966; *see* GAZETTE OF THE SUPREME SOVIET OF THE USSR No. 30, at 597 (1966).

vised person must register with the local organ of militia at his destination.

Administrative supervision is established for terms of from six months to one year. If the behavior of the person under supervision indicates that the established term of supervision is insufficient, it may be extended for another six months, but the total length may not exceed the term provided by law for expungement of records of conviction.

To persons placed under administrative supervision, the following restrictions may be applied: confinement to their homes during certain hours; placing certain locations off limits to them; prohibition of travel outside the local area except on business trips; and compulsory visits to the militia department from one to four times a month.

Such restrictions may be applied in full or in part or modified as appropriate.

Violations of the rules of administrative supervision may be punished by administrative or criminal penalties.

CHAPTER V

SUBSTANTIVE CRIMINAL LAW

S. G. KELINA

Section 1. CRIMES

1.1 Sources of Criminal Law

CRIMINAL RESPONSIBILITIES in the Soviet Union can attach only to acts prohibited by criminal codes, so that criminal punishment can be imposed only for violations of the criminal law and not for violations of any other normative legislation. This principle is reflected in Article 3 of the Criminal Law Fundamentals of the USSR and the Union Republics (hereafter referred to as CL Fundamentals) which states, "Only a person guilty of committing a crime, that is, one who has either intentionally or carelessly committed a socially dangerous act provided for by the criminal law, shall be subject to criminal responsibility and punishment.[1]

The Supreme Court of the USSR in its directive of March 18, 1963, "On strict observance of laws by courts at trials of criminal cases," stressed the need for unconditional observance of the rule: "Courts shall meet the requirements of the criminal legislation accurately and constantly. . . . Actions shall be adjudged criminal in full correspondence with the law providing criminal responsibility for such actions, and deviations from this requirement are not permitted.[2]

Court precedent is not a source of the criminal law in the USSR. The Supreme Court of the USSR and the supreme courts of the union republics have the right to interpret legislation in two ways.

First, such courts may examine a specific criminal case through

1. The Criminal Law Fundamentals were adopted on December 25, 1958, by the Supreme Soviet of the USSR; see GAZETTE OF THE SUPREME SOVIET OF THE USSR No. 1, Item 6 (1959).
2. COLLECTED DECISIONS OF THE PLENUM OF THE SUPREME COURT OF THE USSR 1924-1973, at 284 (1974).

their power of supervision, and it is natural that such supreme court decisions serve as examples to lower courts on interpretations and application of the law. However, the courts' judgments cannot refer to such decisions but only to the underlying criminal law.

Second, the Plenum of the Supreme Court of the USSR has the right to issue to lower courts directives on problems of applying legislation (Art. 9, Decree of the Supreme Court of the USSR).[3] Plenums of the supreme courts of the union republics have the same right. This right is often exercised and frequently consists of commentaries on exceptionally complex and controversial questions on the application of criminal legislation. Such commentaries are developed with the help of scholars. Courts may refer to such directives in their subsequent judgments, not as legal sources, but as official interpretations of the law by an organ charged with such a function by the legislature. The only source of Soviet criminal law is the law itself, in which all the necessary attributes of a crime are defined and measures of punishment are specified.

Basic criminal laws in force are the CL Fundamentals and the penal codes of the union republics.

The CL Fundamentals constitute the law on the federal level, which aims at preserving the integrity of the criminal law regulations throughout the Soviet State on questions of great significance. The CL Fundamentals do not stipulate responsibilities for particular crimes. They are divided into four parts: General Provisions, Crime, Punishment, and Assignment of Punishment or Relief from Punishment.

The Fundamentals are incorporated into the texts of the penal codes of all the union republics and are the basis for the general part.

Each union republic has its own penal code, which is used by practitioners for definitions of specific crimes and assignment of punishment. All new criminal laws—both federal and republican—must be incorporated into the codes. That is why Article

---

3. Decree of the Supreme Court of the USSR, adopted on February 12, 1957; *see* Gazette of the Supreme Soviet of the USSR No. 4, Item 85 (1957).

4 of the PC reads: "All persons who have committed a crime on the territory of the RSFSR are responsible as per this present Code."[4] Similar provisions are included in the penal codes of all other union republics.

The fact that there are fifteen penal codes in the USSR leads to the question of how these codes are applied territorially. The general principle is contained in Article 4 of the CL Fundamentals which states: "All persons who have committed crimes on the territory of the USSR shall be subject to responsibility under the criminal laws in force at the place of the crime." Thus, acts are to be judged by the penal code of the union republic within whose territory they were committed. In cases where a person has committed several crimes on the territories of several union republics, he is responsible under penal codes of each republic within whose territory the criminal actions took place.

For example, Golovenko visited schools and collected money from the students for an organization of tours to visit other cities, then he kept the money for himself. He was convicted for his fraudulent actions under Part 2, Article 147 of the Russian Federation Penal Code, Part 2, Article 144 of the Byelorussian SSR Penal Code, Part 2, Article 147 of the Azerbaidjan SSR Penal Code, and Part 2, Article 143 of the Ukrainian SSR Penal Code.[5]

1.2. Structure of the Criminal Codes

The PC, like the penal codes of other union republics, is not large and comprises only 269 articles. All new laws are incorporated into the penal codes. Thus, the Presidium of the Supreme Soviet Decree of April 19, 1973, "On responsibility for high-jacking of an aircraft,"[6] was incorporated into the PC as Article 213(2).

The PC is subdivided into two parts: the General and the Special. The General Part consists of sixty-three articles, grouped into six chapters: general provisions (Arts. 1-3), scope of appli-

---

4. *See* Gazette of the Supreme Soviet of the USSR No. 40, Item 591 (1960).

5. Bulletin of the Supreme Court of the RSFSR No. 1, at 12 (1971).

6. Gazette of the Supreme Soviet of the USSR No. 1, Item 3 (1973).

cation (Arts. 4-6), crime (Arts. 7-19), punishment (Arts. 20-36), assignment of punishment and relief from punishment (Arts. 37-57), and compulsory measures of medical and educational nature (Arts. 58-63).

The Special Part of the PC deals with the elements of specific crimes and measures of punishment for particular crimes. The structure of the Special Part is based on the interest protected; each chapter contains descriptions of crimes directed against the same object: persons, property, the system of justice, and so on. Such a clear system of organization makes it possible for even nonprofessionals to deal with the code.

The order of the chapters of the Special Part reflects the social importance of the areas of social relations protected under them. The Special Part of the PC consists of twelve chapters: state crimes [Arts. 64-88(2)], crimes against socialist property (Arts. 89-101), crimes against life, health, freedom, and integrity of persons (Arts. 102-131), crimes against political and labor rights of citizens (Arts. 132-143), crimes against personal property (Arts. 144-151), economic crimes (Arts. 152-169), breaches of trust (Arts. 170-175), crimes against justice (Arts. 176-190), crimes against the order of administration [Arts. 190(1)-205(2)], crimes against public security, public order, and public health (Arts. 206-230), crimes relating to local customs (Arts. 231-236), and military crimes (Arts. 237-69).

One should note that Soviet scholars have expressed the opinion that the sequence of subjects within the code should be amended, so that after the first chapter (crimes against the state) would be crimes against persons rather than crimes against socialist property.[7] "All for the benefit of the people, everything for a man," is the goal of the Communist Party of the Soviet Union, which emphasizes that the main purpose of the criminal law is protection of persons and their rights. This explains why the rights of citizens and their guarantees are described in Section II of the new Constitution, immediately after the social structure and policy of the USSR.

---

7. *See, e.g.,* Setting and Development of Soviet Criminal Law 41 (1973; Volograd).

In formulating descriptions of specific crimes, the legislature tries first of all to be extremely precise, then to be concise and use easily understood language. That is why a great part of the PC's provisions (54.9 percent) are descriptive in character. In cases where attributes of a punishable action cannot be completely enumerated within a code article because they are too numerous or they are described in detail in other acts not of a criminal law nature or are subject to frequent changes, the legislature uses so-called blanket dispositions. Such provisions comprise 26.2 percent of all enumerations of crimes and are used to cover such crimes as traffic violations (Arts. 211, 85 PC) or breaches of regulations (Art. 140).

When a person is charged under an article utilizing a blanket disposition, it is necessary to prove not only the presence of all the attributes specified by the penal code in his actions but also to show clearly what regulation was broken.

The Supreme Court terminated the case of Nekhoroshev on the grounds of the absence from the act in question of the elements of a crime. Nekhoroshev, while driving, had knocked down a boy riding a bicycle, but he did not break any traffic rules. The accident took place because of the victim's behavior, when he darted unexpectedly onto the road on a hill.

When composing a sanction, the legislature tries to make the punishment fully correspond to the gravity of the crime. At the time, the court is given a chance to consider thoroughly all the peculiarities of the specific crime and person who committed it when choosing a measure of punishment.[8]

That is why the PC, as well as the penal codes of the other union republics, do not contain automatic or inflexible punishments. All sanctions of the PC are either relatively determined (45.8 percent) or alternative (54.2 percent). They present an opportunity for the court to choose not only the degree but also the kind of punishment. For example, the punishment for cheating customers under Article 156 of the PC may be deprivation of liberty for the term of up to two years, corrective labor for up to one year, or withdrawal of the right to work at commercial enterprises.

---

8. Bulletin of the Supreme Court of the USSR No. 3, at 13-15 (1967).

Frequency of the practical application of the articles of the penal codes are determined by the dynamics and structure of criminality. Among the "most popular" penal code articles is that concerning hooliganism—a crime similar to vandalism. Article 206 of the Penal Code of the USSR defines it as "Actions rudely violating social order and expressing obvious disrespect towards the society." For instance, Shaculenko was punished for hooliganism after he, in a state of drunkenness, abused the administrator of dormitories who reprimanded him, and after he left the dormitory he threw an iron pipe through the window, aiming at the television set in the recreation room, where people were watching a television program.[9]

Hooliganistic acts as a rule are performed in the state of drunkenness and in public places—in the street, park, cinema, restaurants, public transport, etc. Lately, hooliganism accounts for 20 to 30 percent[10] of all crimes.

Among the PC articles which are rarely applied is the article assigning criminal responsibility for willful nonpayment of alimony: "Willful non-payment of the alimony assigned by the court in order to maintain minor children, or adult but disabled children depending on a person, is punished by deprivation of liberty for a term of up to one year or corrective labor for a term of up to one year" (Art. 132 PC). "Willful non-payment of alimony assigned by the court in order to maintain disabled parents is punished by corrective labor for a term of up to one year, or social censure or other means of social influence" (Art. 123 PC).

Such conflicts among relatives are predominantly handled as civil cases, criminal action being possible only when "willful" (meaning long-term, inexcusable) nonpayment takes place. Such cases are rare. Thus, the courts of one region of the RSFSR convicted 6.3 percent of offenders under Article 122 of the PC, and under Article 123 only a few persons during 1972 to 1976.[11]

Another rarely used provision is the article of the PC covering

---

9. Bulletin of the Supreme Court of RSFSR No. 2, at 11 (1977).

10. Criminology 374 (1976; Moscow, "Juriditcheskaya Literatura" Publ. House).

11. Soviet Justice No. 19, at 21 (1977).

"fictitious information added to state reports and presentation of other intentionally distorted information concerning the fulfillment of plans" (Art. 152 of the PC). The danger of such actions lies in the violation of the principles of planned economy, leading to chaos, inefficiency, and waste of people's goods. The motivation for such crimes may vary from a misunderstanding of interests of an enterprise to an attempt to conceal unsatisfactory results of production to personal interest, which is often combined with misappropriation. Thus, the chairman of an inter-kolkhoz construction organization, *Nalivaiko,* was convicted under Article 152(1) of the PC for misappropriation of socialist property. The man had added fictitious data regarding work not done for the sum of 347,400 rubles on nine construction sites in order to create a picture of successful plan fulfilling. Based on this report, workers and employees of his organization received illegal bonuses amounting to 12,900 rubles from the state.[12]

Such cases are rare in judicial-investigatory practice. For example, only 13 percent of all persons convicted for economic crimes (alcohol brewing, speculation, defrauding customers, illegal gambling, fictitious reports, illegal commercial mediation, etc.) were convicted in 1976 under Article 152 of the Penal Code in the Byelorussian SSR.[13]

Section 2. DIRECT CRIMINAL RESPONSIBILITY

2.1. Elements of Criminal Conduct

The basis for criminal responsibility is defined in Article 3 of the CL Fundamentals. It is copied without alteration by all the penal codes of the union republics (Art. 3 of the PC). This penal law norm corresponds to Article 5 of the CP Fundamentals which reads: "No criminal case may be initiated, and one initiated shall be subject to termination, (1) in the absence of the event of a crime, (2) in the absence, in the act, of the elements of a crime. . . ."

This norm strengthens the important principle of Soviet law that criminal responsibility may arise only from a commission or omission defined as criminal by law. No other behavior—not

12. Bulletin of the Supreme Court of the USSR No. 1, at 33 (1978).
13. II Criminal Law of the USSR, Special Part, at 217 (1978; Minsk).

an intention to commit a crime in future, unorthodox attitudes or conduct, or discontent with one or more laws or regulations —can be a ground for criminal responsibility, unless directly forbidden by the penal code as criminal.

What action is qualified as criminal by the Soviet criminal law? This question is answered in Article 7 of the CL Fundamentals, copied by all penal codes of the union republics. It reads:

> *Article 7. The Concept of Crime*
> A socially dangerous act (commission or omission) provided for by the criminal law, which infringes the Soviet social or state system, the socialist economic system, socialist property, the person or the political, labor, property and other rights of citizens, or any other socially dangerous act provided for by the criminal law, which infringes the socialist legal order, shall be deemed to be a crime. . . .

An analysis of Articles 3 and 7 of the CL Fundamentals permits the following conclusion about the three elements of a crime recognized by the Soviet law: The socially dangerous action must be prohibited by the law and must be committed intentionally or by carelessness.

These are the same elements advanced in criminal law theory. As an example, one may take a definition given by A. A. Piontkovsky: "Crime is a socially dangerous, antilegal, guilty, punishable action, encroaching upon the Soviet social or state system, socialist economic system, socialist property, person, political, labor, property and other rights of citizens or infringing the socialist legal order."[14]

SOCIAL DANGER

The element of social danger is the most important one for understanding the essence of a crime. This element is foremost in the mind of the legislature in classifying an action as criminal. Actions which cause damage to the state, the public, or an individual, of such a kind or degree that it cannot be remedied by any other means, are declared criminal.

In some cases, an action is classified as criminal because other,

---

14. II COURSE OF SOVIET CRIMINAL LAW 25 (1970; Moscow, "Nauka" Publ. House).

less strict, measures have proved ineffective in curtailing such actions. Thus, for example, criminal responsibility under Article 156(1) of the PC for breaking regulations on the sale of alcohol (to minors, during prohibited hours, at prohibited places, etc.) arises only when violations are repeated within one year of an earlier fine or other administrative or public sanction.

It is natural that a recognition of a certain action as socially dangerous depends on the class, political, and ethical concepts of the legislature. Such concepts may change with changing socioeconomic, political, or other conditions.

The trend to gradually narrow the scope of criminal actions, excluding from their number those that can be dealt with by disciplinary, administrative, or public influence, is characteristic in the Soviet State.

The process of decriminalization manifests itself clearly in the adoption of the present PC in 1960, in which more than sixty actions of the previous code were excluded. Naturally, elimination of actions which have lost their social danger is not the only trend. A parallel process is criminalization of actions which have come to require criminal law measures to combat them.

In this connection, during recent years the PC was enlarged with norms covering encouraging minors to engage in drinking, repeated drunken driving (1972), pollution of sea water with chemicals dangerous to public health (1974), drug abuse (1974), etc.

The social danger of an action recognized as a crime is its most important element not only for the legislature but also for those applying the law, because the law forbids a mechanical application of criminal law norms. Conversely, it demands evaluation of the social danger of an action, though it formally corresponds to the indicia of a crime. If such an action is outwardly similar to a crime but in fact is of little significance, resulting in little social danger, such an action is not recognized as a crime. Part 2, Article 7 of the CL Fundamentals states "A commission or omission, even one formally containing the indicia of an act which is prohibited by the criminal law, but which by reason of its insignificance does not represent a social danger, shall not be deemed to be a crime."

Insignificance that excludes social danger is often connected with small actual damage. For example, Glagoliev was charged in an automobile accident in which his vehicle collided with another while he was driving under the influence of alcohol. It was a careless action resulting in damages of about 304 rubles. In spite of the fact that Article 211, Part I of the PC provides for criminal responsibility for violations of traffic regulations that result in accidents involving people and substantial material loss, the court found Glagoliev's actions not criminal on the ground that damages of 304 rubles was an insufficient basis for recognizing his actions as socially dangerous. Having terminated the case because of the absence of the elements of a crime, the court characterized Glagoliev's conduct as an administrative offense (driving while intoxicated) and decided the issue of compensation for the damage.[15]

PROHIBITED BY LAW

The second element of a crime is that the commission or omission be directly prohibited by the criminal law. The principle of *nullum crimen sine lege* was confirmed legally in 1958 when Article 7 of the CL Fundamentals, since adopted by the penal codes of all the union republics, was amended to include this requirement.

This constituted a rejection of the principle of crime-by-analogy, well known in previous criminal legislation. The reasons for the prior principle of crime by analogy were, first, the lack of necessary experience in combatting crime in the world's first socialist state, and second, the complicated class struggle characteristic of the early period of the construction of socialism, when the legislative bodies of the young proletarian state were unable to foresee all possible forms of resistance by their class enemies.

It should be noted that crime-by-analogy was tightly restricted by the law. Article 16 of the Penal Code of the RSFSR of 1926

15. BULLETIN OF THE SUPREME COURT OF THE RSFSR No. 3, at 14 (1974).

provided that analogy could be applied only where no law existed upon which to base responsibility for the given action. This
meant that analogy could not be applied to assign a more serious
punishment than that already provided by law. The law also provided that only a norm providing responsibility for *similar*
crimes could be applied. In addition, it should be noted that
from the very beginning an analogy was meant to be applied
only in exceptional cases.[16] Thus the principle of crime by
analogy was never a means for subverting the law.

In practice, crimes-by-analogy were never widely used. M. M.
Isaev, one of the authors of the university textbook *Criminal
Law,* who studied the application of analogy during its thirty-
year period of existence, wrote in 1948 that "analogy application in practice is not on the increase, but on the contrary is becoming more and more limited."[17]

INTENTIONAL OR CARELESS

The third element of the Soviet criminal law is the appropriate *mens rea:* a socially dangerous and illegal action or omission
may be deemed to be a crime only if it was committed intentionally or by carelessness. This requirement of the law is consistently emphasized by the Supreme Court of the USSR. Its decision, "On strict observance of the laws by courts when considering criminal cases," states "Courts shall pay special attention
to a thorough examination of the subjective side of a committed crime. Harmful consequences, irrespective of their gravity,
can incriminate a person only if they were intended or were
committed by carelessness."[18]

Often the text of the law indicates a particular *mens rea* requirement. Thus, Articles 102 and 103 of the PC provide for
punishment of intentional homicide, Article 106 of the PC for
homicide by carelessness, Articles 108 and 109 of the PC provide

---

16. "As a general rule, punishment and other measures of social defense may
be applied by courts only for actions specified in the Penal Code. Exclusions
from this rule are allowed in very exceptional cases. . . ." From a circular letter
of the Peoples' Commissariat for Justice of the RSFSR on the coming into force
of the penal code; *see* WEEKLY OF SOVIET JUSTICE No. 21-28, at 30 (1922).

17. CRIMINAL LAW, General Part 246 (1948; Moscow, "Jurizdat" Publ. House).

18. *Supra* note 2.

for punishment of intentional battery, while Article 114 of the PC covers batteries committed by negligence. In other cases, the law may contain an indirect indication as to the *mens rea* required. For instance, Article 154 of the PC provides punishment for speculation, buying, and reselling goods in order to make a profit. The text of the law leads in judicial theory and practice to the conclusion that speculation is a crime only when it is done intentionally.

If the law requires that an act be intentional to be criminal, the absence of such an intent excludes criminal responsibility. The judicial collegium on criminal cases of the Supreme Court of the USSR reversed the conviction of A. Aliev on the grounds of the absence of the elements of a crime where he had signed some forged documents not knowing of their falsity. The decision of the collegium states that A. Aliev cannot bear the responsibility under Article 170 of the PC since a breach of trust is an intentional crime.[19]

The concepts of forms of intention are provided by law as follows: "A crime shall be deemed to be committed intentionally when the person who has committed it was conscious of the socially dangerous nature of his act or anticipated its socially dangerous consequences and willed or consciously allowed such consequences to ensue" (Art. 8 of the CL Fundamentals, Art. 8 of the PC).

The law differentiates two types of intention, direct and indirect. If a person was conscious of the socially dangerous nature of his actions, anticipated possible consequences, and willed them to ensue, it is a direct intention. Such crimes as stealing, fraud, bribery and rape contain a direct intention.

If a person is conscious of the socially dangerous nature of his act and anticipated the possible consequences but does not will them to ensue, it is an indirect intention. R. Rogov was convicted for homicide with an indirect intention when, in an intoxicated state, he fired shots into a room full of people. He did not wish to kill anybody but consciously created such a possibility.[20]

19. BULLETIN OF THE SUPREME COURT OF THE USSR No. 6, at 36 (1970).
20. VII COURSE OF SOVIET CRIMINAL LAW 292, *supra* note 14.

Determination of the kind of intention in the actions of a person does not influence determination of the gravity of punishment because it is difficult to say which kind of intention is more dangerous. Crimes with an indirect intention usually occur unexpectedly, without preparation, but a very high degree of indifference towards harmful consequences is often connected with a very great harm and testifies, as a rule, to deep antisocial attitudes.

Nevertheless, bodies applying the law pay much attention to correct qualification of the intention, since in some cases a crime can be committed only with a direct intention, and consequently, the absence of such an intention excludes a criminal responsibility. For example, for consumer fraud to be a crime under Article 156 of the PC, it is necessary to establish that the accused person incorrectly measured or priced with a direct intention. Direct intention is a necessary component of all crimes where the legislature includes a special goal of the offender as one of the essential elements of the crime.

Soviet law does not recognize other types of intention, such as premeditation or transferred intent, but such types of intention are differentiated in criminal law doctrine and are sometimes noted by the courts in hearing specific cases. For instance, when cases of intentional homicide tried by the courts of the Primorsky territory were studied, it was noted that 62.5 percent of the cases involved unpremeditated intention, and 37.5 percent, premeditated intention.[21]

The great majority of the cases included in the PC require only intention. According to Zlobin and Nikiforov, intentional crimes constitute 78 percent of all crimes in the PC, and 55 percent of them require a direct intention.[22]

The concept of the *mens rea* of carelessness is provided by Article 9 of the CL Fundamentals (Art. 9 of the PC):

A crime shall be deemed committed by carelessness where a person who has committed it anticipated the possibility of socially

21. P. S. Daguel, *Criminological Significance of the Subjective Aspect of Crime* Soviet State and Law No. 11, at 88 (1966).

22. G. A. Zlobin & B. S. Nikoforov, Intention and Its Forms 48 (1972; Moscow, "Juridicheskaya Literatura" Publ. House).

dangerous consequences ensuing from his commission or omission, but thoughtlessly relied on their being prevented or failed to anticipate the possibility of socially dangerous consequences ensuing, although he could and should have anticipated them.

Criminal responsibility for crimes of carelessness as a rule occurs only where it is connected with grave consequences. The number of crimes of carelessness included in Soviet legislation is considerably smaller than that of intentional ones. According to Zlobin and Nikiforov, 14 percent of the crimes in the PC require only carelessness and 8 percent can be committed by either carelessness or intention.[23]

Carelessness is a less dangerous form of guilt. Persons who commit crimes of carelessness constitute a lesser social danger compared to those who commit intentional crimes. This is reflected in the criminal sanctions. Thus, intentional homicide without special circumstances is punished under Article 103 of the PC by deprivation of liberty for a term of three to ten years, while a homicide by carelessness under Article 106 of the PC provides a punishment of deprivation of liberty for a term of up to three years or corrective labor for a term of up to one year.

Considering the difference of the degrees of social danger of persons who commit intentional or careless crimes, and consequently the differences in measures and means necessary for their correction and re-education, the Decree of the Presidium of the Supreme Soviet of the USSR of February 8, 1977 established special corrective labor colonies for persons who commit crimes of carelessness for the first time.[24]

The law recognizes two types of careless guilt. The graver of the two is criminal recklessness, which in the majority of cases is connected with a conscious breaking of established rules, when a person anticipated a possibility of dangerous consequences to his action but thoughtlessly hoped to avoid them. This type of guilt is common in traffic offenses.

The other type of carelessness is criminal negligence. Crim-

23. *Supra.*
24. GAZETTE OF THE SUPREME SOVIET OF THE USSR No. 7, Item 116 (1977). Such colony settlements are described in the next chapter.

inal negligence occurs when a person does not anticipate the possible consequences of his behavior but should and could have anticipated them. Soviet penal law supports firmly the principle of subjective incrimination, that is, charging a person with criminal responsibility only for such consequences, as he not only should anticipate but also could anticipate. The subjective criterion of carelessness—"could have"—included in the law side by side with the objective one—"should have"—makes it necessary to consider the individual qualities of an accused person: his experience, knowledge, age, professional training, etc., as well as the exact circumstances of the action. For example, in the trial of surgeon Shuryguin, a forensic medical expert established that Shuryguin had given a patient a lethal dose of *chlorous ethelene nascosis*. Such an error was found to be based not on carelessness by the surgeon, but on his experience. The case was terminated because of the absence of the elements of a crime.[25]

In another case, the Plenum of the Supreme Court of the USSR found there was no intention or carelessness in the actions of Borisov who, wishing to play a practical joke, threw a bucket of liquid at a person standing next to a stove and the liquid proved to be gasoline. During the investigation, it was established that the bucket full of gasoline was in the corridor, among similar buckets full of water, that all looked exactly the same, and that Borisov did not know and could not know that the bucket he chose was full of gasoline and not water. The Plenum came to the conclusion that Borisov did not and could not anticipate the consequences that took place in reality, and found him not guilty.[26]

The elements just discussed constitute, in their entirety, the *corpus delicti* of crimes in the Soviet Union. The absence of any of these elements of the *corpus delicti* means the absence of crime and, consequently, the absence of grounds for criminal responsibility.

CATEGORIES OF CRIMES

The last subject that should be mentioned in connection with

25. F. J. BERDICHIEVSKY, CRIMINAL RESPONSIBILITY OF MEDICAL STAFF FOR BREACHES OF PROFESSIONAL TRUST 23 (1973; Moscow).

26. BULLETIN OF THE SUPREME COURT OF THE USSR No. 4, at 21 (1976).

the concept of crime in Soviet criminal law is the categories of crimes.

In principle, there exists a unique concept of crime, as described in Article 7 of the CL Fundamentals. Article 7(1) of the CL Fundamentals singles out the category of "grave crimes." This article is included in all the codes of the union republics. About fifty crimes of particularly great social danger are included in this category. These are intentional crimes, punished with capital punishment, or with deprivation of liberty for long terms. Among them are especially dangerous crimes against the state, banditry, smuggling, damaging communication lines or transportation facilities, aggravated robbery, and intentional homicide. The commission of a crime qualified by the law as grave has several consequences. First, a person convicted of a grave crime shall be directed to the corrective labor colonies of a stricter regime, and after serving the punishment shall be subject to an administrative control.[27] In some cases, the fact that a person was convicted for a grave crime influences the qualification of his next crime. For example, persons who were convicted for grave crimes and then commit an assault on an administration representative in their places of confinement are guilty of a state crime, under Article 77(1) of the PC. Other persons, for the same actions, would be guilty only of a crime against the person.

The law also uses the terms "nonsignificant crime" and "crime of not great social danger." In accordance with Article 51 of the PC, a "nonsignificant crime" can be transferred for consideration by a comrades' court, and if a person has committed "a crime of no social danger" he can be relieved from criminal responsibility altogether and transferred to the supervision of social organizations, the case can be transferred to a juvenile commission, or criminal punishment can be replaced by administrative measures. These two categories of crimes are not formalized, and the law does not contain a list of "nonsignificant crimes" or "crimes of no great social danger."[28] These qualifica-

27. Decree on Administrative Supervision by Organs of Militia Over Persons Released from Places of Confinement, adopted by the Presidium of the Supreme Soviet of the USSR on June 12, 1970.

28. GAZETTE OF THE SUPREME SOVIET OF THE USSR No. 24, Item 206 (1970).

tions depend on the individual circumstances of each case.

Criminal law theory assigns considerable significance to qualification of crimes. Many authors believe that the degree of gravity of a crime should determine the type and degree of sanction to be applied and suggest that five kinds of crimes should be distinguished:

1. particularly grave crimes, including those punishable by capital punishment or deprivation of liberty for terms of more than ten years;
2. grave crimes;
3. crimes which are not grave;
4. crimes of no great social danger;
5. nonsignificant crimes.[29]

2.2. Persons Criminally Responsible

Only natural persons—USSR citizens, foreigners, or stateless persons—are subject to criminal responsibility. Actions on behalf of entities which are legal persons may give rise to criminal responsibility, but only the natural persons actually performing them. Thus, Article 152 of the PC stipulates that a director, chief-engineer, or chief of the technical control body of an enterprise will be responsible for repeated mass production of poor quality products. An employee charged with supervising safety measures will be responsible for accidents resulting from violations of safety regulations that cause injuries to people or other grave consequences (Art. 140 of the PC).

To be responsible for a crime a natural person must possess two qualities: age and capacity.

AGE

The age for criminal responsibility is provided in Article 10 of the CL Fundamentals. As a rule, the age for criminal responsibility is sixteen. However, for certain crimes enumerated

---

29. An exception is the Penal Code of the Georgian SSR, which defines as having "little significance" any criminal action for which the sanctions do not exceed one year of deprivation of liberty and which defines as having "great social danger" any criminal action punished by the law with a penalty of deprivation of liberty for the term exceeding three years.

in Article 10 of the PC (part 2), the age for criminal responsibility is fourteen. This age of responsibility is established for homicide, intentional battery, rape, assault with intent to rob, theft, malicious hooliganism, and others. In composing this list the legislature considered, first, the danger of the actions, which even an adolescent of fourteen must realize. It is necessary to note that all crimes for which criminal responsibility begins at fourteen are intentional crimes, with the sole exception of homicide by carelessness.

However, not all persons who have reached the age of responsibility and who commit crimes are held criminally responsible. On the contrary, about 25 to 33 percent of juvenile delinquents guilty of crimes are relieved from criminal responsibility and their cases are transmitted by the investigator, procurator, or court to the juvenile commissions.[30] Such commissions are established at the executive committees of the Soviets of People's Deputies.[31] They are composed of the deputies of the local Soviet and representatives from trade unions, Komsomol organizations, and public education, public health, social insurance, etc.[32]

The grounds for relieving a juvenile from criminal responsibility and transferring his case to a juvenile commission are provided in Article 10 of the PC (part 4). Such grounds may be that the crime is of no great social danger, that the person is under eighteen, and that the possibility exists of correcting such a person's behavior without applying a criminal law punishment.

Where such grounds exist, the court itself may assign a measure of an educational nature to a juvenile in accordance with part 3, Article 10 of the PC, by terminating the case and assigning, in its conclusion, one of the compulsory measures of an educational nature enumerated in Article 63 of the PC.

---

30. *See* A. B. Sakharov, *Crime Classification,* QUESTIONS OF CRIME COMBATTING No. 17, at 42-54 (1972) and CRIMINOLOGY 285 (1976) which is a textbook for law schools.

31. Decree on Juvenile Commissions Existing in the RSFSR, adopted by the presidium of the Supreme Soviet of the RSFSR on June 3, 1967; *see* GAZETTE OF THE SOVIET OF THE RSFSR No. 23, Item 536 (1967).

32. Goals, functions, and activities of juvenile commissions are described in Chapter IV, Section 3.

The directive Decision of the Plenum of the Supreme Court of the USSR of December 3, 1976, "On practice of the courts in application of legislation to cases of juvenile delinquents and the latter's involvement in criminal or other antisocial activities" reads:

> It is necessary to exclude cases of ungrounded assignations of deprivation of liberty to juvenile delinquents for offenses not presenting great social danger, and when their (juveniles') correction and re-education can be achieved without an isolation from society by means of compulsory measures of an educational nature provided by Articles 10 and 63 of the Penal Code of the RSFSR and the corresponding articles of the penal codes of the union republics.[33]

Studies show that compulsory measures of an educational nature are most often used in cases of thefts of state or personal property, hooliganism, robberies, and thefts of vehicles. Indications of the possibility of correction by means only of compulsory measures of an educational nature include such factors as the crime's being a first offense, deep repentance, a positive attitude toward study or work, compensation of the damage, and other such circumstances.

Compulsory measures of an educational nature in lieu of criminal responsibility may also be applied to those juvenile delinquents who have shown a degree of mental retardedness.

CAPACITY

The second quality which a natural person guilty of a crime must possess to be subjected to criminal responsibility is capacity. The law does not define the concept of capacity. It is formulated by criminal law theory, taking as a source Article 11 of the CL Fundamentals dedicated to incapacity. "Capacity is the ability of a person to account for his actions and to govern them, and connected with it, an ability to be responsible for commission of socially dangerous acts," according to N. S. Leikina and N. P. Grabovskaya.[34] Article 11 of the CL Fundamentals states, "A person who at the time of the commission of a socially dangerous act was in a state of incapacity, that is, was unable to ac-

---

33. BULLETIN OF THE SUPREME COURT OF THE USSR No. 1, at 17-25 (1977).
34. I COURSE OF SOVIET CRIMINAL LAW 269 (1968; Leningrad U. Publ. House).

count for his actions or to govern them in consequence of a chronic mental illness, temporary mental derangement, mental deficiency, or other such condition, shall not be subject to criminal responsibility."[35]

Criminal law theory concludes that the state of incapacity can be established when there are two elements present: a medical one and a psychological one, the latter sometimes being called the legal element. The medical element is established if the person is suffering from a detectable mental disease or is in a mentally abnormal state. However, it is well known that not all mental disorders, even chronic diseases, are accompanied by a constant deficiency of mental functions. That is why the law stipulates that a person may be deemed to lack capacity if he not only possesses the medical aspect of incapacity but also, at the moment of the commission of the act, could not account for or govern his actions.

To establish incapacity, however, it may be sufficient to establish that a person did not realize consciously the socially dangerous nature of his actions or could not govern them, even if he fully realized their actual character. This sometimes happens with epileptics and drug addicts as well as mental incompetents. To determine the question of capacity, a panel of forensic medical experts is appointed.

Persons deemed by the court to lack capacity are not subjected to criminal responsibility. If the court finds that the nature of a mental disease of a person and the degree of the social danger of the committed action require application to that person of compulsory medical treatment, the court's sentence will be to place the person in a mental hospital. Conversely, if the nature of the disease and the gravity of the committed offense do not require application to such a person of compulsory measures of a medical character, he may be ordered to treatment as an outpatient.

Thus, the Rostoy regional court annulled the sentence of a People's Court concerning the application of compulsory treatment to Sh. Shakulenko, deemed to lack capacity though he had committed a homicide. At the moment of the homicide, he was

---

35. BULLETIN OF THE SUPREME COURT OF THE RSFSR No. 8, at 12-13 (1970).

in a state of alcoholic delirium and could not account for his actions or govern them. However, alcohol delirium is not a mental disease, and there was no basis for sending Sh. Shakulenko for compulsory treatment.

The grounds for placing a person who is deemed to lack capacity in a mental hospital are provided in Articles 58 and 59 of the PC. The manner of such placement is regulated by the "Instruction on the manner of application of compulsory treatment and other measures of a medical nature to persons suffering from mental diseases who have committed socially dangerous acts."[36]

Mental hospitals of a general type, which are under the Ministry of Health, provide treatment for persons who were deemed to lack capacity and need medical treatment and compulsory medical care. If such a person, by the very nature of his actions, presents a definite danger to society, he is sent to a mental hospital of a special type, under the Ministry of Interior, where the inmates are kept under security.

A compulsory treatment lasts until the ill person is cured or ceases to be dangerous to society. Every six months inmates undergo a medical re-examination in order to determine their medical condition. If the condition improves, the medical report is submitted to the court, which may decide to terminate the treatment or to change the type of compulsory medical treatment (Art. 60 of the PC).

Criminal responsibility of diplomatic representatives of foreign countries and other persons enjoying immunity is to be decided by diplomatic means.[37] Other foreigners who have committed crimes within the territory of the USSR shall be subject to responsibility under the criminal laws in force at the place of crime.

---

36. The instruction was adopted on February 14, 1967 by the Ministry of Health of the USSR upon agreement of the Supreme Court of the USSR, the Procurator-General of the USSR, and the Ministry of Interior of the USSR; see BULLETIN OF THE SUPREME COURT OF THE USSR No. 4, at 37-39 (1967).

37. Persons enjoying immunity are defined by the Decree on Diplomatic and Consular Representatives of Foreign States in the Soviet Union, adopted on May 23, 1966; see GAZETTE OF THE SUPREME SOVIET OF THE USSR No. 22, Item 317 (1966).

Section 3. INDIRECT RESPONSIBILITY AND INCHOATE CRIMES

3.1. Preparation and Attempt

In determining the conditions for criminal responsibility for preparation of a crime or for complicity in a crime, Soviet legislation is based on the general principles of criminal responsibility described above. This means that an incomplete crime or complicity in a crime may cause criminal responsibility only where the committed actions are socially dangerous and provided for by the criminal law. If some actions performed as a preparation for a crime, an attempt to commit a crime, or in complicity are of little significance, they are not deemed to be criminal, and a criminal case is not initiated, and if one is already initiated, it shall be terminated under part 2, Article 7 of the CL Fundamentals.

At the same time, preparatory activities and complicity have their own peculiarities, which affect the criminal responsibility of persons who perform such actions. That is why the law regulates separately the conditions of criminal responsibility for the preparation of a crime and for complicity.

Soviet criminal law theory distinguishes four stages in the commission of a crime: an intention, a preparation, an attempt, and a complete crime. An intention is not yet an activity expressed in socially dangerous actions. That is why an intention is not criminally punishable. Criminal responsibility begins at the stage of the preparation of a crime. An exception to this rule is a threat as a special manifestation of intention. The criminal code provides for criminal responsibility for a threat of murder (Art. 207 of the PC) and for a threat to an official or a social worker made with the purpose to stop or influence their activity (part 1, Art. 193 of the PC).

Article 15 of the CL Fundamentals defines preparation as "procurement or adaptation of means or instruments or any other intentional creation of conditions for the commission of a crime." Preparatory actions are usually performed in a very early stage of the crime commission and, although in principle the law provides responsibility for them, in practice they are rarely punishable.

Attempts are much more frequent in judicial practice. For example, of 100 cases of homicides heard by the Moscow City Court, none contained charges of preparation, but 14 percent involved attempted homicide.[38] Article 15 of the CL Fundamentals defines an attempted crime as an intentional action directed immediately toward the commission of a crime, where the crime has not been brought to completion for reasons not depending on the will of the guilty person.

As an example, it is useful to consider I. Igumnov's conviction for attempted homicide. He started a quarrel with his neighbor while in a state of severe intoxication. During this quarrel, he shot five times with bird-shot through a veneer door. Although the shots caused only light injuries to the two victims, the court found the actions of Igumnov were directed toward commission of a homicide, the failure of which to occur was against the will of the guilty person.[39]

The law itself contains an indication that an attempt or a preparation can take place only in connection with an intentional crime. A question concerning the possibility of an attempt in cases of both direct and indirect intention has arisen in judicial practice. The Supreme Court's answer to the question was given in the context of homicides. The directive Decision of the Plenum of the Supreme Court of June 27, 1975, reads: "In the spirit of Article 15 of the Fundamentals of Criminal Legislation of the USSR, Union and Autonomous Republics, an attempted homicide is possible only with a direct intention, that is, in a case where the guilty person's actions testified to the fact that he had anticipated the occurrence of the death, wished it to happen, but it failed through circumstances independent from his will."[40] Lower courts use this directive of the USSR Supreme Court not only in cases of homicide, but also when hearing other cases of attempted crimes, excluding the possibility of an attempted crime of indirect intention.

The law does not contain a definition of a completed crime.

---

38. A. A. HERZENSON, CRIMINAL LAW AND SOCIOLOGY 68 (1970; Moscow, "Juridicheskaya Literatura" Publ. House).

39. BULLETIN OF THE SUPREME COURT OF THE RSFSR No. 8, at 516 (1970).

40. BULLETIN OF THE SUPREME COURT OF THE USSR, No. 4, at 8 (1975).

Criminal law theory defines it as an action possessing all the elements of a *corpus delicti*. If the law includes the occurrence of consequences in the *corpus delicti*, then the crime is completed only when these consequences occur. Criminal law theory labels such *corpae delictorum* "material." They are homicide, battery, theft, robbery, fraud, and many others. However, some crimes are described in the law in such a way that they are completed from the moment of the commission or omission of a certain action, irrespective of the occurrence of consequences. Such *corpae delictorum* are labelled "formal." Failute to report and concealment are such crimes. An assault with the intention to rob is described as a formal *corpus delicti* since the crime is completed at the moment of the assault when it is accompanied by the requisite intent (Art. 146 of the PC). The legislature constructs formal *corpus delicti* in two situations: if consequences are difficult to show (as in the case of a failure to report) or if the crime is so dangerous that it is necessary to punish the commission of an action even if the criminal goal is not achieved (as in the case of an assault with intent to rob).

Soviet law does not contain an obligatory mitigation of punishment for preparation or attempt. The court decides this according to its discretion when examining a particular case, but Article 15 of the CL Fundamentals contains a principle indicating that a court should take into consideration the nature and degree of the social danger of the actions committed by the guilty person, the degree of realization of the criminal intention, and the causes preventing completion of the crime when pronouncing a sentence. Since criminal consequences never occur at an attempt or a preparation, these types of criminal activities are punished more mildly than completed crimes.

3.2. Abandonment of Criminal Attempt

A criminal action may be interrupted before completion by either a voluntary act of the person who began it or by independent factors. The law provides that "a person who has voluntarily abandoned the completion of a crime shall not be subject to criminal responsibility" (Art. 16 of the CL Fundamentals, Art. 16 of the PC).

It is necessary to establish two circumstances for this provision to apply. First, the abandonment must be total, and not merely a provisional suspension, with an intent to complete the crime later, under more favorable conditions. Second, the abandonment must be voluntary. Voluntariness may involve any motive, from pity for the victim to fear of being caught.

Studies of judicial practice show that the majority (up to 70 percent)[41] of voluntary abandonments occur in cases of rape. In one of the cities of the RSFSR during a period of five years, 16.3 percent of all cases involving rape were not completed because of the voluntary abandonment.[42]

Voluntary abandonment may occur at any stage of the commission of the crime before completion. Actions after completion of the crime directed at compensation of the damage, however, do not eliminate criminal responsibility. Such acts as returning stolen property, calling a doctor for the victim, etc., are regarded by the law as mitigating circumstances (Art. 38 of the PC), which do not eliminate responsibility but are taken into consideration by the court in sentencing.

3.3. Complicity

The concept of complicity is described in Article 17 of the CL Fundamentals (Art. 17 of the PC): "Intentional joint participation by two or more persons in the commission of a crime shall be deemed to be complicity." Thus, complicity is established only when two or more persons acted not only intentionally but also jointly. This second requirement is the most important and probably the most complicated for practitioners. This requirement means that accomplices' activity is a special form of a crime in which each participant accounts for both his own actions and also for the other participants' actions which were aimed at reaching a common criminal goal.

The degree of coordination among accomplices may vary. It is the highest when a crime is committed by a group of people based on a prior agreement or by a criminal organization. The

---

41. K. A. PANKO, VOLUNTARY ABANDONMENT OF CRIME IN SOVIET CRIMINAL LAW 126 (1975; Voronezh).

42. *Supra.*

coordination among the accomplices may appear both before or at the moment of the commission of the crime. A coordination is a necessary characteristic for complicity, and without it, participants in a crime may not be deemed accomplices. A person cannot be considered an accomplice if, because of his age, a mental disease, or other reasons, he was deceived, misinformed, or for any other reason did not realize the socially dangerous nature of his actions or those of other participants in the crime.

Thus, the USSR Supreme Court did not find complicity in homicide in the actions of Telnov, who saw a man running and tripped him. It turned out that the man had been running from attackers and this fall cost him his life. However, since Telnov had not been a witness to the quarrel between the murderers and the victim and had not known the reason for the chase, the court could not find the coordination necessary for a complicity.[43]

The law (as one can see from Art. 17 of the CL Fundamentals and Art. 19 of the PC) provides for responsibility for complicity only in intentional crimes. The responsibility of each participant is determined independently. For example, Watchman Djoshuganov, who permitted a car carrying stolen goods to leave a factory, was not deemed to be an accomplice to the theft, since it was established that his only guilt was failure to compare the documents presented to him with the actual contents of the car. Djoshuganov was convicted under Article 93 of the Penal Code of the Azerbaijan SSR for neglect of duties (criminal negligence towards the safety of state and social property).[44]

The law (Art. 17 of the CL Fundamentals) describes characteristics of different types of accomplices with special attention to their roles in the crime. Of all the types of accomplices—perpetrator, instigator, accessory, and organizer—the latter is the most dangerous. A person who has organized the commission of a crime or has directed its commission shall be deemed to be an organizer. An instigator, that is a person who has incited the commission of a crime, is also a dangerous person, though in practice, they are rare, comprising only 1 to 3 percent of all ac-

43. BULLETIN OF THE SUPREME COURT OF THE USSR No. 3, at 6-8 (1975).
44. BULLETIN OF THE SUPREME COURT OF THE USSR No. 4, at 46-47 (1976).

complices.[45] They are especially dangerous where minors are involved in the commission of a crime. In this connection, a special norm was introduced into the PC (Art. 210), which provides criminal responsibility for an independent crime, contributing to the delinquency of a minor, which includes inciting juveniles to commit crimes or engage in drinking, begging, prostitution, or gambling. The Supreme Court repeatedly reminds lower courts of the necessity to thoroughly examine the role of adults in cases of juvenile delinquency. The Directive of the Plenum of the USSR Supreme Court of December 3, 1976 explains that involvement of minors into criminal or other antisocial activity may be accomplished by a variety of ways, including physical or moral force, persuasion, threat, bribes, or deceit.[46]

Complicity often involves actions of an accessory. Accessories are those who have promoted the commission of a crime by advice, instruction, providing means, or removing obstacles, or by promising beforehand to conceal the criminal, the instruments and means for commission of the crime, or criminally acquired articles.

Persons guilty of failure to report or of concealment after-the-fact are not deemed to be accessories. Such persons are responsible for independent criminal actions, appearing in the law as crimes against justice [Arts. 189 and 190 of the PC; Arts. 88(1) and 88(2) of the PC concerning failure to report and concealment of state criminals]. It is necessary to mention that Soviet law punishes failure to report and concealment only in cases of very grave crimes. A full list of such crimes is presented in the Special Part of the PC.

The criminal law acknowledges a relative independence of each accomplice. It is natural that all accomplices be held responsible for a crime, but there is no automatic link. If the accomplices agreed upon, for example, a simple robbery, and the perpetrator went beyond the agreement and used violence, only the perpetrator is responsible for such actions, which are called an excess of a perpetrator. The other accomplices are responsible

45. EFFECTIVENESS OF CRIMINAL LAW APPLICATION 43 (1973; Moscow "Juridicheskaya Literatura" Publ. House).
46. BULLETIN OF THE SUPREME COURT OF THE USSR No. 1, at 17-28 (1977).

only for instigation or accessory acts. If the perpetrator's actions constitute a repeated theft, which is a more serious crime (part 2, Art. 144 of the PC), such a more serious crime is attributable to an instigator or accessory if they were fully aware of the perpetrator's prior crimes.

For example, Klepikov suggested to Shuvalov that they visit an acquaintance of his who brewed spirits at home, but never mentioned that he intended to kill her. When in the victim's house, Klepikov took out his knife; Shuvalov became frightened and ran away. The murder took place in his absence, but afterwards Klepikov made Shuvalov search for money in the victim's house. The judicial collegium on criminal affairs of the USSR Supreme Court examined the case and established that Shuvalov took part only in the theft of money. Klepikov's actions were qualified as a homicide and assault with intent to rob and Shuvalov's as accessory to a theft.[47]

Soviet law does not divide accomplices into types as first or second degree. The law gives the court discretion to evaluate the danger of each accomplice and assign an appropriate punishment. The law reads: "In assigning punishment, the court must take account of the degree and nature of participation of each of the accomplices in the commission of the crime" (Art. 17 of the CL Fundamentals, Art. 17 of the PC).

It is natural that the perpetrator usually is assigned a stricter punishment than an accessory. As far as an instigator or an organizer is concerned, in some cases they receive stricter punishment than the perpetrator of the crime.

Section 4. DEFENSES

4.1. Self-Defense

The main characteristic of a crime in Soviet criminal law is social danger. If this characteristic is not present, an action ceases to be a crime even if it bears an external similarity to a crime.

The law stipulates two circumstances which exclude social danger of an action, and whose presence negates criminality even if

---

47. Bulletin of the Supreme Court of the USSR No. 3, at 22-23 (1976).

the action results in harmful consequences. They are self-defense (also called necessary defense) and necessity.[48]

Legal conditions for self-defense are regulated by Article 13 of the CL Fundamentals (Art. 13 of the PC). This norm's application in practice is discussed in the Decision of the Plenum of the USSR Supreme Court of December 4, 1969, "Practice of courts in the application of legislation on necessary defenses."[49]

The law defines the necessary defense as "protecting the interests of the Soviet State, social interests, or the person or rights of the defender or of another person against a socially dangerous infringement, by causing harm to the infringer, provided that no action in excess of those required for necessary defense has been committed."

Necessary defense is interpreted in the Soviet criminal law as a circumstance excluding criminal responsibility, as a right of the citizens for defense, as law-abiding behavior, and a special form of crime combatting. This position was formulated in the above-mentioned decision of the Plenum of the Supreme Court of the USSR: "Actions of such a kind resulting from the indefeasable right of the citizens for defense do not contain the elements of crime and do not present any social danger but, on the contrary, contribute to the strengthening of proper socialist legal order, and just consideration of such cases contributes to participation in crime combatting."

The law stresses only one aspect—that the requirements of necessary defense should not be exceeded. Criminal law theory presents a more detailed elaboration of the conditions characterizing both the assault and the defense. An assault which is socially dangerous and which has begun but has not been completed, and which is real and not imagined by the defender, gives rise to the right of defense. The defense is legal if its object is to protect

---

48. Some scholars of criminal law note other circumstances of a similar type. Thus, they consider having the victim's consent, acting pursuant to a professional duty, and execution of an order by a subordinate person, in addition to self-defense and necessity, as circumstances that exclude a social danger, but the law does not formally recognize such circumstances. *See* II COURSE OF SOVIET CRIMINAL LAW 393-401 (1968; Leningrad U. Pub. House).

49. *Supra* note 2, at 356-363.

the rights and interests of the defender, or other persons, organizations, establishments, or the state. The defender may inflict harm only to the person who is attacking and not to any third party, and he must not exceed the limits of necessity.

In practice, the right of necessary defense is used to protect one's life, health, or property, and occasionally to protect other objects.

The Supreme Court of the USSR has directed the lower courts to assess the actions committed as necessary defense, bearing in mind that such actions must not be a means of taking the law into one's own hands. At the same time, the actions of persons attacking and defending cannot be compared mechanically. The one who attacks is the initiator of the event, so that the defender, being forced to react, may not always judge the situation correctly.

The Plenum of the USSR Supreme Court explained that the right for defense may be realized not only at the moment of an assault but also when assault is imminent. The right of self-defense is also valid when the person assaulted could have run away but did not. The Supreme Court has pointed out that this corresponds to the "principles of Soviet morality and socialist consciousness."

The most complicated question concerns the existence or non-existence of an excess by the defender. As Article 13 of the CL Fundamentals states: "Clear disproportion between the defense and the nature and danger of the infringement shall be deemed to be an excess of necessary defense. . . ." Making the provision more precise, the Plenum of the USSR Supreme Court explained that a defender's actions which are not caused by either the nature or the danger of an assault, or by the real situation, and which result in great harm to the assailant, are deemed to be in excess of necessary defense.

For example, the actions of Khumarian, who mortally wounded Tarposhian, were qualified as an excess of necessary defense. Khumorian and Tarposhian were married to two sisters, but their attitude toward one another was very negative. Once during a quarrel Tarposhian wounded Khumarian with a knife. He was convicted and sentenced for this act. After his release, he returned home and met Khumarian, blamed him for his misfortunes, and slapped his face. During the fight which followed, Khumarian stabbed Tarposhian with a kitchen knife. Tarposhian died within a few minutes. The court qualified Khumarian's actions as originating as necessary defense but involving means which were beyond those appropriate to the character of the assault.[50]

Actions qualified by the law as an excess of necessary defense are deemed to be a crime. However, because such actions are provoked by a socially dangerous assault, they are usually qualified as a crime with extenuating circumstances (part 6, Art. 38 of the PC). Causing death or grave bodily injury to an assailant through an excess of necessary defense is provided for in Articles 105 and 111 of the PC and is punished more mildly than comparable actions committed by carelessness.

4.2. Necessity

The concept of necessity is described in Article 14 of the CL Fundamentals (Art. 14 of the PC) as "An action which, while falling within the indicia of an act provided for in the criminal law, has been committed in a state of dire necessity—that is, in order to eliminate a danger threatening the interests of the Soviet State, social interests, or the person or rights of the given person or another citizen—shall not be a crime, where in the given circumstances such danger was greater than the harm caused."

This definition contains two conditions, that there be a danger causing dire necessity and that the actions be committed in order to eliminate such a danger.

The source of danger is not limited to an assault but can be natural phenomena (flood, fire), an assault by a wild beast, or wrongful actions of people, such as causing a dangerous traffic situation. As distinguished from necessary defense, the harm is done here not to the source of the danger but to a third party. The harm is inevitable, the only possible way to avoid the dan-

---

50. BULLETIN OF THE SUPREME COURT OF THE USSR No. 4, at 44-46 (1976).

ger. If there was another course of action that would have prevented the danger without causing harm, there is no state of dire
necessity.

The most important condition for the legality of actions in
dire necessity mentioned in the law is that the harm caused be
smaller than the one that would have occurred as a result of the
danger. For example, the Supreme Court of the USSR found
Shmik not guilty where he had found a person on the road who
had been badly beaten and, in order to get medical help, com-
mandeered a vehicle and damaged it while using it. The Supreme Court qualified Shmik's actions as based on dire necessity,
and the harm caused to the vehicle was deemed to be smaller
than that which could have occurred if Shmik had left the victim without medical help.[51]

Section 5. PUNISHMENT

5.1. Purpose of Punishment

The Soviet State acknowledges punishment as an important
means of combatting crime but it is not the only one and not
even the main one. The principal means for eliminating crime
are those affecting the material and cultural level of the Soviet
people, the improvement of all the units of the State structure,
the education of the Soviet people in respect for law and rules
of the socialist way of living, and the creation of a complex system of measures for prevention of crimes.[52]

The Soviet State applies punishment only in extreme cases because punishment is contradictory in nature. It is a necessary and
useful means of combatting crime but at the same time it causes
negative results, adversely affecting the convict's family, breaking established social links, and placing the convict for a long
time in a milieu of antisocial attitudes.

That is why the Communist Party Program of 1919 called for

---

51. BULLETIN OF THE SUPREME COURT OF THE USSR No. 6, at 46-47 (1965).
52. The Plenum of the Supreme Court of the USSR adopted a directive on
"Further improvement of judicial activities in crime prevention" on December 3,
1977, in which lower courts' attention was drawn to a series of deficiencies in
the prophylactic significance of judicial practice; *see* BULLETIN OF THE SUPREME
COURT OF THE USSR No. 1, at 11-17 (1977).

gradual replacement of punishment with measures of an educational nature. This provision was advocated by V. I. Lenin and it is included in the present Program of the Communist Party of the Soviet Union "in the end, to replace measures of criminal punishment by measures of social influence and education."

Soviet criminal law is developing in this direction, slowly but steadily reducing the scope of criminal actions, replacing punishments of deprivation of liberty with other measures not involving isolation of the convicted person from society, and narrowing the area of actual application of punishment by broadening grounds for relief from criminal responsibility.

These trends are clearly expressed in the Decree of the Presidium of the USSR Supreme Soviet of February 8 and 15, 1977,[53] and decrees adopted in the union republics during the first part of 1977.[54] They excluded from the list of crimes repeated petty hooliganism and buying, selling, and exchanging large quantities of currency or valuable papers. These actions, which were qualified before as criminal, are now punished by administrative measures.

These decrees also abruptly reduced the number of persons assigned punishment for commission of crimes. This goal was achieved by enlarging the number of cases where a person is relieved from criminal responsibility for a crime and subjected instead to administrative measures (Art. 43 of the Fundamentals, parts 3 and 4) or to discipline by courts.

Reducing the number of persons who are actually subjected to punishment by deprivation of liberty was achieved by means of a broader basis for applying conditional punishment of deprivation of liberty with compulsory labor. Another new article [39(1) of the CL Fundamentals] serves the same purpose, providing for suspension of sentences, to give a chance to minors to avoid actually serving the punishment if they meet certain requirements during the suspension period.

---

53. GAZETTE OF THE SUPREME SOVIET OF THE USSR No. 7, at 116-121; No. 8, at 137 (1977).

54. Decree of the Presidium of the Supreme Soviet of the RSFSR of February 3, 1977, "Alterations and recognition as obsolete of certain legislative acts in the RSFSR"; *see* GAZETTE OF THE SUPREME SOVIET OF THE RSFSR No. 6, at 129 (1977).

Finally, these decrees enlarged opportunities for early release. Article 44(2) has been introduced into the CL Fundamentals to create a new type of conditional early release, conditional release with compulsory labor. Amendments to Articles 44 and 44(1) of the CL Fundamentals substantially reduced the number of people who are ineligible for early conditional release.

In determining the essence of a punishment Soviet scholars of criminal law distinguish the following characteristics: (a) punishment is a measure of state enforcement, expressing a negative assessment of particular behavior; (b) punishment may be awarded only for criminal behavior; (c) punishment is awarded only by a court sentence provided by Article 160 of the Constitution of the USSR and Article 3 of the CL Fundamentals; and (d) the legal consequence of a punishment is a record of conviction.[55]

A distinguishing peculiarity of punishment under Soviet criminal law is complete rejection of retribution as a purpose of punishment. This was legally confirmed in even earliest acts of socialist criminal law. Article 10 of the directive "Initiatives on criminal law of the RSFSR of 1919"[56] stated: "As a defensive measure, punishment must be expedient but at the same time devoid of torture and extra suffering."

These ideas have been reflected consistently in subsequent legislation and are confirmed now by Article 20 of the CL Fundamentals, where the purposes of punishment are defined:

> *Article 20. The Purposes of Punishment*
> Punishment shall not only be chastisement for a committed crime but shall also have the aim of correcting and re-educating convicted persons in the spirit of an honest attitude toward work, strict observance of the laws, and respect for the rules of socialist community life and also of preventing the commission of new crimes by convicted person and other persons.
> Punishment shall not have the purpose of inflicting physical suffering or degrading human dignity.

Thus, punishment in the Soviet criminal law has two purposes. The more important one is prevention of further crimes by the

---

55. I. S. Noĭ, Essence and Functions of Criminal Punishment 45 (1973; Saratov).

56. CL RSFSR No. 60, at 590 (1919).

offender and is achieved by means of correction and re-education of convicts in the spirit of a respect for law and the socialist way of living, by raising their educational level, professional training, etc.

5.2. Forms of Punishment

Soviet criminal law contains a great variety of measures applied as punishments. This variety allows individualized punishment corresponding not only to the gravity of the crime committed but also to individual peculiarities of the offender.

Article 21 of the PC lists eleven forms of punishment:

1. deprivation of liberty (see Chapter VI, Section 3);
2. exile (see Chapter VI, Section 2.3);
3. restricted residence;   ba¹
4. corrective labor without deprivation of liberty (see Chapter VI, Sections 2.1 and 2.2);
5. deprivation of the right to hold certain offices or engage in certain activities;
6. fines
7. discharge from an office;
8. an order to compensate damages;
9. social censure;
10. confiscation of property;
11. reduction in military or other rank.

It is obvious that the frequency of application of the various forms of punishment is not the same. Deprivation of liberty is comparatively frequent both in legislation and in practice. However, this type of punishment does not predominate. Half of all sanctions, affecting more than half of all convicts, are measures of punishment not connected with deprivation of liberty.[57] The USSR Supreme Court, in its directives to lower courts, consistently calls for a differentiated approach to assigning types of punishment; only dangerous criminals must be isolated from society, while other offenders may generally be assigned punishments not connected with deprivation of liberty.

The Plenum of the USSR Supreme Court, in its decision of

---

57. Punishment Without Deprivation of Liberty 20 (1972; Moscow).

March 26, 1976, "On raising the level of justice administration in the spirit of the decisions of the XXV Congress of the Communist Party of the Soviet Union" states: "Persons who have committed grave crimes and recidivists willfully rejecting the way of correction and leading an antisocial, parasitic life shall be subjected to the application of strict measures provided for by the law. At the same time, it is necessary to eliminate from practice deficiencies connected with ungrounded assignment of deprivation of liberty to persons who have committed crimes presenting no social danger."[58]

Capital punishment is not included in the list of punishments of Article 21 of the PC because this measure has always been regarded by Soviet criminal law as exceptional and provisional. The Soviet State has repeatedly abolished it. The first decree abolishing capital punishment was adopted on the second day of the October Revolution, October 26, 1917.[59] However, historical conditions have not yet permitted complete rejection of this measure.

Present legislation (Art. 22 of the CL Fundamentals, Art. 23 of the PC) permits application of the death penalty as "an exceptional measure of punishment pending its final abolition." The law provides for application of the death penalty, by firing squad, for crimes against the state, for hijacking of aircraft, for rape under especially aggravating circumstances such as group rape or rape of a minor, and for some other crimes. However, in practice in recent years, the death penalty has been applied only for intentional homicide.[60]

The law never provides the death penalty as the sole possible punishment for a crime. Persons who at the time of the commission of a crime have not attained the age of eighteen years and women who are pregnant at the time of the commission of the crime or at the time judgment is rendered may not be sentenced to death.

---

58. Bulletin of the Supreme Court of the USSR No. 3, at 10 (1976).
59. CL RSFSR No. 1, at 10 (1917).
60. I. I. Gorielik & I. S. Tischkevich, Issues of Criminal Law (General Part) in the Practice of the Supreme Court of the Byelorussian SSR 42 (1973; Minsk).

Deprivation of liberty can be assigned only for definite terms. Soviet criminal law has never provided for life imprisonment. The maximum term for deprivation of liberty under Article 23 of the CL Fundamentals is ten years; for especially grave crimes and for especially dangerous recidivists in cases provided by the law the term is not more than fifteen years. The minimum term for deprivation of liberty is established by the penal codes of the various union republics (under the PC it is three months).

Since the great majority of crimes committed in the USSR are not grave and do not present a great social danger, short terms of deprivation of liberty prevail. In the Moldavian SSR, for instance, data indicates that the persons sentenced to deprivation of liberty for terms of under one year constituted 3 to 4 percent of the total number of convicted persons; from one to three years, 38 to 40 percent; and from three to five years, 25 to 27 percent. Thus, the great majority of the persons sentenced to deprivation of liberty (more than 70 percent) were assigned to terms of confinement of five years or less.[61]

Corrective labor (Art. 27 of the PC) is the most common alternative to deprivation of liberty. This measure consists of sentencing a person who has committed a crime to pay a certain portion of his salary (from 5 to 20 percent) to the state for a fixed period. As a rule, this person continues to work where he did before. If the person does not work and for some other reasons, this measure may be accomplished by having the agency charged with its execution assign the person a job at some local enterprise.

Corrective labor constitutes 19 to 22 percent of the sanctions of the penal codes of the union republics, and in practice is applied to 22 to 25 percent of offenders.[62] Usually, this measure brings positive results: the recidivism rate does not exceed 9.2 percent and is decreasing.[63]

When assigning a fine (Art. 30 of the PC), the law considers not only the gravity of the crime but also the material condi-

---

61. Questions of Crime Combatting No. 10, at 15 (1969).
62. *Supra* note 57, at 21.
63. *Supra* note 57, at 54.

tions of the convict. Thus, a regional court of Belgorod reduced a fine from 250 to 25 rubles for Myslivtseva, who was convicted of brewing spirits in her home, in view of the fact that she lived on a pension and this was her first conviction.[64]

Fines constitute about 10 percent of all sanctions. They can be applied only when included by the law in the measures of punishment for the particular crime. The law prohibits replacing a fine with deprivation of liberty or deprivation of liberty with a fine. If it is impossible to exact a fine, the court may replace it with corrective labor without deprivation of liberty.

Other measures of punishment occupy a very small place both in legislation and in judicial practice.

5.3. Sentencing

In assigning a punishment, courts are concerned with fairness, in making the punishment fit the crime and the offender. The principles which orient the courts are those of humanism, justice, expediency, and individualization of punishment.

The Plenum of the USSR Supreme Court, in its directive of December 3, 1976, "Further improvement of judicial activities in crime prevention" writes "Only a just sentence may contribute to socialist law consciousness. That is why courts, when choosing the type and degree of punishment, must be guided by the principle of individualization, consider the nature and degree of the social danger of the crime, personal characteristics of the offender, and circumstances both mitigating and aggravating responsibility."[65]

The main principles for punishment assignment are described in Article 32 of the CL Fundamentals (Art. 37 of the PC), which states that the court shall assign a punishment within the limits established by the articles of the law (providing for responsibility for the crime) in strict accordance with the provisions of that article, norms of the General Part, and socialist law consciousness.

The law enumerates aggravating and mitigating circumstances.

---

64. BULLETIN OF THE SUPREME COURT OF THE RSFSR No. 9, at 16 (1963).
65. BULLETIN OF THE SUPREME COURT OF THE USSR No. 1, at 13 (1977).

One should note that the list of the aggravating circumstances (Art. 39 of the PC) is exhaustive and cannot be expanded by interpretation. On the other hand, the list of the mitigating circumstances (Art. 38 of the PC) is not exhaustive and the law authorizes the court to recognize other circumstances as mitigating.

Among mitigating circumstances, the law names voluntary compensation of damages, commission of a crime in consequence of grave personal or family problems or under the influence of a threat or coercion, commission of a crime by a minor or a pregnant woman, sincere repentance, and voluntary surrender. Having established mitigating circumstances, the court may reduce the punishment within the limits of the law applying to the offense. The court also has the right to go beyond the minimum sanction provided for the law and assign a milder measure if there are unique circumstances (Art. 43 of the PC). In practice, such mitigation of punishment usually takes place when there are several simultaneous mitigating circumstances. Very often, courts refer to a positive attitude of the person, his having dependents, his advanced age, or his participation in the Great Patriotic War (World War II).

Aggravating circumstances are repeated crime; commission of a crime by an organized group; commission of a crime from avaricious or other base motives; commission of a crime against a young, aged, or helpless person; commission of a crime with extreme brutality; commission of a crime presenting a public danger; and committing a crime in the state of intoxication, etc.

The judicial collegium of the Supreme Court of the RSFSR examined the case of Goloshchapov, who had been accused of rape, and held as improper the trial court's considering as aggravating circumstances his refusal to admit guilt and unwillingness to speak. The judicial collegium indicated that such circumstances are not provided for in Article 39 of the PC.[66]

The most significant aggravating circumstance is repeated crime. The Special Part of the Penal Code contains twenty articles in which repeated offenses constitute an element the addition of which qualifies an act as a more serious crime. Persons

---

66. BULLETIN OF THE SUPREME COURT OF THE RSFSR No. 4, at 9 (1965).

who have been previously convicted are isolated from first-time offenders in confinement. Persons who have been convicted repeatedly for grave crimes may be recognized by the court as especially dangerous recidivists (Art. 231 of the LC Fundamentals, Art. 241 of the PC).[67]

A person may be deemed an especially dangerous recidivist if he has been previously sentenced to deprivation of liberty for an especially dangerous crime against the State; banditry; making or offering counterfeit money or securities under aggravating circumstances; violating rules on currency handling under aggravating circumstances; stealing state or social property on an especially large scale; assault with intent to seize state, social, or personal property under aggravating circumstances; intentional homicide; or rape. If a person was sentenced previously three or more times to deprivation of liberty for malicious hooliganism or if while serving a sentence for a grave crime a person committed a new crime for which the sentence is a deprivation of liberty for a term of not less than five years, he is also considered an especially dangerous recidivist.

Whether to designate a convicted person as an especially dangerous recidivist is discussed by the court during sentencing and its determination is reflected in the sentence. Factors considered include previous convictions, the personality of the offender, the degree of social danger, and motivations of previous crimes and the offender's role in their commission. Based on these considerations, the court may refuse to deem a person an especially dangerous recidivist even if he meets the formal criteria. The court does not consider convictions for crimes committed before the person reached eighteen years of age or convictions which have been expunged or cancelled.

Deeming a person as especially dangerous recidivist is of great practical importance. Such persons are sent to corrective labor establishments with a strict regime or to colonies with a special regime (Art. 23 of the CL Fundamentals, Art. 24 of the PC),

67. A practical application of these norms is discussed in the Directive of the Plenum of the Supreme Court of the USSR of June 25, 1976, on "Practice of judicial application of legislation on combatting recidive crimes"; *see* BULLETIN OF THE SUPREME COURT OF THE USSR No. 4 (1976).

may not obtain a conditional early release [Art. 44(1) of the CL Fundamentals, Art. 53(1) of the PC], and after serving punishment are subject to administrative supervision.[68] Also, the commission of a further crime by such a person is sometimes regarded as qualifying as a more serious crime. For example, Article 102 lists, as a separate classification, homicide committed by an especially dangerous recidivist and part 3, Article 144 lists theft committed by an especially dangerous recidivist. Another factor aggravating responsibility is commission of a crime by a person in the state of alcoholic intoxication (par. 10, Art. 39 of the PC).

Aiming at the prevention of crimes connected with alcoholism or drug addiction, the law (Art. 62 of the PC) gives the court the right to apply both punishment and compulsory medical treatment. Such treatment may be assigned only if it has been established by medical experts that the offender is an alcoholic or a drug addict.[69] Persons sentenced to deprivation of liberty undergo treatment at the place of their confinement.

Section 6. REDUCTION OF CRIMINAL RESPONSIBILITY AND PUNISHMENT

6.1. Reduction and Dismissal of Charges

As has already been mentioned, the aim of punishment is correction and re-education of the offender as well as deterring crime commission by other members of society. If this goal may be achieved without application of punishment or by compulsory educational measures in lieu of punishment, or if the goal already has been achieved, Soviet law allows for relieving the offender from criminal responsibility or punishment.

The CL Fundamentals and the penal codes of the union re-

---

68. GAZETTE OF THE SUPREME SOVIET OF THE USSR No. 24, at 206 (1960).

69. The Directive of the Plenum of the Supreme Court of the USSR of September 26, 1975 on "Judicial practice of application of legislation and decisions of the Plenum of the Supreme Court of the USSR directed against drunkenness and alcoholism" provides that a medical commission's conclusion must contain an indication whether the person is an alcoholic or a drug addict and needs compulsory medical treatment, and whether there is any doubt about it; see BULLETIN OF THE SUPREME COURT OF THE USSR No. 6, at 12-16 (1975).

publics provide a whole system of different types of relief from criminal responsibility.

If punishment is not required for correction of an offender but his correction requires the efforts of a labor collective or a social organization, agencies of justice may relieve him from criminal responsibility and apply measures of *social influence*. In such a situation, after the criminal case is terminated the matter may be brought to a comrades' court or to a juvenile commission, or the person may be transferred to the supervision of a labor collective or social organization. This type of relief from responsibility was applied, for example, to Bogachev, who was a first-time offender accused of stealing a fur coat from his mistress.[70]

The comrades' courts try only insignificant offenses. Sometimes transfer of a case to such courts is provided for among the sanctions of the Special Part of the PC. Such provisions are contained in Art. 97 (misappropriation of a lost article), Art. 112 (minor battery), Art. 123 (not supporting one's parents), and some others.

The activities of comrades' courts in the RSFSR are regulated by a new law adopted by the decision of the Presidium of the Supreme Court of the RSFSR of March 11, 1977.[71] Studies of the comrades' courts have shown that they are effective in educating citizens, contributing to labor discipline, defending socialist property, and carrying on a successful struggle against antisocial activities. This was the foundation for a Decree of the Presidium of the Supreme Soviet of the USSR of February 8, 1977, "Further improvement of the comrades' courts work,"[72] which contains a recommendation to the union republics to expand the competence of such courts.

Relief from criminal responsibility resulting in a transfer of a case to a juvenile commission (Art. 43 of the CL Fundamental; part 4, Art. 10 of the PC) is possible if the crime has been committed by a person who has reached the age of crim-

---

70. BULLETIN OF THE SUPREME COURT OF THE USSR No. 2, at 9-10 (1975).
71. GAZETTE OF THE SUPREME SOVIET OF THE RSFSR No. 12, Item 254 (1977).
72. GAZETTE OF THE SUPREME SOVIET OF THE USSR No. 7, Item 121 (1977).

inal responsibility but is still under eighteen, the offense is of no great social danger, and the person may be corrected without punishment.

Relief from punishment resulting in a social supervision (Art. 43 of the CL Fundamentals, Art. 52 of the PC) is possible when the crime committed presents no great social danger, the guilty person has admitted his guilt and shown sincere repentance, and a social organization or a labor collective petitions to take this person under its supervision. Such relief is conditional, the offender being required to prove his correction by exemplary behavior and an honest attitude towards work during the period of one year. If he does not, the collective may withdraw its petition, and the criminal procedure recommences.

As a rule, relief from criminal responsibility with application of measures of social treatment produces good results. A study of such relief in Eastern Siberia for a period of thirteen years has shown that only 3.2 percent of those relieved from criminal responsibility committed additional crimes during the period of one year after the relief.[73]

The Decision of the Presidium of the Supreme Court of the USSR of February 8, 1977[74] introduced a new type of relief from criminal responsibility: a relief or replacement of punishment with measures of an administrative nature (Art. 43 of the CL Fundamentals, Art. 501 of the PC). This form of relief is possible if the crime does not present a great social danger, is punishable by a maximum penalty of one year or less of deprivation of liberty, and it is shown that correction and re-education may be achieved without punishment. If such relief is applied by the agencies of preliminary investigation (with the procurators' consent), they terminate the case and direct it to a single judge. If such relief is applied by the court at trial, the full court upon termination of the case assigns an administrative penalty.

In addition, relief from criminal responsibility occurs upon the expiration of the period provided under the applicable statute of limitations (Art. 41 of the CL Fundamentals, Art. 48 of

73. S. G. KELINA, THEORETICAL PROBLEMS OF RELIEF FROM CRIMINAL RESPONSIBILITY 4-5 (1974; Moscow, "Nauka" Publ. House).

74. GAZETTE OF THE SUPREME SOVIET OF THE USSR No. 7, Item 116 (1977).

the PC). Moreover, the law allows such relief if the situation has changed so that the crime consequently has lost its socially dangerous nature, or the person who committed the crime ceased to be socially dangerous (part 1, Art. 43 of the CL Fundamentals; part 1, Art. 50 of the PC). Such relief was applied to Ivanov who, while on a train, had stolen a conductor's wrist watch, because some time later he was recruited for the Army and proved to be an honest person.[75]

Several types of relief from punishment are provided for in the norms of the Special Part of the Penal Code: relief from criminal responsibility for high treason by a USSR citizen who was recruited by a foreign intelligence service, if he has not performed any assignments and voluntarily reported his connection with the foreign intelligence service to the authorities (part B, Art. 64 of the PC); a relief from criminal responsibility for bribery, if the person was forced to offer the bribe, but after giving it, voluntarily reported it (notes to Art. 174 of the PC); a relief from criminal responsibility for illegal possession of firearms, if the person voluntarily surrenders them (notes for Art. 218 of the PC).

6.2. Suspended Sentences

Soviet criminal law provides several forms of complete relief from punishment by a conditional sentencing (Art. 38 of the CL Fundamentals, Art. 44 of the PC), a conditional punishment of deprivation of liberty with compulsory labor [Art. 23(2) of the CL Fundamentals, Art. 24(2) of the PC], a suspension of the punishment for a minor [Art. 39(1) of the CL Fundamentals, Art. 46(1) of the PC], expiration of the period of limitation of the sentence (Art. 42 of the CL Fundamentals, Art. 49 of the PC), or suspension of punishment for a military man during war (Art. 39 of the CL Fundamentals, Art. 46 of the PC). A person may be completely relieved from punishment if, because of his faultless behavior subsequent to the crime, the court finds him no longer a danger to society (part 2, Art. 43 of the CL Fundamentals; part 2, Art. 50 of the PC).

---

75. COLLECTED DECISIONS OF PRESIDIUM AND RULINGS OF JUDICIAL COLLEGIUM OF THE SUPREME COURT OF THE RSFSR ON CRIMINAL CASES 23-24 (1960; Moscow, "Gosyurizdat" Publ. House).

Conditionally convicted persons under Article 38 of the CL Fundamentals comprise 25 to 27 percent of all persons sentenced to punishments not involving deprivation of liberty;[76] persons conditionally punished with compulsory labor comprise 20 percent of those sentenced to deprivation of liberty for terms of up to three years.[77]

Article 38 of the CL Fundamentals provides that where—in considering punishment in the form of deprivation of liberty or corrective work—the court, taking into consideration the circumstances of the case and the personality of the offender, becomes convinced that it would be inappropriate for the guilty person to serve such punishment, it may decree a conditional nonapplication of the punishment. The law does not contain any formal limitations to sentences of conditional punishment.

The Plenum of the Supreme Court of the USSR, having examined the practice of conditional sentencing, indicated in its decision of March 4, 1961 that a conditional sentence should not, as a rule, be applied to persons guilty of grave crimes, and the courts should be very cautious when deciding to assign a conditional punishment to a person who has been convicted previously.[78] In practice, conditional punishments are assigned for minor crimes and to the less active participants in minor crimes. Frequently, conditional punishment is assigned to juveniles and persons who have committed crimes of carelessness, such as causing traffic accidents.

A conditional punishment consists of assigning the offender to a probation period of from one to five years, during which he must not commit any further intentional crime punishable by deprivation of liberty.

The court may place a conditionally sentenced person under the supervision of a social organization or a labor collective. Such a procedure usually produces good results: whereas recidivism among all conditionally punished persons is 11.4 percent, among those under such supervision the rate is 7.2 percent.[79]

---

76. Soviet State and Law No. 3, at 117 (1972).
77. Soviet Justice No. 21, at 2 (1974).
78. *Supra* note 2, at 399-401.
79. Socialist Legality No. 7, at 27 (1969).

The Decision of the Presidium of the Supreme Soviet of the USSR of June 12, 1970[80] introduced a new type of conditional punishment—a replacement of deprivation of liberty with compulsory labor. This decision was codified on February 8, 1977, in a new article of the CL Fundamentals, 23(2), providing wider grounds for relief from actual execution of punishment of deprivation of liberty.[81]

Conditional punishment with compulsory labor may be applied when there are the following grounds:

a. a person is convicted for the first time;

b. the crime is one for which the punishment would be deprivation of liberty for up to three years if the commission was intentional and up to five years for a crime of carelessness;

c. the nature of the crime and its social danger, the offender's personality, and other circumstances make it likely that correction and re-education of the person may be achieved without his isolation from society, but that conditions of compulsory work and supervision over his behavior are required. The term of compulsory work is equal to that of the punishment that would otherwise have applied, except that a person who has served half of the term may qualify for conditional early release.

A study of 1,000 cases of this type of relief has shown that 32.7 percent of such cases involved hooliganism, 21.4 percent thefts of state or personal property, and 11.2 percent traffic violations.[82]

Suspension of sentences for a minor is a new type of complete relief from punishment in Soviet criminal law. It was introduced by a Decree of the Presidium of the Supreme Soviet of the USSR of February 15, 1977.[83] This type of relief is similar in nature to probation in American criminal law. Suspension is applied to a minor, convicted for the first time for a crime punishable by a term of up to three years. The court should take into consideration the nature of the crime, the personality of

---

80. GAZETTE OF THE SUPREME SOVIET OF THE USSR No. 24, at 205 (1970).
81. GAZETTE OF THE SUPREME SOVIET OF THE USSR No. 7, at 116 (1977).
82. SOCIALIST LEGALITY No. 9, at 65 (1973).
83. GAZETTE OF THE SUPREME SOVIET OF THE USSR No. 8, at 136 (1977).

the accused, and the possibility for his correction and re-education without being isolated from society.

6.3. Forms of Parole

Soviet criminal law provides for two types of conditional early release from punishment. One is a traditional type governed by Articles 44, 44(1), and 45 of the CL Fundamentals [Arts. 53, 53(1), 54 of the PC]. The second type was introduced by a Decree of the Presidium of the Supreme Soviet of the USSR on February 8, 1977.[84] It is governed by Article 44(2) of the CL Fundamentals [Art. 53(2) of the PC] and involves conditional early release with compulsory labor.

A general conditional early release may be assigned to persons sentenced to a punishment of fixed duration: to deprivation of liberty, exile, restricted residence, corrective labor, or service in a disciplinary battalion. It also may be applied to persons sentenced conditionally to deprivation of liberty with compulsory labor [Art. 44 of the CL Fundamentals, Art. 53(2) of the PC].

The law sets forth two grounds for conditional early release: serving a part of the term of punishment and correction of the person as proved by his good behavior and honest attitude towards work. When such conditions are present, the remaining part of the term may be replaced by a milder punishment (for example, deprivation of liberty replaced by exile).

The Supreme Court of the USSR, in its directive of October 19, 1971, "On judicial practice of conditional early release from punishment and replacement of the remaining term of punishment with a milder one," indicated that "A decision on whether a convict has been corrected must be based on a study of multifaceted data concerning the convict's behavior during the term of his confinement, and not only during the period immediately before the request. It is particularly necessary to consider information about the convict's observation of the corrective labor establishment regime, his attitude towards work and study, and his participation in social life."[85]

The smallest punishment after which there can be a right for

---

84. Gazette of the Supreme Soviet of the USSR No. 7, at 116 (1977).
85. *Supra* note 2, at 419.

a conditional early release is determined by the law. It depends on the gravity of the crime committed, with the general rule being not less than half of the term, but for grave crimes and for persons convicted repeatedly, two-thirds of the term must be served, and for persons who have committed especially grave crimes, three-fourths (Art. 44 of the CL Fundamentals, Art. 53 of the PC). These terms are reduced if the crime was committed by a person under eighteen, in which case they are, respectively, one-third, one-half, and two-thirds of the term of punishment (Art. 45 of the CL Fundamentals, Art. 55 of the PC).

Conditional early release is assigned by the court. A request is submitted jointly by the administration of the establishment where the punishment is executed and the oversight commission of the executive committee of the local Soviet.[86]

The All-Union Institute for Study of Causes and Development of Measures for Crime Prevention presents data showing that 44 percent of the convicts released from confinement in 1965 were released after serving their full term, and 36.5 percent were released under conditional early release.[87]

The term of the probation period is equal to the remaining part of the original term of punishment. The law has only one requirement to be met by the released person, that he not commit a new intentional crime punishable by deprivation of liberty during the probation period.

In general, conditional early release brings about good results. The recidivism rate among those who are conditionally released is usually 1.5 to 2 times lower than among those who served the whole term of punishment.[88] Placing the relieved person under the supervision of a collective of working people proves to be especially successful (part Art. 44 of the CL Fundamentals).

The law identifies a rather narrow class of people who cannot be conditionally released. These are especially dangerous recidivists, persons convicted of aggravated homicide, and persons

---

86. Organization, composition, and functions of the agency are described in Chapter VI, Section 1.

87. EFFECTIVENESS OF CRIMINAL LAW MEASURES IN COMBATTING CRIME 174 (1968; Moscow, Nauka Publ. House).

88. *Supra* at 175.

whose death penalty was replaced by a deprivation of liberty because of an amnesty or pardon [Art. 44(1) of the CL Fundamentals, Art. 53(1) of the CP]. These limitations do not affect convicts who committed crimes at an age under eighteen. All such persons are eligible.

The second type of conditional early release is conditional early release with compulsory labor, introduced on February 8, 1977 by Article 44(2) of the CL Fundamentals.

Two requirements must be met in order to apply this type of the conditional release: the serving by the convict of a part of the term, and his behavior must allow the court to come to the conclusion that further correction and re-education of the person can be achieved without his isolation from society, though it is advisable to maintain a measure of control over him.

The law does not limit the application of this type of conditional early release according to the gravity or nature of the crime. It may be applied to all able-bodied adult convicts, including those to whom general conditional early release is prohibited by law. The gravity of the crime does, however, determine the minimal terms necessary for requesting such relief. These terms are defined by the law as one-third, one-half, two-thirds, and three-fourths of the punishment assigned by the court. Conditional early release with compulsory labor is also assigned by the court. It consists of transferring the convict to work, and obliging him to observe labor discipline, public order, and special rules of residence. One day of work is counted as a day of serving punishment.

CHAPTER VI

EXECUTION OF SENTENCES

V. P. SHUPILOV

Section 1. GENERAL PRINCIPLES

1.1. The Concept of Corrective Labor

EXECUTION OF PUNISHMENT in the USSR is governed by the corrective labor law, which is based on the Constitution of the USSR and the constitutions of the union republics.

Article 14 of the new Constitution of the USSR states: "The source of the growth of social wealth and the well-being of the people, and of each individual, is the labor, free from exploitation, of the Soviet people." Article 60 of the Constitution goes further, saying: "It is the duty of, and a matter of honor for, every able-bodied citizen of the USSR to work conscientiously in his chosen, socially useful occupation, and strictly to observe labor discipline. Evasion of socially useful work is incompatible with the principles of socialist society." These constitutional principles are of great importance for corrective labor legislation, since a rationally organized system of labor plays a major role in the correction and re-education of convicts in the USSR. Consequently, the entire body of regulations governing correction and re-education is called the corrective labor law.

The Fundamentals of Corrective Labor Legislation of the USSR and the Union Republics (hereafter referred to as CLL Fundamentals) were adopted on July 11, 1969.[1] Article 2 of the CLL Fundamentals provides that corrective labor legislation exists on both the federal and union republic levels. An example of legislation by union republics is the Decree on Oversight Commissions. Such commissions administer nongovernmental control over the activities of agencies and organizations charged with the execution of court sentences of persons sentenced to deprivation of liberty, exile, restricted residence, and corrective

1. GAZETTE OF THE SUPREME SOVIET OF THE USSR No. 29, Item 247 (1968).

labor. Decrees on these commissions were approved by the presidiums of the Supreme Soviets of the union republics, and thus have become one of the sources of the corrective labor law.[2] The theory of the corrective labor law divides all corrective labor measures into compulsory, restrictive, and mandatory. The first two categories govern the manner and conditions for execution of punishment, define convicts' responsibilities, and establish the limitations to which convicts are subject during their sentences. Restrictive and mandatory norms apply to both convicts and agencies executing their punishment. For example, persons sentenced to deprivation of liberty are kept in custody and under surveillance. By the court sentence, they must be kept in places of confinement, but it is the duty of the administration of the place of confinement to provide for both guarding and controlling them.

Mandatory norms are directed mainly to the administration of agencies executing punishment. At the same time, some norms, such as those establishing rules for voluntary or social groups of convicts, may be viewed as being mandatory in nature.

The goal of corrective labor legislation, as stated in Article I of the CLL Fundamentals, is to effect punishment for offenses and also to correct and reform offenders in the spirit of a conscientious attitude toward work, strict observance of the laws, and respect for the rules of socialist community life, preventing commission of new crimes both by the convicts and by other persons, thus promoting eradication of crime.

1.2. Principles of Implementation

It is possible to focus on the principles which are the foundation of the policy on execution of criminal punishment in the USSR: strict observance of socialist legality, ample involvement of the public in re-education of convicts, humanism, compulsory socially useful work by convicts, individualization of punishment execution, and differential application of the means and

---

2. Yu. M. Tkachievsky, Soviet Corrective Labor Law 17-18 (1971; Moscow U. Pr).

methods of correction and re-education in the spirit of collectiveness and initiative of convicts.

Strict observance of legality in executing a criminal punishment calls for regularity in the activities of agencies charged with punishment execution in order to create the necessary conditions for achievement of the goals of corrective labor. This requirement means guaranteeing constant observance of the rights of convicts while they are in confinement, while ensuring that the convicts fulfill the duties assigned to them. The goal of correction and re-education is equally impaired by neglect of either of these conditions.

The importance of observance of legality is emphasized in all the corrective labor codes of the union republics. For example, Article 10 of the Corrective Labor Code of the RSFSR (hereafter referred to as the CLC) states:

> All activities of corrective labor institutions and agencies executing court sentences of exile, restricted residence, and corrective labor without deprivation of liberty are based on strict observance of the law. Officers of such institutions and agencies are responsible for law observance in such activities.
>
> Persons who are serving punishment must obey constantly the rules defining the manner and conditions of their punishment.

Procurator's supervision is called upon to guarantee strict observance of legality. Article 10 of the CL Fundamentals stipulates that supervision of the strict observance of the law during the execution of sentences of deprivation of liberty, exile, restricted residence, and corrective labor without deprivation of liberty shall be exercised by the Procurator-General of the USSR and the procurators subordinate to him in accordance with the "Ordinance on the supervisory powers of the Procurator's Office of the USSR." In exercising supreme supervision over the observance of the law in the name of the State, the procurator shall be obliged to take timely measures to prevent and eliminate any breaches of the law and to bring the guilty to account. The administration of corrective labor institutions shall be obliged to carry out decisions and proposals of the procurator concerning observance of rules for serving of sentences contained in the CLL Fundamentals.

The procurator is given broad powers in this area, including the right to suspend any decisions by the administration of a place of confinement that contradict the law; the right to present the administration of places of confinement with binding orders concerning the proper standards for living conditions of convicts; and the right to free from custody any person kept illegally in a place of confinement. These powers are applicable in all places of confinement for all categories of convicts.

In accordance with Articles 33 to 37 of the "Ordinance on the supervisory powers," the procurator shall systematically visit places of confinement; see that only persons placed into custody pursuant to a procurator's order or a court decision are kept in such places and only for the term stipulated by law or court sentence; release from custody anyone who has been arrested or kept in custody illegally; supervise the observance of laws on convicts' care and prevent both granting of unfounded privileges and infringements of convicts rights; inspect first-hand the orders and instructions of the administration and suspend any that are contrary to the law and file protests against them; see to it that the administration properly transmits complaints and petitions of convicts to the officials and agencies to whom they are addressed and that responses to them are delivered promptly to the convicts; examine the complaints and petitions of convicts and inform authors of his assessment of them; charge those who have broken the law with criminal responsibility; evaluate the grounds for requests for conditional early releases from confinement which are presented in court; report and comment on practices within places of confinement and initiate questions which may contribute to further improvement in correction and education of convicts; discover and eliminate ungrounded penalties against convicts and application of measures prohibited by law or contrary to human dignity; and secure compliance with the requirement that socially useful labor be provided for all able-bodied convicts.

To enable the procurator to perform these important functions, he is also empowered to visit all correctional institutions at any time with unimpeded access to all areas; to examine documents serving as the ground for deprivations of liberty; to personally question convicts to check on the legality of activities of the administration affecting their regime and living conditions; and to demand explanations from officials of the administration concerning any breaches of the rules for the keeping of convicts.

Execution of criminal punishment involves a punitive element in that certain requirements and restrictions are imposed on convicts. However, Article I of the CLL Fundamentals emphasizes the humanistic aspect of punishment. Punishment is not aimed at physical suffering or offense to human dignity. Some suffering and deprivation is inevitable but may be permitted only to the extent necessary for achievement of the goals of punishment.

In accordance with Article 9 of the CLL Fundamentals, activities of agencies executing punishment are subject to both State and nongovernmental control. Social representatives see that punishment execution is humanistic and that corrective institutions' processes are directed in the long-term to correction of convicts and toward their rehabilitation.

An important role in nongovernmental control over corrective labor institutions is played by oversight commissions. The "Ordinance on oversight commissions of executive committees of district and city Soviets of People's Deputies of the RSFSR" was adopted by the Presidium of the Supreme Soviet of the RSFSR on September 30, 1965.[3] It was later amended by a decree of the Presidium of October 1, 1970, "On establishing oversight commissions of executive committees of cities', regions', and territories' Soviets of People's Deputies and under councils of ministers of autonomous republics and amendments and additions to the 'Ordinance on oversight commissions.' "[4] Similar ordinances were adopted by the various union republics at approximately the same time.

Oversight commissions are social bodies composed of a chairman, deputy chairman, secretary, and five to eight members, all approved by the corresponding Soviet or council of ministers.

---

3. GAZETTE OF THE SUPREME SOVIET OF THE RSFSR No. 40, Item 990 (1965); GAZETTE OF THE SUPREME SOVIET OF THE RSFSR No. 41, Item 832 (1970).

4. Adopted on December 18, 1970; *see* GAZETTE OF THE SUPREME SOVIET OF THE RSFSR No. 51, Item 220 (1970).

Because such commissions exercise nongovernmental control over activities of agencies charged with execution of punishments and may, when necessary, bring to court or to Procurator's Offices cases involving conduct of such institutions, neither the Ministry of the Interior nor the courts nor the Procurator's Offices are represented on them.

Oversight commissions monitor actual conditions in places of confinement and render assistance to agencies executing punishment by organizing and directing activities of individuals and social organizations participating on a voluntary basis in re-education of convicts.

The right to examine the grounds for refusal of jobs to persons from places of confinement is a very important function of the commissions. If such an examination shows that a person has been refused a job at an enterprise solely because he has served punishment, the commission takes immediate measures to put an end to such an illegal practice. Administrations of offices, enterprises, and organizations must inform the commission of measures they have taken to remedy deficiencies cited in the commission's decision within two weeks. The decision of the oversight commission may be appealed to the corresponding executive committee of a Soviet or to the council of ministers of an autonomous republic, whose decisions are then final.

Nongovernmental control over application of corrective and educational measures for minors is accomplished by commissions on juveniles under executive committees of the Soviets. These commissions may submit proposals to enterprises, organizations, and social agencies concerning educational work, vocational training, and job placement, as well as placing minors in educational institutions. They supervise activities of institutions for minors and educational labor colonies for juvenile delinquents. Rights of such commissions are as wide as those of the oversight commissions and their decisions are binding on administrations of educational labor colonies. If an administration fails to comply with decisions of the commission, the commission is authorized to seek disciplinary penalties for the responsible officers.

Wide public participation in the work of agencies executing punishment contributes not only to the strengthening of the humanistic aspect of punishment but also helps in maintaining and developing convicts' social ties, furthering their re-education and eliminating the stigmatizing impact of punishment.

In the course of treatment, due significance is attached to socially useful work. Soviet corrective labor law and practice emphasize the educational impact of labor, which helps to form such positive qualities as teamwork, industriousness, ability to coordinate personal and social interests, desire to be a useful member of the society, and respect for others' work.

Article 27 of the CLL Fundamentals stipulates that each convicted person has a duty to work. The administration of corrective labor institutions is required to assign socially useful labor with due consideration for the work capacity and, if possible, profession of each convict.

Convicted persons shall, as a rule, be enlisted for work at enterprises of corrective labor institutions.

"The economic activity," according to Article 27 of the CLL Fundamentals, "of corrective labor institutions must be subordinated to their main task, that of correction and reform of convicted persons."

The most widespread form of labor of convicts sentenced to deprivation of liberty is at enterprises founded by corrective labor institutions themselves. Creation of its own industrial base provides for full employment of convicts and furnishes necessary equipment for vocational training.

Corrective labor institutions with their own productive bases are more economical. The proximity of the enterprise to the residential zone allows the convicts to save time greatly needed for their studies at school, vocational training courses, advanced learning, or cultural leisure activities.

Work at enterprises under other ministries and departments is also practiced. In such circumstances, convicts kept in one colony may work part of the time in a shop of a large plant and part of the time in construction of an industrial or a residential building.[5]

Wherever a convict works, he always learns the use of modern

---

5. M. A. Efimov, Fundamentals of Soviet Corrective Labor Law 42 (1963; Sverdlovsk).

techniques in order to maintain and develop skills and learn new trades which are useful in the people's economy.

During the work process, much attention is paid to the reform of convicts in the spirit of a conscientious attitude toward work by their involvement in social competition. The competitors strive to achieve such indicia as high productivity, economical use of the raw materials, maintenance of technical specifications in mechanical operations, and maintenance of their instruments and equipment in good condition. The socialist competition indicia permit objective comparison of the results achieved. Socialist labor competition is practical among workers of the same team, same trade, among the teams making up a battalion, and among the battalions of the same institutions. Champions are rewarded according to their achievements.[6]

The work of a convict, according to Article 28 of the CLL Fundamentals, shall be organized in accordance with the observance of labor safety rules stipulated by the Labour Law of the USSR.

Article 29 of the CLL Fundamentals states:

> The work of persons deprived of liberty shall be paid according to quantity and quality at the norms and rates operating in the national economy. The crediting of earnings to convicted persons shall be made with deductions representing partial compensation by them of the expenditure incurred in maintaining corrective labor institutions.
>
> Under the procedure established by the present Fundamentals and the corrective labor codes of the union republics, convicted persons may be employed without remuneration only in the work of improving the place of confinement and adjacent territory and also the work of improving the cultural and living conditions of the convicted persons.

Labor in corrective labor institutions is an efficient means of treatment. All economic activities of the corrective labor institutions are directed to one goal, correction and reform of the convicted persons. This goal requires an *individualization of punishment execution,* a differential application of means and methods of correction and reform.

---

6. *Supra* at 43-44.

General principles of criminal responsibility and punishment individualization are determined by Soviet criminal law norms. The penal code stipulates that convicts shall be awarded punishment within the range of sanctions provided in the Special Part and in compliance with the provisions of the General Part with due consideration of the character and degree of social danger of the crime committed, the offender's personality, and the circumstances of the case.[7]

Soviet corrective labor law theory emphasizes the fact that individualization of punishment execution requires due consideration of each convict's personality, as well as the norms established by the general rules of corrective labor law in choosing among corrective means and methods.[8]

A characteristic feature of treatment policy in the USSR is creation of a spirit of collectiveness and development of initiative in persons serving punishment. By initiative is meant participation by convicts in the educational work conducted in their corrective labor institution. Collectiveness is promoted by properly organizing and leading groups of convicts for accomplishment of various goals within the institution and is an important means of inspiring respect for the principal rules of socialist life, public opinion, and the needs of other persons.

Turning a collective into a basis for the educational process is one of the principles of the Makarenko pedagogical system. Makarenko, a well-known Soviet expert on pedagogy, consistently emphasized that education of both individuals and collectives should be directed by a single goal, so that any influence on the collective is also an influence on the individual. The collective becomes a creative treatment force in such a situation. Obviously, proper use of a collective in reforming convicts requires that it be effectively led and oriented toward proper goals. Likewise, use of the collective must be combined with individual treatment work.

When the administration of punishment-executing agencies

---

7. Described in Chapter V, Section 5.

8. N. A. Struchkov, Soviet Corrective Labor Policy and Its Role in Crime Combatting 176 (1970; Saratov).

does not take steps toward formation of sound collectives, they form spontaneously and acquire a powerful influence. Soviet penitentiary research has shown that such spontaneous groups tend to take the following forms:

1. groups with a positive orientation, which are formed on the basis of a common interest, attitude, or tastes. A person with knowledge or experience in the area of common concern tends to dominate such a group. Groups of this kind may be used by the administration to achieve treatment goals.

2. groups with an indefinite orientation are formed on the basis of similarities in age, profession, or other features. Such groups should be directed by the administration toward a positive orientation.

3. groups with a negative orientation may appear among convicts who engage in similar violations of the regime or have common plans for criminal activities in the future. Such groups tend to coalesce around a "ring leader."[9] It is crucial that the administration of places of confinement take steps to break up such groups.

Within institutions of confinement, the principal autonomous convicts' organization is the council of the collective, consisting of seven to fifteen persons elected by open vote at yearly general meetings of the convicts.[10] The members of the council are the crucial factor influencing their usefulness, since activities of such councils are determined entirely by them. Accordingly, the administration of institutions has the right to disqualify certain nominees for positions on such councils.

The council of the collective directs everyday work of sections and inspires convicts to meet and surpass their production quotas and to develop socialist labor competition. The council also helps the administration to organize and develop technical and vocational training and to improve creativity in work, as well as to enhance the general education of the convicts. It is especially

---

9. Yu. M. Tkachievsky, *supra* note 2, at 96.

10. Y. N. Kalinin, G. B. Utevsky, & A. M. Yakoliev, Soviet Corrective Labor Institutions 60 (1960; Moscow, "Juriditcheskaya Literatura" Publ. House).

active in cultural and sports events, hobbies, and reading programs. Councils have the right to submit petitions to the administration for rewards to deserving members of labor brigades.

Sections of these councils consist of five to seven persons and deal with such concerns as labor competition, production, cultural activities, sports, educational activities, professional training, living conditions, and complaints by convicts.[11]

Councils also organize a section on internal order, which helps the administration maintain discipline and encourage convicts to respect state property. Such sections patrol the institution's grounds after working hours and confront violators, explaining to them the regulations they have broken. If such explanations are not sufficient to end violations, the incident is registered in a log. Persons guilty of repeated violations may be summoned before the council to explain their behavior. The council has no power to apply disciplinary measures but may refer such matters to the administration.

Participation by convicts in such self-governing agencies is a social duty that directs their energy into a useful activity which helps the administration in its efforts to re-educate convicts.

This discussion has by no means covered all of the methods used in reforming convicts but has described the most basic and important mechanisms and approaches.

Section 2. NONCUSTODIAL SENTENCES

2.1. Ordinary Compulsory Labor

V. I. Lenin, in laying the foundations of Soviet criminal policy in the early years of Soviet power, emphasized the need to reduce reliance on deprivation of liberty as a criminal sanction. He urged the following measures:

1. increased use of conditional convictions;
2. increased use of social censure;
3. replacement of deprivation of liberty with compulsory work to be performed while residing at home;
4. replacement of prisons with educational institutions;

---

11. *Supra* at 61.

5. introduction of comrades' courts to handle certain categories of cases.[12]

Any time the goals of punishment can be achieved without isolation of the offender from society, punishment without deprivation of liberty is preferable. Among the significant, long-term alternatives to deprivation of liberty are corrective labor, conditional sentencing to deprivation of liberty with compulsory work, and exile.

Corrective labor is the most frequently applied of these alternatives. For example, according to the PC, corrective labor may be awarded in 149 situations. About 25 percent of all persons sentenced serve this type of penalty.[13]

Article 5 of the CLL Fundamentals stipulates that corrective labor without deprivation of liberty is executed by agencies of the Ministry of Interior of the USSR and the ministries of interior of the union republics.

Corrective labor agencies of ministries of interior are divided into city, district, and interdistrict departments, which are directly responsible for execution of this type of punishment.

Corrective labor departments have the following responsibilities:

a. personal registration of those who are awarded this penalty;

b. organization of job-finding for persons so sentenced and supervising those who are sentenced to corrective labor at the place of their work;

c. participation in the organization of educational work with persons serving this kind of punishment;

d. supervision over the manner of work of such persons in enterprises and establishments, ensuring proper deduction of the specified amount from offenders' salaries for transfer to the state account, and rewarding and disciplining persons serving punishment, as well as presentation to the court of documents on persons who willfully evade work;

---

12. V. I. LENIN, 36 COMPLETE WORKS 408.

13. CORRECTIVE LABOR LAW 395-396 (1971; Moscow, "Juriditcheskaya Literatura" Publ. House).

e. presentation to courts of documents for conditional early release of the persons who have been sentenced to corrective labor, or for substitution of milder punishment;

f. organization through the militia of searches for persons who have been sentenced to corrective labor but whose location is unknown.[14]

The departments register the term of serving corrective labor. In accordance with Article 42 of the PC, the term of serving corrective labor is counted by months. A month is served if the offender worked on all working days. Periods of illnesses, pregnancy, and maternity leaves confirmed by medical documents are also counted.

Article 43 of the CLL Fundamentals stipulates that correction and reform of persons serving a sentence of corrective labor without deprivation of liberty is effected through their participation in socially useful work. Thus, labor is recognized as the most important means for correction of convicts.

The first step in handling an offender is registration, which includes summoning the convict to the department where the current legislation on corrective labor is explained to him, especially rights and responsibilities of the person serving punishment.

Officers then periodically visit the enterprises where convicts work, meet with them and with the enterprise administration and comrades of the convicts, and try to find the causes of discipline breaches, if there are any. If necessary, the officers summon convicts to the department, visit their homes, and speak to the members of their families.

A convict is assisted in learning a trade if he had none before. If necessary, experienced workers establish a patronage over the convicts. Patrons are appointed by social organizations and carry on their work till the end of the term of punishment.

Corrective labor possesses a certain punitive element. In accordance with Article 44 of the CLL Fundamentals, deductions from the salary of persons sentenced to corrective labor without deprivation of liberty are made for the benefit of the state during the term of sentence in amounts fixed by the court sentence

---

14. *Supra* at 397.

(within the range of 5 to 20 percent). The deductions are made from gross earnings and without regard for any claims on the convict under writs of execution.

During the entire term of serving the sentence of corrective labor without deprivation of liberty, convicted persons may not be dismissed from their jobs at their own request without permission of the organs in charge of execution of this type of punishment.

Time spent serving a sentence of corrective labor is not generally included in the general record of work of the convict, and a special entry is made in his labor book. However, if he has done work and shown exemplary behavior during the term of serving corrective labor, this term may be included in his general labor record pending a court decision in accordance with legislation of the union republic.

Persons sentenced to corrective labor without deprivation of liberty do not get annual leaves while serving the term of punishment but may be paid for sick days or maternity leaves.

Convicts who have proved their reform by exemplary behavior and honest attitude towards labor and education may be granted conditional early relief or the remaining term of punishment may be replaced by a milder penalty.

In cases of willful evasion of work by convicted persons in serving their sentences, the organ in charge of the execution of this type of punishment may request the court to replace the remaining part of the sentence with a sentence of deprivation of liberty, in accordance with Article 45 of the CLL Fundamentals.

Evasion may take various forms, such as leaving work without permission or absence from work for significant periods of time without a proper excuse. As a rule, a person is considered as evading work if the break in his work lasts fourteen days.[15]

Research conducted by Soviet criminologists establishes that recidivism among persons who have served corrective labor is not great. According to selective studies made by the researchers of the Federal Institute for Study of Causes and Development of

---

15. EFFECTIVENESS OF CRIMINAL LAW MEASURES IN COMBATTING CRIME 137 (1968; Moscow, Nauka Publ. House).

Measures for Crime Prevention, during the period of three years after serving corrective labor, only 9 percent of such persons commit new crimes and are sentenced by the court[16] and the majority of them are persons who had a prior conviction when they were sentenced to corrective labor. Considering this circumstance, courts usually award such a penalty only to first-time offenders.

A study of eighty-eight Peoples' Court cases concerning persons sentenced to corrective labor has shown that 8 percent were in court for the first time, 97.1 percent were working or studying, and more than 76 percent had families.[17] It is therefore possible to conclude that this punishment is sufficiently effective for the great majority of persons sentenced to corrective labor. In cases where the court questions the sufficiency of the penalty of corrective labor for a given offender, the court may sentence him to conditional deprivation of liberty with compulsory labor.

2.2. Compulsory Labor as a Condition for Suspended Sentence

This measure of punishment is provided by Article 23(2) of the CLL Fundamentals. It states that conditional punishment in the form of deprivation of liberty with compulsory labor may be awarded to an able-bodied adult sentenced for the first time to deprivation of liberty for an intentional crime punishable by a term of up to five years.[18]

When such a measure is applied by the court, the convict must remain a resident of the designated district and work at the place assigned.

Restricted liberty lies in choosing the place and character of work and the convict's obligation not to leave the limits of the administrative district. This is an important punitive element of conditional punishment of deprivation of liberty with compulsory labor which distinguishes this measure from corrective labor.

---

16. *Supra* at 142.

17. Yu. B. Melnikova, *Corrective Labor and Short Terms of Deprivation of Liberty*, PUNISHMENT WITHOUT DEPRIVATIONS OF LIBERTY 53 (1972; Moscow, "Juriditcheskaya Literatura" Publ. House).

18. GAZETTE OF THE SUPREME SOVIET OF THE USSR No. 7, Item 116 (1977).

Conditional punishment may be replaced by actual deprivation of liberty, not only if the convict commits a new crime but also if he fails to comply with the regulations during the period of compulsory labor. Such failures may be (1) evasion of work at the place assigned by the organ charged with the punishment execution; (2) systematic or deliberate breaches of labor discipline or public order; or (3) systematic or deliberate breaches of the rules of residence.

An evasion occurs when the subject refuses to work, does not report to work, or after having worked for some time, leaves. An absence from work without a proper excuse for several days in succession may be considered in some cases an evasion of work.[19]

Persons serving conditional punishment with compulsory labor have all rights of citizens of the USSR except as expressly limited by law. They fully enjoy the benefits of legislation. In cases where a convict violates labor discipline or public order, he is subjected to disciplinary or administrative responsibility. In case of systematic or multiple breaches of labor discipline or public order, conditional sentencing may be replaced by confinement in a corrective labor institution.[20]

Persons who are sentenced conditionally periodically report to the Ministry of Interior. Their visits may be from one to four times a month. Convicts may not leave the bounds of the administrative district where they work without special permission of the appropriate organ of the Ministry of Interior. In exceptional cases, under Article 3 of the CLL Fundamentals, when a convict's behavior is exemplary and his attitude toward work honest, such a person may be allowed to leave the boundaries of the district on business, for a vacation, or other good reasons with joint permission of the enterprise administration and the organ of the Ministry of the Interior.

A systematic breach of the rules of restricted residence can be a basis for replacement of the penalty with deprivation of liberty. Such a decision can be made by the court located at the

---

19. I. M. GALPERIN & S. B. ROMAZIN, AWARDING OF CONDITIONAL PUNISHMENT WITH COMPULSORY LABOR OF CONVICTS 32 (1971; Moscow).

20. *Supra* at 34.

place of work of the convict. The court's decision is final and not subject to appeal or protest by means of supervision.

The Plenum of the Supreme Court of the USSR, having analyzed judicial practice on the problem in its Statement of December 23, 1970, has drawn all courts' attention to the fact that, during examination of materials on the replacement of conditional punishment with compulsory labor, one must thoroughly consider all the circumstances connected with the convict's evasion of work, as well as breaches of discipline and public order, or established rules of living. The Statement of the Plenum underlines especially the fact that a transfer of such a person to a place of confinement under a court sentence may take place only when such breaches are of a malicious or systematic nature, and the prior measures applied to him failed. The Plenum recommends that courts study information from the places of work of the persons considered and meet with representatives of social organizations, enterprises, administrations and oversight commissions of the local Soviets of People's Deputies.[21]

Persons serving conditional punishment with compulsory labor, as well as other categories of convicts, are involved in social and professional education and educational work. Studies have shown that the educational work assigned is in many respects identical to that applied in the execution of corrective labor. Conditionally sentenced convicts, like other convicts, may be assigned patrons who are honored workers with advanced skills. An important organizational role in treatment work belongs to the administration and social organizations of enterprises and construction projects where convicts work. The effectiveness of such efforts is enhanced if such agencies cooperate with organs of the Ministry of Interior, Procurator's Office, and courts.

Recent research by Soviet legal scholars shows improvement of not only the forms of individual work with convicts but also of collective work with them. Such forms now include more frequent lectures, group discussions, and meetings with enterprise administrations and law enforcement officials during which con-

---

21. BULLETIN OF THE SUPREME COURT OF THE USSR No. 1, at 12 (1971).

victs' questions are answered. Use of conversations with groups of convicts depends on the character of the crimes committed by members of the group. Often convicts themselves take the floor and analyze causes of their crimes.[22]

Research has also shown that conditional punishment with compulsory labor is generally a rather effective measure. Recidivism among convicts subjected to this type of sentence is most common among those with prior convictions for hooliganism and theft of personal property, so extra care is now taken with such convicts.[23] Overall, the recidivism rate among those sentenced to this form of punishment is about the same as for those sentenced to corrective labor.

In consideration of this high level of effectiveness, the Presidium of the Supreme Soviet of the USSR in its statement of February 8, 1977, "On amendments and additions to criminal legislation of the USSR," narrowed the range of convicts ineligible for such punishment. Article 23(2) of the CL Fundamentals, enacted in response to this statement, provides that compulsory labor cannot be applied to:

1. persons sentenced for especially dangerous state crimes, banditry, homicide (except where certain mitigating factors are present), rape committed by a group or resulting in serious injury, rape of a minor, or especially malicious hooliganism;

2. persons sentenced to compulsory treatment for alcoholism or drug addiction as well as to punishment for a crime, or those who have not completed a course of treatment for a venereal disease;

3. convicted foreigners or stateless persons.[24]

2.3. Exile

Exile is listed second, right after deprivation of liberty, in the list of punishments in Article 21 of the CL Fundamentals. This testifies to the fact that the legislature views it as the second gravest type of punishment.

---

22. K. Pavlischev, N. Beliakin, & S. Kashtahov, *Legal Education of Conditionally Sentenced and Conditionally Relieved Persons*, SOCIALIST LEGALITY No. 11, at 31 (1976).

23. *Supra* at 30.

24. GAZETTE OF THE SUPREME SOVIET OF THE USSR No. 7, Item 116 (1977).

Article 40 of the CLL Fundamentals provides that persons sentenced to exile shall serve punishment in designated localities, being sent there at state expense within ten days after such a sentence takes legal effect. If escorted to the place of exile, traveling time of a convict is counted against his sentence with one day under escort counting as three days in exile.

Exiled persons are assigned socially useful work and given political and educational training as part of their reform.

Within the bounds of the administrative district assigned as a place of exile, a convict is free to choose his own place of residence, but departures from that district are permitted only in accordance with the corrective labor codes of the various union republics.

Article 6 of the CLL Fundamentals provides that lists of localities for exile be compiled by the Council of Ministers of the USSR and councils of ministers of the union republics. Sites selected are generally remote, serving as places that remove convicts from milieu where they are inclined to commit crimes.

Exile may be applied either as a single main penalty or in addition to another penalty, for terms of from two to five years. It may not be applied to persons under the age of eighteen, pregnant women, or women with children under the age of eight.

Corrective labor codes of the union republics require that a person sentenced to exile register upon his arrival in the district with the local organ charged with execution of this type of punishment. Thereafter, he must register from one to four times a month and give three days advance notice of any change in his place of residence or work.

Officers of the organ charged with execution of exile periodically check for convicts' presence at their places of work and residence, investigate their behavior, and when necessary, call convicts to their offices for consultations.

The corrective labor codes of the union republics also provide that convicts under sentence of exile may be permitted temporary leaves beyond the limits of the place of exile under the following circumstances: as a reward for good behavior and an honest attitude toward work, for a yearly vacation; when summoned by an educational institution for state examinations or to defend a diploma, for the necessary period; for special medical treatment; and upon death or grave illness of a close relative, for ten days plus transportation time; and for business trips.

In such cases, time spent outside the place of exile nevertheless counts toward completion of the sentence.

Exiled persons may work where they choose, but socially useful work is required as part of their sentence and opportunities may be limited by the local employment conditions.

Exiled convicts are paid like other citizens doing similar work, and Article 83 of the CLC and comparable articles of codes of union republics oblige local Soviets of People's Deputies to find employment for exiled convicts within fifteen days of their arrival. If a suitable job cannot be found, the convict may be transferred to another place of exile.

An exiled person who evades socially useful work is notified officially of his responsibility for such conduct and if he does not undertake work, he may be charged with criminal responsibility under Article 209(1) of the PC and comparable articles of the codes of other union republics.[25]

For violations of rules governing exile, the organ in charge of execution of sentences may issue warnings, reprimands, or orders limiting a convict's freedom of movement for periods of up to six months. Such penalties may be appealed to the chief of the organ imposing them.

As rewards for good behavior and an honest attitude toward work, convicts may receive a commendation, early release from a prior penalty, or permission to leave the place of exile for yearly vacation.

The corrective labor codes of the union republics, *e.g.*, Article 85 of the CLL Fundamentals, provide the opportunity for a convict to request a court to replace his remaining term of exile with a conditional early release or some other milder punishment if the convict has demonstrated that he has been reformed. Such decisions are within the power of the court at the place of exile.

25. COMMENTARY ON THE CORRECTIVE LABOR CODE OF THE RSFSR 211 (1973; Moscow, "Juriditcheskaya Literatura" Publ. House).

Studies at the Federal Institute for Study of Causes and Development of Measures for Crime Prevention show that 1 percent of all persons sentenced are sentenced to exile as a main or additional punishment.[26] Persons who were awarded exile as a main punishment were primarily persons guilty of nonsupport of children or of vagrancy. These studies have shown that exile was assigned in only 7 percent of all cases for nonsupport and 5 percent for vagrancy.[27]

The recidivism level among persons sentenced to exile is approximately twice as high as among persons sentenced to corrective labor, with persons sentenced for vagrancy being the worst recidivists. In most cases, the new crime was either identical to that for which the sentence of exile was imposed (46 percent) or very similar to it (40 percent).[28]

In view of this, there is a clear trend in all the union republics to reduce reliance on exile as a sentence. In some union republics it is already restricted to extraordinary cases.

Section 3. CUSTODIAL SENTENCES

3.1. Corrective Labor Institutions

The convict population in corrective labor institutions is heterogeneous. In order to provide for differential treatment for each category of convicts, to eliminate negative influences of one category on another, and in consideration of age, sex, degree of social danger of crimes committed, and criminal records of individuals, corrective institutions of different types have been established.

Article II of the CLL Fundamentals states that three types of corrective labor institutions are established in all the union republics: corrective labor colonies, prisons, and educational labor colonies. In turn, corrective labor and educational labor colonies are subdivided into several types.

In accordance with Article 23 of the CLL Fundamentals, male adults may serve sentences of deprivation of liberty in corrective

---

26. S. A. Shlykov & O. I. Garsikho, *Exile*, PUNISHMENT WITHOUT DEPRIVATION OF LIBERTY 39 (1972; Moscow, "Juriditcheskaya Literatura" Publ. House).

27. *Supra* at 42.

28. *Supra* note 26, at 47.

labor institutions with a general regime, a reinforced regime, a special or strict regime, and in settlement colonies.

Prisons have two regimes, general and strict. CLL Fundamentals provide for five types of corrective labor colonies: corrective labor colonies of general regime, reinforced regime, strict regime, special regime, and settlement colonies. These types of colonies differ from each other by both the composition of convicts serving punishment and the degree of the restriction of their rights. The highest degree of restriction is characteristic for colonies of special regime, where the conditions for keeping convicts are close to those in prisons. The lowest degree of restriction is in corrective labor settlement colonies, where the convicts are kept without guards under the administration's supervision. Corrective labor colonies of general, reinforced, and strict regime have similar rules of isolation in all of them; all the convicts are lodged in unlocked hostels and can move freely about the living zone of the colony. The colony territory is surrounded by a special fence.

If international terminology were used to characterize places of confinement, colonies of a special regime as well as prisons are institutions of a closed type. Colonies of general, reinforced, and strict regime, as well as educational labor colonies, are of a semiopen type. Settlement colonies should be considered as open institutions.

Assignment of men to various corrective labor colonies is as follows: Those being sentenced for the first time for crimes which are not grave are sent to colonies with a reinforced regime; those who are either convicted of especially dangerous crimes against the state or who have prior convictions leading to sentences of deprivation of liberty are placed in colonies with a strict regime; and those who are deemed especially dangerous recidivists are sent to colonies with a special regime.

Women are assigned to two types of corrective labor colonies. Colonies of a reinforced regime receive women who are deemed especially dangerous recidivists or whose sentence of capital punishment was commuted by way of pardon or amnesty. Other women are assigned to institutions of a general regime.

Settlement colonies are special types of corrective labor institutions. Persons convicted for crimes of carelessness are sent directly to such institutions and other convicts who have served part of their sentences in colonies of strict, reinforced, or general regimes may be transferred to such institutions if they have shown signs of correction.

Article 20 of the CLL Fundamentals defines the characteristics of the regime in corrective labor settlement colonies. Convicts are kept under surveillance, but without guards; have the right of free movement within the colony from the waking signal to the retirement signal; may, with permission of the administration, travel without surveillance outside the territory of the colony, but within the surrounding administrative area, for their work or studies; may wear ordinary civilian clothes, carry money and other valuables; may, with the permission of the administration, buy a home and set up a household with their families within the colony's territory.

Convicts from any type of corrective labor institution who are assigned to a settlement colony may be kept in a single such colony.

Corrective labor colonies are the predominant type of corrective labor institution for keeping adults sentenced to deprivation of liberty. Assignment to prisons is rather rare in the USSR. Article 23 of the CL Fundamentals provides that assignment to prisons is appropriate for especially dangerous recidivists and persons over eighteen who have committed prior grave offenses and have been sentenced to terms of more than five years. However, in the vast majority of cases where prison is assigned, it is assigned for only a part of the term, and the offender is transferred to a corrective labor colony for the remainder of the term.

According to Article 14 of the CLL Fundamentals, a convict may be transferred from a colony to a prison for a malicious violation of the regime of the colony. In exceptional cases, persons sentenced for the first time to deprivation of liberty for crimes which are not grave who were assigned to corrective labor colonies of a general regime may, with their consent, be assigned to do household work at a prison.

Article 15 of the CLL Fundamentals specifies that persons sentenced for the first time to imprisonment and persons transferred from a strict prison regime shall be kept under a general regime. A strict regime shall be applied to persons who have previously served a term of imprisonment, persons sentenced to prison for crimes committed in places of confinement, persons transferred from colonies to prison and persons transferred to a strict regime as a penalty in accordance with statutory procedure. The period for keeping a person under a strict regime ranges from two to six months.

Minors serve punishment in educational labor colonies. Male minors are kept in educational labor colonies of two types: general and reinforced regimes. General regime colonies are assigned for minors sentenced for the first time to deprivation of liberty for crimes that are not grave, or sentenced for the first time for crimes that are grave but for a term of three years or less. More dangerous male minors are kept under a reinforced regime. All female minors are kept under a general regime.

Convicts who reach the age of eighteen are transferred to corrective labor colonies of a regime corresponding to the regime of their educational labor colony.

In the interest of integrity in the corrective process or for completion of educational programs of minors, they may be permitted to remain in an educational labor colony beyond their eighteenth birthday, but not beyond the age of twenty.

The type of corrective labor or educational institution to which a convict is assigned is fixed by his court sentence.

The Plenum of the Supreme Court of the USSR has drawn the attention of lower courts to the fact that the legally established criteria for assigning an offender to a particular type of institution include prospects for improvement and reform of the offender as well as concern for prevention of further crimes by the offender.[29]

In determining the type of corrective labor institution to as-

---

29. Decision of the Plenum of the Supreme Court of the USSR of **October 19, 1971** on "Practice of assignment by courts to different types of corrective labor institutions of persons sentenced to deprivation of liberty"; *see* COLLECTED DECISIONS OF THE PLENUM OF THE SUPREME COURT OF THE USSR 1924-1973, at 370 (1974).

sign to an offender, the court is to consider the nature of the social danger of the crime committed and whether the offender has previously been convicted. At the same time, criminal legislation of the union republics (Art. 24 of the PC) permits a court, depending on the nature and social danger of the crime committed, the offender's personality, and other circumstances, to adopt a reasoned decision assigning convicts who are not deemed to be especially dangerous recidivists to colonies of any type other than a special regime. In the same way, convicted male minors may be placed in educational colonies of a general rather than strict regime.

Commenting on these provisions, the Plenum of the USSR Supreme Court, in its decision of June 19, 1961, emphasized the necessity for courts to observe the general criteria established by Article 92 of the CL Fundamentals on punishment assignment, including factors mitigating criminal responsibility or aggravating it. On the basis of these considerations, a court may assign an offender to a milder or stricter regime than that generally provided for such an offense, except for colonies of a special regime, which are reserved for especially dangerous recidivists and persons whose sentence of capital punishment was commuted by way of pardon or amnesty. A reasoned decision is required.

Article 17 of the CLL Fundamentals provides that persons sentenced to deprivation of liberty are generally to serve their entire sentence within a single institution in order to create more favorable conditions for rehabilitation. Article 17 permits transfers between colonies of the same type of regime in cases of illness or a radical change in the size or the nature of the work performed by the convict and in other extraordinary circumstances.

Transfers to colonies of less strict regimes is permitted under Article 33 of the CLL Fundamentals for convicts who have demonstrated that they have chosen to reform.

Transfers to stricter regimes are also permitted. According to Article 34 of the CLL Fundamentals, convicts who maliciously violate rules of the regime under which they are kept may be so transferred. Such transfers may take the form of a revocation of an earlier transfer in the other direction or be a provisional transfer from a colony to a prison. Transfer from an educational labor colony with a general regime to a corrective labor colony with a reinforced regime is also possible and is not limited in duration.[30]

Decisions on transfers between regimes are made by the court where the convict is serving punishment, upon the recommendation of the administration of the institution.

Article 6 of the CLL Fundamentals sets forth the main principles governing assignment of persons sentenced to deprivation of liberty to various types of corrective labor colonies. It provides that persons sentenced to deprivation of liberty for the first time shall, as a rule, serve their sentence within the union republic where they resided prior to their arrest or conviction. In exceptional cases, however, where more successful correction appears likely if they are sent further away, they may be sent to a corresponding institution in another union republic.

Persons who previously have served sentences of deprivation of liberty, persons whose death sentences have been commuted by way of pardon or amnesty, persons who are been convicted of especially dangerous crimes against the State, and convicted aliens and stateless persons shall be sent to serve their sentences in corrective labor institutions set aside for these categories of offenders, regardless of the union republic in which they resided previously.

In the absence of an appropriate corrective labor institution in the union republic where they resided prior to arrest or conviction, women, persons requiring special medical treatment, and minors sentenced to deprivation of liberty may be sent to serve their sentences in a corrective labor institution of another union republic.

3.2. Legal Status of Convicts in Custody

The legal status of a person sentenced to deprivation of liberty is governed by the corrective labor law. Legal norms based on the very essence of deprivation of liberty establish a series of

---

30. COMMENTARY ON THE CORRECTIVE LABOR LAW FUNDAMENTALS OF THE USSR AND THE UNION REPUBLICS 135 (1972; Moscow, "Juriditcheskaya Literatura" Publ. House).

specific responsibilities and limitations and regulate the rights of a convict during his punishment.

Every convicted person, whether he serves punishment in a colony or in a prison, must obey the rules of the corrective labor institution to which he is assigned.

The particular circumstances of execution of criminal punishment in the form of deprivation of liberty dictates some limitations of constitutional rights, including guarantees of the immunity of homes and privacy of correspondence. Personal effects of the convicts, premises where they live, and they themselves may be searched at any time. In accordance with Article 19 of the CLL Fundamentals, convicted persons are not allowed to keep money, valuables, or certain other objects. Money and valuables found on a person are removed and, as a rule, confiscated on the basis of a reasoned decision of the chief of the corrective labor institution approved by a procurator.

Convicts are unable to directly send and receive correspondence. Article 26 of the CLL Fundamentals, regulating convicts' rights regarding correspondence, states that convicts may receive letters without restrictions.

The number of letters which convicts may send is limited by the following norms: in corrective labor colonies with a reinforced regime, not more than three letters a month; with a strict regime, not more than two letters; and with a special regime, one letter a month; and in prison, for those of a general regime, one letter a month and for those of a strict regime, one letter every two months.

Persons serving sentences in corrective labor colonies with a general regime, in corrective labor settlement colonies, and in educational labor colonies may send letters without restriction. Correspondence is not allowed among convicts serving sentences of confinement unless they are relatives. Convicted persons have the right to lodge complaints with, and make statements and send letters to, state organs, social organizations, and officials. Complaints, statements, and letters of convicts are dispatched to their destination and examined in accordance with the procedure prescribed by the law. Replies from such officials and organizations should be delivered to the convicts within three days of their arrival at the institution.

The postage for sending complaints and statements is paid by the convict-author unless he has no money, in which case the expenses are paid by the corrective labor institution. On request, a convict is entitled to receive paper and pens to write a complaint or a statement.

Persons in corrective labor colonies, after serving half of their sentence, are allowed to receive up to three parcels a year delivered by mail or in person. The weight of a parcel should not exceed five kilograms. Convicts may receive such parcels from anyone.

Persons serving sentences in educational labor colonies are allowed to receive parcels from the moment of their arrival, up to six parcels a year delivered by mail or in person.

The law does not link the convict's right to receive parcels with good behavior. Thus, persons sentenced to imprisonment are not allowed to receive parcels, regardless of their behavior. In corrective labor settlement colonies, the number of parcels that can be received is not limited.

Convicts, irrespective of the type of their corrective labor institution, are allowed to buy books and magazines from the bookshops within their institution without restriction.

Convicts in corrective labor colonies who for disciplinary reasons are transferred to cells in colonies of a general, reinforced, or strict regime or to a solitary cell in a colony of a special regime are not allowed to receive parcels as they are kept under the same regime as convicts in prisons.

Convicts, according to Article 24 of the CLL Fundamentals, are allowed two types of visits: brief visits of up to four hours with relatives and friends in the presence of a representative of the institution, and prolonged visits, up to three days with right of living together, which are allowed only with close relatives.

In the course of a year, visits are allowed as follows: in corrective labor colonies with a general regime, three brief and two prolonged visits; with a reinforced regime, two brief and two prolonged; with a strict regime, two brief and one prolonged; with a special regime, one brief and one prolonged; in educational labor colonies with a general regime, six brief ones; with a reinforced regime, four brief ones; in prisons, prisoners on a general regime, two brief visits; in corrective labor settlement colonies, without restriction.

For good behavior and a conscientious attitude toward work, a person who has served not less than one-half of his sentence may be allowed additionally, in the course of a year, in corrective-labor colonies, one prolonged visit and, in the absence of close relatives, one brief visit; in educational labor colonies with a general regime, after serving one-quarter of the sentence, six brief visits; in colonies with a reinforced regime, after serving one-third of the sentence, two brief visits.

The law stipulates that prolonged visits are allowed only with close relatives, but the CLL Fundamentals do not contain a list of relatives who are deemed to be "close." Such a list is provided in Article 37 of the PC. Among close relatives with whom the convict is allowed to have a prolonged visit are parents, children including adopted children, brothers and sisters, grandparents, grandchildren, and spouse.

Visits are allowed with no more than two adults simultaneously, who may bring minor children of the convict with them.

The right to choose among visitors belongs to the convict. Visits of representatives of patron organizations and newsmen are not counted.

Life, health, honor, and integrity of the personality of a convicted person are protected by the State, as are those of all citizens of the USSR.

Equal rights of all convicts, irrespective of their nationality, race, or sex, are provided for in places of confinement. Convicts have the right to speak their own language and write letters and complaints in it.

Persons deprived of liberty are guaranteed the constitutional rights of freedom to practice any religious cult or to conduct antireligious propaganda.

Persons deprived of liberty enjoy the constitutional right to work. Under conditions of deprivation of liberty, socially useful work for convicts provides the basis for their correction and re-education.

Article 27 of the CLL Fundamentals states that each convict has the duty to work. The administration of corrective labor institutions is duty-bound to ensure the enlistment of convicted persons in socially useful labor with due consideration for their work capacity and, if possible, profession. Persons serving sentences in corrective labor colonies with a special regime are, as a rule, employed on arduous jobs.

After their release, persons who became disabled while serving their sentences in places of confinement have the right to a pension in accordance with the legislation of the USSR.

The rules of labor protection and safety established by the labor legislation extends to the labor of persons sentenced to deprivation of liberty, irrespective of the type of corrective labor institution where they are serving their sentences. Convicts employed in health-hazardous jobs as designated by Article 63 of the Labor Law are provided with means of individual protection, special footwear and clothing, as well as free milk and special food to prevent diseases. The administration of corrective labor institutions should arrange to teach convicts safe handling of mechanisms and machinery as well as other potentially dangerous materials. General guidelines of trade unions and agencies for labor protection and safety rules of trade unions, as well as guidelines of the agencies of State sanitary supervision on sanitary conditions of work, are binding on the administration of corrective labor institutions.

The chief of the enterprises of corrective labor institutions and his deputies for production are responsible for labor protection and safety. The engineer on safety rules is responsible for supervising observance of labor protection law.

In the exceptional case that convicts are employed not at the enterprises of the corrective labor institution but at the enterprises of other departments, the administration of the latter is responsible for the state of the sanitary conditions, labor protection, and safety.[31]

The work of persons deprived of liberty is remunerated according to Article 29 of the CLL Fundamentals, according to the

31 *Supra* at 107-108.

quantity and quality of the norms and rates operating in the national economy. The crediting of earnings to convicts is made with deductions representing partial compensation by them of the expenditure incurred in maintaining corrective labor institutions. Persons serving sentences in corrective labor colonies and prisons refund from their earnings the cost of their food and clothing, except the cost of work clothes.

The economic activity of corrective labor institutions must be subordinate to their main task, that of the correction and reform of convicted persons.

An eight-hour working day is established for convicted persons. They are given one free day a week.

A refusal of the convict to work is considered one of the sharpest violations of the regime.

Under the procedure established by the present CLL Fundamentals, convicted persons may be employed without remuneration only in the work of improving the place of confinement and adjacent territory, and also the work of improving the cultural and living conditions of the convicts. Among such work are cleaning up the area and planting greenery, setting up recreation areas and sports fields, and repairing of living quarters and recreation facilities. Such activities as road construction and construction of living quarters or other buildings are not deemed to be work of improving cultural and living conditions.[32] Such work is remunerated.

Article 41 of the CLC and corresponding articles of the codes of the union republics permit such unpaid work by convicts, as a rule, after working hours. The duration of the work should not exceed two hours.

Convicted persons, like all Soviet citizens, enjoy the right to general education and vocational instruction. At the moment of the CLL Fundamentals' adoption there was compulsory eight-year education in the USSR. The same rule applied in corrective labor institutions. Article 31 of the CLL Fundamentals states that compulsory general educational eight-year schooling for convicted persons is to be provided in corrective labor institu-

---

32. *Supra* note 30, at 111.

tions.[33] Compulsory vocational training is organized for convicted persons who have no trade. The enrollment of convicted persons over the age of forty in general educational studies and of invalids in vocational training is at their request.

It is the direct responsibility of the administration of corrective labor institutions to provide convicted persons a real opportunity to study at school. Thus, the schedule of work and other activities should be arranged in such a way as to make it possible to attend classes.

Now that the USSR has introduced compulsory schooling of ten years, efforts are underway to found ten-year schools in corrective labor establishments. Although not much time has passed since introduction of compulsory ten-year schooling, many corrective labor institutions already provide convicts the opportunity to complete ten years of schooling.

Schools of corrective labor institutions use the same curriculum as general evening schools established for people who work and study at the same time. Persons who complete ten or eight years of schooling receive diplomas or certificates adopted by the USSR Ministry of Education for all school graduates. Since all education is free of charge in the USSR, convicted persons receive their education on the same basis.

Vocational training of convicts is organized in accordance with the general rules of education established for training and advanced training of workers directly at an enterprise. Convicts' learning of trades may be either full-time or part-time. They may be taught individually, in a group, or at special courses and vocational schools.

When learning individually, a person is apprenticed to a highly qualified worker. He may be attached to a foreman and included in a team in which the team leader is responsible for the teaching. When the team method is applied, special student teams of convicts are organized. The teams may vary in number depending on the nature of the trade, material and technical base, and other circumstances. Such teams, in accordance with

33. One should bear in mind that the new Constitution of the USSR adopted on October 7, 1977 has established universal compulsory secondary education, *i.e.*, ten years of schooling (Art. 45).

their curricula, perform certain work at enterprises or construction-sites under the leadership of experienced team instructors.

Teaching convicts more complicated trades is accomplished at special vocational technical school (hereafter referred to as VTS) at corrective labor institutions of the agencies of ministries of interior of the union republics.

Persons serving punishment in places of confinement are provided with living quarters conforming to the requirements of sanitation and hygiene.

Convicts are assigned individual sleeping places and bed linen. They receive clothing, underwear, and footwear according to the season and the climate of the place.

Convicted persons receive adequate food. Article 36 of the CLL Fundamentals states that food rations vary depending on local climatic conditions, the location of a corrective labor institution, the nature of the work done by the convicts, and their attitude towards work. Persons placed in a penal or disciplinary isolation ward, in a punishment cell, in premises of the cell type, or in solitary confinement in colonies with a special regime receive food at reduced rations.

Pregnant women, nursing mothers, minors, and ill persons are provided with better accommodations and other amenities and are given higher food rations.

Convicted women who approach their work conscientiously and observe the requirements of the regime may be allowed by the administration of a corrective labor institution, upon agreement with the supervisory commission, to live outside the colony during a maternity leave until the child reaches the age of two.

Convicts released from work because of illness, pregnant women, and nursing mothers receive food free of charge for the period they are released from work. Minors and invalids are also given food and clothing free of charge.

The requisite medical institutions are set up in places of confinement. Under Article 37 of the CLL Fundamentals, treatment and prevention of diseases and antiepidemic work is organized and conducted in places of confinement in accordance with health legislation.

3.3. Treatment

The participation of convicts in political and educational activities is encouraged and taken into account in ascertaining the extent of their correction and reform.

Organization and conduct of the treatment among convicts is regulated by the norms of the corrective labor law. These norms stipulate general conditions, but the choice of concrete forms of such work, its methods and means, lies within the competence of the administration of the corrective labor institutions.

Forms and means of treatment of convicts are diversified. The corrective labor codes of the union republics, as a rule, stipulate the following types: labor competition; commenting on Soviet legislation; agitation work; culture and sports activities; and individual work with a person, conducted on the basis of a personality study, considering the crime committed, age, education, trade and other characteristics.

Political educational work with persons deprived of liberty is carried out in different ways, depending on the type of corrective labor institution and its regime.

The basic unit for treatment work is a detachment of convicts. The detachments are formed on two bases: work and residence. The detachment has a unified productive task, so usually all teams constituting a detachment work in the same shop or the same section. This helps to build up an integrated collective of the enterprise. Usually, members of a detachment have adjoining accommodations. The detachments take care of this area, and plant flowers, trees, etc. The allocation of living quarters and land to a detachment contributes to the development of integrity of the interests of the convicts, who carry on the work of improving their living conditions, repairing the rooms where they rest, etc.

The number of members in a detachment depend on the qualitative composition of the convicts and opportunities to conduct educational work with them. In some settlement colonies a detachment may include 150 persons; in colonies of a general regime, 100 persons, in colonies of reinforced and strict regime, not more than 100; in colonies of special regime, up to 50 persons. In educative labor colonies, detachments usually include 100 persons.[34]

The detachment has a chief, who has a higher pedagogical or legal education and a practical work experience with convicts. The detachment chief combines the properties of an administrator with those of an educator and leader in the work. The chief is assisted in his work by a council of detachment educators, consisting of (besides himself) the chief of the workshops where the convicts work, foremen directing the work of the teams constituting the detachment, technical section controllers, norm controllers, and other representatives of engineering services. The councils of treatment are collegial bodies in operation.

The chief of detachment knows the profession of the convict, the state of his health, his wish to do a certain kind of work, and any wish he may have to learn a certain trade. All this enables him to set up the teams constituting the detachment with a maximum consideration of the interest of the convicts and the enterprise.

As a rule, labor competition in a colony is conducted among detachments. Quarterly, the detachments make certain labor commitments, in public or in writing. Such labor commitments contain economic indexes, such as fulfillment of plan tasks, growth of labor productivity, improvement of quality, reduction of production costs, observance of safety rules, rationalization of work, and safe maintenance of instruments and equipment.

Besides production target, the commitments include such items as involvement of all members who do not have a secondary school education in studies; involvement in vocational training of all convicts who know no trade; advancement of labor qualifications and learning related trades; maintenance of living quarters in perfect order; development of the territory adjacent to the detachment's quarters; attendance at political studies, lectures, and other mass events by all the convicts; reading of library books; active participation in the social life of the team, detachment, and the whole colony; strict observance of the re-

---

34. Yu. M. TKACHIEVSKY, *supra* note 2, at 137.

gime; and other goals. These items are then considered when the competition is scored.

The accounting of the commitments' results and computation of the final score is accomplished by sections of the convicts: collectives under leadership of the corrective labor institution administration. The champions of the competition are encouraged materially, as well as morally by writing their names on the list of names at the honor board of the colony, etc. The degree of the convicts' participation in labor competition is one of the important indications used by the corrective labor institution administration in deciding whether a convict has chosen the way of correction.

Explanatory and agitation work is conducted in all colonies among all convicts. Groups for such studies consist of fifty persons. Convicts at approximately the same level of education are selected for each group. Each group uses a fixed room and has a monitor, who prepares the materials and the room for studies and registers the attendance.

Studies are conducted by permanent teachers on issues of internal affairs and international events. The classes are conducted in the form of seminars, with main topics being announced to the convicts in advance, as well as a list of recommended literature, which is usually placed on the information stand of the detachment.

Lectures on connected subjects are used to explain more complicated problems. Convicts are not allowed to deliver lectures or reports on political, ethical, or legal subjects.[35]

Living premises of the convicts in all colonies are fitted with loudspeakers. This permits broadcast of both general and local programs for educational purposes. A movie projector in each colony permits showing of newsreels containing examples of the proper attitude toward labor and facts about regime violations, grants and refusals of conditional early release, letters from relatives, and addresses by exconvicts to their comrades.

All these forms of work are supplemented by group and individual conversations with convicts, different aspects of interrelations in small groups, and additional information on some

35. Yu. M. Tkachievsky, *supra* note 2, at 227-228.

matters of internal or foreign policy which are of interest to the convicts.

An important place in the individual work with a convict is occupied by his preparation for release. Chiefs of detachments do their best during the whole term of the convict's sentence to help him maintain his relations with his family and the collective where he worked prior to conviction.

Three months before the punishment expires or a conditional early release begins, the corrective labor institution administration explores the possibilities of finding a job for the convict.

It should be emphasized that the USSR practice of re-socialization of exconvicts does not encounter the stigmatization process much discussed in Western criminological literature.[36] Labor collectives as a rule treat the released person kindly and help him to enter a normal labor life. The process is simplified by the fact that serving the punishment is a preparation for the process of labor relations which the exconvict encounters upon his release.

Soviet criminological literature contains a number of research findings on the recidivism level among persons who served their punishments in corrective labor colonies. Data from a ten-year study of an average corrective labor colony, mentioned in Klochkov's[37] survey, are most impressive. Over a ten-year period the recidivism level among persons released from colonies is 8.4 percent. In cases where the released person is assigned a patron at the enterprise where he is employed after release, the recidivism level is lower yet.

36. M. A. Efimov, *supra* note 5, at 84.

37. V. V. Klochkov, Criminal Policy and Main Trends in Application of Punishment of Deprivation of Liberty in the USSR 23 (1977; Moscow, All-Union Institute of Study of Causes and Development of Measures for Crime Prevention). This has also been published in French.

CONSTITUTION (FUNDAMENTAL LAW) OF THE UNION OF SOVIET SOCIALIST REPUBLICS*

ARTICLE 4. The Soviet state and all its bodies function on the basis of socialist law, ensure the maintenance of law and order, and safeguard the interests of society and the rights and freedoms of citizens.

State organizations, public organizations and officials shall observe the Constitution of the USSR and Soviet laws.

ARTICLE 5. Major matters of state shall be submitted to nationwide discussion and put to a popular vote (referendum).

ARTICLE 34. Citizens of the USSR are equal before the law, without distinction of origin, social or property status, race or nationality, sex, education, language, attitude to religion, type and nature of occupation, domicile, or other status.

The equal rights of citizens of the USSR are guaranteed in all fields of economic, political, social, and cultural life.

ARTICLE 35. Women and men have equal rights in the USSR. Exercise of these rights is ensured by according women equal access with men to education and vocational and professional training, equal opportunities in employment, remuneration, and promotion, and in social and political and cultural activity, and by special labour and health protection measures for women; by providing conditions enabling mothers to work; by legal protection, and material and moral support for mothers and children, including paid leaves and other benefits for expectant mothers and mothers, and gradual reduction of working time for mothers with small children.

ARTICLE 39. Citizens of the USSR enjoy in full the social, economic, political, and personal rights and freedoms proclaimed and guaranteed by the Constitution of the USSR and by Soviet laws. The socialist system ensures enlargement of the

---

* Adopted at the Seventh (Special) Session of the Supreme Soviet of the USSR, Ninth Convocation, on October 7, 1977.

rights and freedoms of citizens and continuous improvement of their living standards as social, economic, and cultural development programmes are fulfilled.

Enjoyment by citizens of their rights and freedoms must not be to the detriment of the interests of society or the state, or infringe the rights of other citizens.

ARTICLE 54. Citizens of the USSR are guaranteed inviolability of the home. No one may, without lawful grounds, enter a home against the will of those residing in it.

ARTICLE 56. The privacy of citizens and of their correspondence, telephone conversations, and telegraphic communications is protected by law.

ARTICLE 60. It is the duty of, and a matter of honour for, every able-bodied citizen of the USSR to work conscientiously in his chosen, socially useful occupation, and strictly to observe labour discipline. Evasion of socially useful work is incompatible with the principles of socialist society.

ARTICLE 151. In the USSR justice is administered only by the courts.

In the USSR there are the following courts: the Supreme Court of the USSR, the Supreme Courts of Union Republics, the Supreme Courts of Autonomous Republics, Territorial, Regional, and city courts, courts of Autonomous Regions, courts of Autonomous Areas, district (city) people's courts, and military tribunals in the Armed Forces.

ARTICLE 152. All courts in the USSR shall be formed on the principle of the electiveness of judges and people's assessors.

People's judges of district (city) people's courts shall be elected for a term of five years by the citizens of the district (city) on the basis of universal, equal and direct suffrage by secret ballot. People's assessors of district (city) people's courts shall be elected for a term of two and a half years at meetings of citizens at their places of work or residence by a show of hands.

Higher courts shall be elected for a term of five years by the corresponding Soviet of People's Deputies.

The judges of military tribunals shall be elected for a term of five years by the Presidium of the Supreme Soviet of the

USSR and people's assessors for a term of two and a half years by meetings of servicemen.

Judges and people's assessors are responsible and accountable to their electors or the bodies that elect them, shall report to them, and may be recalled by them in the manner prescribed by law.

ARTICLE 153. The Supreme Court of the USSR is the highest judicial body in the USSR and supervises the administration of justice by the courts of the USSR and Union Republics within the limits established by law.

The Supreme Court of the USSR shall be elected by the Supreme Soviet of the USSR and shall consist of a Chairman, Vice-Chairmen, members, and people's assessors. The Chairmen of the Supreme Courts of Union Republics are ex officio members of the Supreme Court of the USSR.

The organisation and procedure of the Supreme Court of the USSR are defined in the Law on the Supreme Court of the USSR.

ARTICLE 154. The hearing of civil and criminal cases in all courts is collegial; in courts of first instance cases are heard with the participation of people's assessors. In the administration of justice people's assessors have all the rights of a judge.

ARTICLE 155. Judges and people's assessors are independent and subject only to the law.

ARTICLE 156. Justice is administered in the USSR on the principle of the equality of citizens before the law and the court.

ARTICLE 157. Proceedings in all courts shall be open to the public. Hearings in camera are only allowed in cases provided for by law, with observance of all the rules of judicial procedure.

ARTICLE 158. A defendant in a criminal action is guaranteed the right to legal assistance.

ARTICLE 159. Judicial proceedings shall be conducted in the language of the Union Republic, Autonomous Republic, Autonomous Region, or Autonomous Area, or in the language spoken by the majority of the people in the locality. Persons participating in court proceedings, who do not know the language in which they are being conducted, shall be ensured the right to become fully acquainted with the materials in the case; the services of an interpreter during the proceedings; and the right to address the court in their own language.

ARTICLE 160. No one may be adjudged guilty of a crime and subjected to punishment as a criminal except by the sentence of a court and in conformity with the law.

ARTICLE 161. Colleges of advocates are available to give legal assistance to citizens and organisations. In cases provided for by legislation, citizens shall be given legal assistance free of charge.

The organisation and procedure of the bar are determined by legislation of the USSR and Union Republics.

ARTICLE 162. Representatives of public organisations and of work collectives may take part in civil and criminal proceedings.

ARTICLE 163. Economic disputes between enterprises, institutions, and organisations are settled by state arbitration bodies within the limits of their jurisdiction.

The organisation and manner of functioning of state arbitration bodies are defined in the Law on State Arbitration in the USSR.

ARTICLE 164. Supreme power of supervision over the strict and uniform observance of laws by all ministries, state committees and departments, enterprises, institutions and organisations, executive-administrative bodies of local Soviets of People's Deputies, collective farms, co-operatives and other public organisations, officials and citizens is vested in the Procurator-General of the USSR and procurators subordinate to him.

ARTICLE 165. The Procurator-General of the USSR is appointed by the Supreme Soviet of the USSR and is responsible and accountable to it and, between sessions of the Supreme Soviet, to the Presidium of the Supreme Soviet of the USSR.

ARTICLE 166. The procurators of Union Republics, Autonomous Republics, Territories, Regions and Autonomous Regions are appointed by the Procurator-General of the USSR. The procurators of Autonomous Areas and district and city procurators are appointed by the Procurators of Union Republics, subject to confirmation by the Procurator-General of the USSR.

ARTICLE 167. The term of office of the Procurator-General of the USSR and all lower-ranking procurators shall be five years.

ARTICLE 168. The agencies of the Procurator's Office exercise their powers independently of any local bodies whatsoever, and are subordinate solely to the Procurator-General of the USSR.

The organisation and procedure of the agencies of the Procurator's Office are defined in the Law on the Procurator's Office of the USSR.

FUNDAMENTALS OF CRIMINAL PROCEDURE OF THE USSR AND THE UNION REPUBLICS*

SECTION I

GENERAL PROVISIONS

ARTICLE 1. *Legislation on Criminal Procedure*

The procedure in criminal cases shall be determined by the present Fundamentals and by other laws of the USSR and the codes of criminal procedure of the Union Republics promulgated in accordance therewith.

ARTICLE 2. *The Tasks of Criminal Procedure*

Soviet criminal procedure shall have the task of speedy and complete detection of crimes, the conviction of the guilty persons, and the assurance of correct application of the law, so that every person who has committed a crime shall be subjected to just punishment, and no innocent person shall be charged with criminal responsibility or convicted.

Criminal procedure must help to consolidate socialist legality, prevent and eradicate crime and educate citizens in a spirit of undeviating observance of Soviet laws and respect for the rules of socialist community life.

ARTICLE 3. *The Duty of Initiating Criminal Cases and Detecting Crimes*

The court, the procurator, the investigator and the agency of inquiry shall have the duty, within their terms of reference, to initiate a criminal case in every instance in which indicia of a

---

* The Law of the Union of Soviet Socialist Republics of December 25, 1958, on the approval of the Fundamentals of Criminal Procedure of the USSR and the Union Republics as decreed by the Supreme Soviet of the Union of Soviet Socialist Republics; *see* GAZETTE OF THE SUPREME SOVIET OF THE USSR No. 1, Item 15 (1959).

crime have been discovered, and to take all the measures provided for by the law to establish the event of the crime, and the persons guilty of committing it, and to punish them.

ARTICLE 4. *The Impermissibility of Prosecution Otherwise Than on the Grounds and in Accordance with the Procedure Established by the Law*

No person may be prosecuted as an accused otherwise than on the grounds and in accordance with the procedure established by the law.

ARTICLE 5. *Circumstances Which Rule Out Criminal Proceedings*

No criminal case may be initiated and one initiated shall be subject to termination:

1) in the absence of the event of a crime;

2) in the absence, in the act, of the elements of a crime;

3) upon the expiry of the periods of limitation;

4) in consequence of an act of amnesty, where it has abolished the application of punishment for the act committed, and also in view of the pardon of individual persons;

5) with respect to a person who has not, at the moment of commission of a socially dangerous act, attained the age at which, according to the law, criminal responsibility is possible;

6) upon reconciliation of the victim with the accused, in the instances provided for by the legislation of the Union Republics;

7) in the absence of a complaint from the victim, where the case may be initiated only upon his complaint, with the exception of instances where the legislation of the Union Republics gives the procurator the right to initiate a case even in the absence of a complaint from the victim;

8) with respect to a deceased person, with the exception of instances where proceedings in the case are necessary to rehabilitate the deceased or to re-open the case with respect to other persons on the strength of newly discovered circumstances;

9) with respect to a person concerning whom there is a judge-

ment, under the same accusation, which has taken legal effect.

Where the circumstances indicated in par. 1, 2, 3 or 4 of the present Article come to light at the stage of judicial examination, the court shall carry on the examination to its end and shall decree a judgement of acquittal or a judgement of conviction with release of the convicted person from punishment.

A case may not be terminated on the grounds indicated in par. 3 and 4 of the present Article, where the accused objects to this. In such instance, proceedings in the case shall be continued in the usual manner.

ARTICLE 6. *Immunity of the Person*

No person may be subjected to arrest otherwise than by a decree of the court or with the sanction of the procurator.

The procurator shall have the duty immediately to release any person illegally deprived of liberty or being detained in custody for more than the term provided for by the law or by a judgement of the court.

ARTICLE 7. *Administration of Justice Only by the Court*

Justice in criminal cases shall be administered only by the court. No person may be deemed guilty of the commission of a crime and subjected to criminal punishment otherwise than by a judgement of the court.

ARTICLE 8. *Administration of Justice on the Principle of Equality of All Citizens Before the Law and the Court*

Justice in criminal cases shall be administered on the principle of equality of all citizens before the law and the court, regardless of their social, property and official status, nationality, race or creed.

ARTICLE 9. *Participation of People's Assessors and Collegiality in the Examination of Cases*

Criminal cases in all courts shall be examined by judges and people's assessors elected in accordance with the procedure established by the law.

The examination of criminal cases in all the courts of first instance shall be made by a bench consisting of a judge and two people's assessors.

The people's assessors shall have equal rights with the person presiding at the judicial session in deciding all matters arising in the examination of the case and in decreeing judgement.

The examination of cases by way of cassation shall be made by benches consisting of three members of the court, and by way of judicial supervision, by benches consisting of not less than three members of the court.

ARTICLE 10. *The Independence of Judges and Their Subordination Only to the Law*

In the administration of justice in criminal cases, the judges and the people's assessors shall be independent and subordinate only to the law. The judges and people's assessors shall decide criminal cases on the strength of the law, in conformity with the socialist concept of justice and under conditions precluding extraneous influence on the judges.

ARTICLE 11. *The Language in Which Judicial Proceedings Are Conducted*

Judicial proceedings shall be conducted in the language of the Union or Autonomous Republic, or the Autonomous Region, and in the instances provided for by the Constitutions of the Union or Autonomous Republics, in the language of the National Area or of the majority of the local population.

Persons taking part in the case who have no command of the language in which the judicial proceedings are being conducted shall be assured of the right to make statements, give testimony, plead in court, and file petitions in their own language, and also to have the services of an interpreter, in accordance with the procedure established by the law.

The investigative and judicial documents shall, in accordance with the procedure established by the law, be handed to the accused in a translation into his own language or into another language of which he has command.

ARTICLE 12. *The Public Nature of the Judicial Examination*

The examination of cases in all the courts shall be open, with the exception of instances where this is contrary to the interests of protecting state secrets.

Moreover, closed judicial examination shall be allowed, upon a reasoned ruling of the court, in the cases of crimes committed by persons who have not attained the age of 16 years, in the cases of sexual crimes, and also in other cases for the purpose of preventing the spread of information concerning the intimate aspects of the life of persons taking part in the case.

The judgements of the courts shall in all instances be publicly pronounced.

ARTICLE 13. *Assurance of the Accused of the Right to Defence*

The accused shall have the right to defence.

The investigator, the procurator, and the court shall have the duty to assure the accused of the possibility of defending himself by the ways and means established by the law against the accusation brought against him, and to ensure the protection of his personal and property rights.

ARTICLE 14. *Comprehensive, Thorough and Objective Scrutiny of the Circumstances of the Case*

The court, the procurator, the investigator and the person conducting the inquiry shall have the duty to take all the measures stipulated by the law for the comprehensive, thorough and objective scrutiny of the circumstances of the case, and to bring out equally the circumstances which convict and which exonerate the accused, and also those which aggravate and which mitigate his guilt.

The court, the procurator, the investigator and the person conducting the inquiry shall not have the right to lay the duty of proof on the accused.

It shall be prohibited to seek to obtain testimony from the accused through the use of force, threats or any other illegal means.

ARTICLE 15. *Circumstances Subject to Proof in Criminal Cases*

In the conduct of the preliminary investigation and the examination of a criminal case in court the following shall be subject to proof:

1) the event of the crime (time, place, mode and other circumstances attending the commission of the crime);

2) the guilt of the accused in the commission of the crime;

3) circumstances, affecting the degree and nature of the responsibility of the accused;

4) the nature and extent of the damage caused by the crime.

ARTICLE 16. *Evidence*

Evidence in a criminal case shall be any facts on the strength of which the organs of inquiry, the investigator and the court may, in accordance with the procedure established by the law, determine the existence or non-existence of a socially dangerous act, the guilt of the person who has committed the act, and any other circumstances of importance for the correct decision of the case.

These facts shall be established: by the testimony of witnesses, the testimony of the victim, the testimony of the suspected person, the testimony of the accused, the findings of the expert, material evidence, the records of the investigative and judicial action and other documents.

ARTICLE 17. *Assessment of the Evidence*

The court, the procurator, the investigator and the person conducting the inquiry shall assess the evidence in accordance with their inner convictions based on a comprehensive, thorough and objective examination of all the circumstances of the case in their aggregate, being guided by the law and the socialist concept of justice.

No evidence shall have predetermined value for the court, the procurator, the investigator and the person conducting the inquiry.

ARTICLE 18. *Challenge to the Judge, the Procurator and Other Participants in the Trial*

The judge, the people's assessor, the procurator, the investigator, the person conducting the inquiry, the secretary of the judicial session, the expert or the interpreter may not participate in the proceedings in a criminal case and shall be subject to challenge where they are personally, directly or indirectly, concerned in the case.

ARTICLE 19. *Supervision of Judicial Activity by the Supreme Court of the USSR and the Supreme Courts of the Union and Autonomous Republics*

Supervision of the judicial activity of the judicial organs of the USSR and also of the judicial organs of the Union Republics shall be exercised by the Supreme Court of the USSR, within the limits established by the law.

The Supreme Courts of the Union Republics and the Supreme Courts of the Autonomous Republics shall exercise supervision of the judicial activity of the judicial organs of their respective Republics.

ARTICLE 20. *Procurator's Supervision in Criminal Proceedings*

Supervision over the strict observance of the laws of the USSR and the Union and Autonomous Republics in criminal proceedings shall be exercised by the Procurator-General of the USSR both directly and through the procurators subordinate to him.

It shall be the duty of the procurator, at every stage of the criminal proceedings, promptly to take all the measures provided for by the law to eliminate any breaches of the law, whosoever may be the source.

The procurator shall exercise his powers in the criminal proceedings independently of any organs or persons in office whatsoever, being subordinate only to the law and guided by the instructions of the Procurator-General of the USSR.

The decrees of the procurator rendered in accordance with the law shall be binding on all institutions, enterprises, organisations, officials and citizens.

THE PARTICIPANTS IN THE TRIAL, THEIR RIGHTS AND DUTIES

ARTICLE 21. *The Rights of the Accused*

The accused shall have the right: to know of what he is accused and to give explanations concerning the accusation brought against him; to present evidence; to enter petitions; to acquaint himself, upon completion of the preliminary investigation with all the material of the case; to have a defence counsel; to take part in the judicial examination in the court of first instance; to make challenges; and to file complaints over the actions and decisions of the investigator, the procurator and the court.

The accused shall have the right to the last word.

ARTICLE 22. *The Participation of the Defence Counsel in Criminal Proceedings*

The defence counsel shall be allowed to participate in the case from the moment the accused has been informed of the completion of the preliminary investigation and has been handed a record of the proceedings in the case to acquaint himself with them. On the procurator's order the defence counsel shall be allowed to participate in the case from the moment the indictment has been presented.

The participation of the defence counsel in the preliminary investigation and the court proceedings shall be mandatory in cases involving crimes by minors, by mute, deaf, blind and other persons who, by reason of their physical or mental deficiencies are unable to exercise their right to defence. In such cases the defence counsel shall be allowed to participate in the case from the moment the indictment has been presented.

In the cases of persons who do not know the language in

which proceedings are conducted or who are accused of committing crimes for which punishment may be assigned in the form of death penalty, the participation of the defence counsel shall be mandatory from the moment the accused is told that the preliminary inquiry is over and when the material of the case is presented to him for acquaintance.

The participation of the defence counsel in the case can also be mandatory in other instances determined by the legislation of the Union Republics.

Advocates, representatives of trade unions and other mass organisations and other persons accorded the right by the legislation of the Union Republics may act as defence counsels.

ARTICLE 23. *The Duties and Rights of the Defence Counsel*

It shall be the duty of the defence counsel to make use of all the ways and means of defence indicated in the law for the purpose of bringing to light the circumstances exonerating the accused or mitigating his responsibility, and to render to the accused all the necessary legal aid.

From the moment the defence counsel has been admitted to participation in the case, he shall have the right: to meet the accused; to acquaint himself with all the material of the case, and to make extracts of any necessary information therefrom; to present evidence; to enter petitions; to participate in the judicial examination; to make challenges; to file complaints against the actions and decisions of the investigator, the procurator and the court. Moreover, with the permission of the investigator, the defence counsel may attend the interrogation of the accused and the conduct of other acts of investigation performed upon the petition of the accused or his defence counsel.

The advocate shall not have the right to abandon the defence of the accused once he has accepted it.

ARTICLE 24. *The Victim*

A person on whom moral, physical or material injury has been inflicted shall be deemed to be the victim.

A citizen who has been declared to be the victim of a crime or his representative shall have the right: to give testimony on the case; to present evidence; to enter petitions; to acquaint himself with the material of the case from the moment of completion of the preliminary investigation; to participate in scrutinising the evidence in the judicial investigation; to make challenges; to file complaints against the actions of the person conducting the inquiry, the investigator, the procurator and the court; and also to file complaints against the judgement or rulings of the court and the decrees of the people's judge.

In the instances provided for by the legislation of the Union Republics, the victim shall have the right, personally or through his representative, to maintain the accusation in the judicial examination.

ARTICLE 25. *The Civil Plaintiff*

A person who has suffered material loss from a crime shall have the right, in the proceedings in a criminal case, to bring against the accused or persons bearing material responsibility for the acts of the accused, a civil suit which shall be examined by the court together with the criminal case.

The civil plaintiff or his representative shall have the right: to present evidence; to enter petitions; to participate in the judicial examination; to request the agency of inquiry, the investigator and the court to take measures to secure the claim entered by them; to maintain the civil suit; to acquaint themselves with the material of the case from the moment of completion of the preliminary investigation; to make challenges; to file complaints against the actions of the person conducting the inquiry, the investigator, the procurator and the court, and also to enter complaints against that part of the judgement or the rulings of the court which relates to the civil suit.

ARTICLE 26. *The Civil Defendant*

Parents, guardians, trustees and other persons, and also institutions, enterprises and organisations which, in virtue of the law, bear material responsibility for the damage caused by the criminal acts of the accused, may be brought to trial as civil defendants.

The civil defendant or his representative shall have the right: to make objections to the suit brought; to give explanations concerning the substance of the suit brought; to present evidence; to enter petitions; to acquaint themselves with the material of the case within the limits established by the law; to participate in the judicial examination; to make challenges; to file complaints against the acts of the person conducting the inquiry, the investigator, the procurator and the court, and also to file complaints against that part of the judgement and the rulings of the court which relates to the civil suit.

ARTICLE 27. *The Duty to Explain and Ensure the Rights of the Persons Participating in the Case*

It shall be the duty of the court, the procurator, the investigator and the person conducting the inquiry to explain to the persons participating in the case their rights and to ensure the possibility of their exercising these rights.

SECTION III

THE INQUIRY AND THE PRELIMINARY EXAMINATION

ARTICLE 28. *The Organs of Preliminary Investigation*

The preliminary investigation in criminal cases shall be conducted by investigators of the procurator's office and also by the procurators of agencies for the protection of law and order, in cases involving crimes whose list shall be established by the legislation of the USSR and the Union Republics, and by investigators of state security agencies, in cases involving crimes provided for by the following articles of the Law on Criminal Responsibility for Crimes Against the State: 1 (high treason), 2 (espionage), 3 (terroristic acts), 4 (terroristic acts against representatives of a foreign state), 5 (sabotage), 6 (wrecking), 7 (anti-Soviet agitation and propaganda), 9 (organising activity designed to commit especially dangerous crimes against the state and also participation in anti-Soviet organisations), 10 (especially dangerous anti-state crimes committed against another working people's state), 12 (divulgence of state secrets), 13 (loss of documents containing state secrets), 15 (smuggling), 16 (mass disorders), 20 (illegal exit abroad and illegal entry into the USSR), 21 (breach of the rules of international flights), 25 (breach of the rules of currency operations), 26 (the part relating to failure to report crimes against the state provided for in Articles 1-6 and 9), 27 (the part relating to concealment of state criminals provided for by Articles 1-6, 9, 15 and 25). Investigators of state security agencies shall also conduct preliminary investigation in criminal cases provided for by par. "a," "b" and "c" of Article 23 (divulgence of military secrets or loss of documents containing military secrets) of the Law on Criminal Responsibility for Military Crimes.

A preliminary inquiry shall be mandatory in cases involving crimes against the state or military crimes and also other crimes whose list shall be established by the legislation of the USSR and the Union Republics.

ARTICLE 29. *The Inquiry*

Agencies of the militia and other legally empowered institutions and organisations and also the commanders of military units or formations and the heads of military institutions shall be organs of inquiry.

The organs of inquiry shall have the duty of taking the necessary operational measures of search to detect the indicia of a crime and the persons who have committed it.

Where there are indicia of a crime for which a preliminary investigation is mandatory, the organ of inquiry shall initiate a criminal case and, being guided by the rules of the law on criminal procedure, shall carry out urgent acts of investigation to establish and fix the traces of the crime: inspection, search, seizure, the taking of evidence, the detention and the interrogation of the suspected persons, and the interrogation of the victims and the witnesses.

The agency of inquiry shall immediately inform the procurator of the discovery of the crime and the start of the inquiry.

In cases where the preliminary investigation is not mandatory the material of the inquiry shall be the ground for an examination of the case in court. In such instances, the agency of inquiry shall submit the material of the inquiry to the procurator, with whose approval the case shall be referred for examination in court.

ARTICLE 30. *The Powers of the Investigator*

In the conduct of the preliminary investigation, the investigator shall independently decide on the lines of the investigation and the conduct of acts of investigation, with the exception of instances where the law provides for obtaining the sanction of the procurator, and shall bear full responsibility for their being legally carried out in good time.

In the event of the investigator's disagreeing with the instructions of the procurator on the prosecution of a person as the accused, on the qualification of the crime and the scope of accusation, on the referral of the case to bring the accused to trial, or the termination of the case, the investigator shall have the right to take the case to the higher procurator, with a written statement of his objections. In such instance, the procurator shall either countermand the instructions of the lower procurator or assign another investigator to conduct the investigation in the case.

The investigator shall, in the cases he investigates, have the right to give assignments and instructions to the agencies of inquiry concerning the conduct of acts of search and investigation and to demand of the agencies of inquiry co-operation in conducting individual acts of investigation. Such assignments and instructions of the investigator shall be binding upon the agencies of inquiry.

The decrees of the investigator rendered in conformity with the law in the criminal cases conducted by him shall be binding on all institutions, enterprises, organisations, officials and citizens.

ARTICLE 31. *Supervision of the Observance of the Laws in the Conduct of the Inquiry and the Preliminary Investigation*

Supervision of the observance of the laws in the conduct of

the inquiry and the preliminary investigation shall be effected by the procurator in accordance with the Ordinance on the Supervisory Powers of the Procurator's Office in the USSR.

The procurator's instructions shall be issued in writing and shall be binding on the investigator and the person conducting the inquiry.

ARTICLE 32. *Detention of a Person Suspected of the Commission of a Crime*

The agency of inquiry or the investigator shall have the right to detain a person suspected of the commission of a crime for which punishment may be assigned in the form of deprivation of liberty only where there is one of the following grounds:

1) where such a person has been caught committing the crime or immediately after its commission;

2) where eye-witnesses, including the victims, have directly identified the person as having committed the crime;

3) where clear traces of the crime have been discovered on the suspected person or on his clothing, in his possession or in his dwelling.

Where there are other facts giving ground to suspect a person of the commission of a crime, he may be detained only in the event the person has attempted to escape or where he has no permanent place of residence or where the identity of the suspected person has not been established.

A person detained on suspicion of the commission of a crime shall have the right to file a complaint against the acts of the person conducting the inquiry, the investigator or the procurator, to give explanations and to enter petitions.

The agency of inquiry or the investigator shall make a record of every instance of detention of a person suspected of the commission of a crime, stating the grounds and motives for which he has been detained and notifying the procurator thereof within 24 hours. It shall be the duty of the procurator to issue his sanction to detain in custody or to release the detained person within 48 hours from the moment of receiving notification of his detention.

ARTICLE 33. *Application of Measures of Preventive Restriction*

Where there are sufficient grounds to assume that the accused, if left at liberty, may go into hiding from investigation or prevent the establishment of the truth in a criminal case or will engage in criminal activity, and also to ensure execution of the judgement, the person conducting the inquiry, the investigator, the procurator and the court shall have the right to apply one of the following measures of preventive restriction with respect to the accused: written undertaking not to leave the place, personal surety or the surety of social organisations, detention in custody and other measures of preventive restriction which may be determined by the legislation of the Union Republics.

In exceptional cases, a measure of preventive restriction may be applied with respect to a person suspected of the commission of a crime even before the accusation is presented to him. In such instance, the accusation must be presented not later than ten days from the moment the measure of preventive restriction is applied. Where the accusation has not been presented within this period, the measure of preventive restriction shall be revoked.

A person detained in custody before the accusation has been presented to him has the right: to file complaints against the acts of the person conducting the inquiry, the investigator or the procurator, to give explanations or to enter petitions.

ARTICLE 34. *Detention in Custody*

Detention in custody as a measure of preventive restriction shall be applied only in cases involving crimes for which the law provides punishment in the form of deprivation of liberty.

With respect to persons accused of the commission of the gravest crimes, whose list shall be established by the law, detention in custody may be applied for no other reason than the danger of the crime.

Detention in custody during the examination of a case may not continue for more than two months. This term may be prolonged only in view of the special complexity of the case by the procurator of the Autonomous Republic, Territory, Region, Autonomous Region or National Area, by the military procurator of a military district or a fleet, to three months, and by the procurator of the Union Republic, and the Chief Military Procurator, to six months from the first day of detention in custody. The term of detention in custody may be further prolonged only in exceptional instances by the Procurator-General of the USSR for an additional term of not more than three months.

ARTICLE 35. *The Conduct of Search and the Procedure Governing the Seizure of Correspondence*

A search may be carried out by decision of the agency of inquiry or the investigator and only with the sanction of the procurator.

In the instances not permitting of delay, a search may be carried out by the agency of inquiry or the investigator without the sanction of the procurator but with subsequent communication to the procurator of the effected search within 24 hours.

The impounding of correspondence and its seizure at postal and telegraph offices may be carried out only with the sanction of the procurator or by a decree of the court.

Search and seizure shall be carried out in the presence of persons specially invited to witness the legality of attendant procedural actions.

SECTION IV

ADJUDICATION OF CASES IN COURTS
OF FIRST INSTANCE

ARTICLE 36. *Committal for Trial*

Where there are sufficient grounds for examining a case in judicial session, the judge shall, without predetermining the question of guilt, issue a decree on the committal of the accused for trial.

In the cases of crimes committed by minors and crimes for which death penalty may be assigned as a measure of punishment and also in the instances where the judge disagrees with the conclusions of the bill of indictment, or where there is need to change the measure of preventive restriction that has been adopted with respect to the accused, the case shall be subject to examination in an administrative session of the court.

In its administrative session, the court shall render a ruling on the committal of the accused for trial or shall return the case for further examination or terminate the proceedings in the case and also decide on the question of the measure of preventive restriction. In the event the accused is committed for trial, the court, in administrative session, may expunge individual sections of the accusation from the bill of indictment or apply a criminal law on a less grave crime, without modifying the formulation of the accusation.

ARTICLE 37. *Direct, Oral and Uninterrupted Nature of the Judicial Examination*

It shall be the duty of the court of first instance, in examining the case, to make a direct scrutiny of the evidence in the case: to interrogate the accused, the victims and the witnesses, to hear the findings of the experts, to view the material evidence, and to have the records and other documents read out in public.

The judicial session in each case shall proceed without interruption, with the exception of the time allotted for rest. It shall not be permitted for the same judges to examine other cases before the completion of the hearing of the case already commenced.

ARTICLE 38. *The Equality of Rights of the Participants in the Judicial Examination*

The accuser, the prisoner, the defence counsel, the victim and also the civil plaintiff, the civil defendant and their representatives in the judicial examination shall enjoy equal rights in presenting evidence, participating in the scrutiny of the evidence and in filing petitions.

ARTICLE 39. *The Participation of the Prisoner in the Judicial Examination*

The examination of a case in a session of the court of first instance shall proceed with the participation of the prisoner, whose presence in court shall be mandatory. Examination of a case in the absence of the prisoner shall be allowed only in exceptional cases, as expressly provided for by the law.

ARTICLE 40. *Participation of the Procurator in the Judicial Examination*

The procurator shall maintain the state accusation before the court, take part in scrutinising the evidence, give conclusions on the questions arising during the judicial examination, and present to the court his considerations concerning the application of the criminal law and the measures of punishment with respect to the prisoner.

In maintaining the accusation, the procurator shall be guided by the requirements of the law and his inner conviction based on the examination of all the circumstances of the case.

Where, as a result of the judicial examination, the procurator becomes convinced that the facts of the judicial investigation have failed to confirm the accusation presented to the prisoner, it shall be his duty to withdraw the accusation and to state to the court his motives of doing so.

The procurator shall have the right to bring a civil suit or to maintain the civil suit brought by the victim where this is required for the protection of state or social interests or the rights of citizens.

ARTICLE 41. *Participation of Public Accusers or Defence Counsels in the Judicial Examination*

Representatives of mass organisations of working people may, by a ruling of the court, be allowed to take part in the judicial examination of criminal cases as public accusers or defence counsels.

ARTICLE 42. *The Limits of the Judicial Examination*

The examination of a case in court shall be conducted only with respect to the accused persons and only under the indictment under which they have been committed for trial.

Changes in the indictment may be made in court where this does not worsen the position of the prisoner and does not infringe his right to defence. Where changes in the indictment entail infringement of the prisoner's right to defence, the court shall refer the case for a fresh preliminary investigation.

ARTICLE 43. *The Judgement of the Court*

The judgement of the court must be legal and valid.

The court shall found its judgement only on the evidence which has been examined in the judicial session.

The court may render a judgement of conviction or of acquittal. The court's judgement of conviction or acquittal must be reasoned.

A judgement of conviction may not be founded on assumptions and shall be rendered only where, in the course of the judicial examination, the prisoner's guilt in committing the crime has been proved. The court shall render a judgement of conviction without assigning any punishment where, by the moment of the examination of the case in court, the act has lost its social danger or the person who has committed it has ceased to be socially dangerous.

A judgement of acquittal shall be rendered in instances where the event of the crime has not been established, where the prisoner's act did not contain the elements of a crime, and also where the prisoner's participation in the commission of the crime has not been proved.

The Supreme Court of the USSR and the military tribunals shall render judgement in the name of the Union of Soviet Socialist Republics, and the courts of the Union Republics, in the name of the Union Republic.

SECTION V

ADJUDICATION OF CASES IN THE CASSATION
AND SUPERVISION INSTANCES

ARTICLE 44. *The Right of Cassation Appeal and Protest
Against the Judgement*

The prisoner, his defence counsel and legal representative, and also the victim shall have the right to appeal against the judgement of the court by way of cassation.

It shall be the duty of the procurator to protest by way of cassation against every illegal or invalid judgement.

The civil plaintiff, the civil defendant and their representatives shall have the right to appeal against that part of the judgement which concerns the civil suit.

A person who has been acquitted by the court shall have the right to appeal by way of cassation against the reasoning and the grounds for the acquittal in the judgement of acquittal.

The time limits for filing and the procedure governing the examination of cassation appeals and protests, and also the procedure governing appeals and protests against the rulings and decrees of the court shall be determined by the legislation of the USSR and the Union Republics.

The judgements of the Supreme Court of the USSR and the Supreme Courts of the Union Republics shall not be subject to appeal or protest by way of cassation.

ARTICLE 45. *Examination of Cases on Cassation Appeal and Protest*

In examining a case by way of cassation, the court shall verify the legality and validity of the judgement on the strength of the material in the case and material additionally presented. The court shall not be bound by the arguments of the cassation appeal or protest and shall verify the case as a whole with respect to all the persons convicted, including those who have not filed appeals and those with respect to whom no cassation protest has been entered.

As a result of the examination of the case by way of cassation, the court shall take one of the following decisions: to leave the judgement unchanged, and the appeal or protest, unsatisfied; to vacate the judgement and refer the case for a fresh investigation or a fresh judicial examination; to vacate the judgement and terminate the case; to change the judgement.

In the examination of the case by way of cassation, the procurator shall give his conclusion concerning the legality and validity of the judgement.

The question on the convicted person's participation in the

session of the court examining the case by way of cassation shall be decided by this court. A convicted person who attends the judicial session shall be allowed to give explanations in all instances.

The defence counsel may participate in the session of the court of cassation instance.

ARTICLE 46. *Impermissibility in the Cassation Instance of Increasing the Convicted Person's Punishment or Applying to Him a Law on a Graver Crime*

In examining a case by way of cassation, the court may mitigate the punishment assigned by the court of first instance or apply a law on a less grave crime but shall not have the right to increase the punishment or apply a law on a graver crime.

The judgement may be vacated in connection with the need to apply a law on a graver crime or because of the mildness of the punishment only in instances where the procurator has brought a protest or the victim has filed an appeal on these grounds.

ARTICLE 47. *Vacation of a Judgement of Acquittal*

A judgement of acquittal may be vacated by way of cassation not otherwise than on the protest of the procurator or on the appeal of the victim or on the appeal of the person acquitted by the court.

ARTICLE 48. *Review by Way of Judicial Supervision of a Court Judgement, Ruling or Decree That Has Taken Legal Effect*

Review by judicial supervision of a court judgement, ruling or decree that has taken legal effect shall be allowed only on the protest of the procurator, the chairman of the court, and their deputies who are duly empowered by the legislation of the USSR and the Union Republics.

The Procurator-General of the USSR, the Chairman of the Supreme Court of the USSR, their deputies, the Chief Military Procurator and the Chairman of the Military Collegium of the

Supreme Court of the USSR, shall, in accordance with their competence, have the right to stay, by way of judicial supervision, the execution of a protested judgement, ruling or decree of any court of the USSR, of a Union and Autonomous Republic, pending decision of the case. The same right with respect to a protested judgement, ruling or decree of any court of a Union Republic and of its constituent Autonomous Republics shall be exercised by the procurator and the Chairman of the Supreme Court of the Union Republic.

Review by way of judicial supervision of a judgement of conviction, a ruling or a decree of the court because of the mildness of the punishment or the need to apply to the convicted person a law on a graver crime and also of a judgement of acquittal or ruling or decree of the court terminating the case, shall be allowed only in the course of one year from their taking legal effect.

As a result of the examination of the case by way of supervision, the court may: leave the protest unsatisfied; vacate the judgement and all the subsequent judicial rulings and decrees and terminate the proceedings in the case or refer it for a fresh investigation or a fresh judicial examination; vacate the cassation ruling and also all the subsequent judicial rulings and decrees where they have been rendered and refer the case for a fresh cassation examination; vacate the rulings and decrees rendered by way of supervision and leave in force, either with or without changes, the judgement of the court and the cassation ruling; make changes in the judgement, ruling or decree of the court.

In the examination of the case by way of judicial supervision, the court may mitigate the punishment assigned to the accused or apply a law on a less grave crime, but shall not have the right to increase the punishment or to apply a law on a graver crime.

The procurator shall take part in the examination of criminal cases by the presidiums of the respective courts to maintain the protest he has entered or to give his conclusions on a case being examined on the protest of the chairman of the court or his deputy.

The court examining a case by way of judicial supervision shall have the right, where necessary, to summon the convicted person to attend the judicial session.

ARTICLE 49. *Grounds for Vacating or Changing the Judgement by Way of Cassation or by Way of Judicial Supervision*

The grounds for vacating or changing the judgement in the examination of a case by way of cassation or by way of judicial supervision shall be these: one-sidedness or incompleteness of the preliminary inquiry or judicial investigation; discrepancy between the court's findings as set out in the judgement and the actual circumstances of the case; essential infringement of the law on criminal procedure; incorrect application of the criminal law; discrepancy between the punishment assigned by the court and the gravity of the crime or the character of the convicted person.

ARTICLE 50. *The Re-opening of Cases Because of Newly Discovered Circumstances*

A judgement that has taken legal effect may be vacated because of newly discovered circumstances.

Review of a judgement of acquittal shall be allowed only within the periods of limitation established by the law for bringing charges of criminal responsibility and not later than one year from the day the new circumstances have been discovered.

ARTICLE 51. *The Binding Nature of the Instructions of Superior Courts*

The instructions of the court examining the case by way of cassation or by way of judicial supervision shall be binding in the additional investigation and in a re-examination of the case by the court.

The court examining the case by way of cassation or by way of judicial supervision shall not have the right to establish or consider as proven facts which had not been established in the judgement or had been rejected by it, nor the right to predetermine the question of whether the accusation has or has not been proved, of whether this or that piece of evidence is authentic or unauthentic or of the superiority of some evidence over other evidence, of the application by the court of first instance of this or that criminal law and of the measure of punishment.

Equally, the court examining the case by way of judicial supervision, in vacating a cassation ruling, shall not have the right to predetermine the conclusions which may be made by the cassation instance in a re-examination of the case.

ARTICLE 52. *Examination of the Case by the Court of First Instance After the Vacation of the Original Judgement*

Following the vacation of the original judgement, the case shall be subject to examination in accordance with the general rules.

Increase of the punishment or application of a law on a graver crime in a fresh examination of the case by the court of first instance shall be allowed only where the original judgement has been vacated because of the mildness of the punishment or in view of the need to apply a law on a graver crime on the cassation protest of the procurator or the appeal of the victim or by way of judicial supervision and also where, in the fresh examination of the case after the vacation of the judgement, circumstances are established testifying to the commission by the accused of a graver crime.

SECTION VI

EXECUTION OF THE JUDGEMENT

ARTICLE 53. *Entry of the Judgement into Legal Effect and Its Execution*

The judgement shall take legal effect upon the expiry of the period for cassation appeal or protest where it has not been appealed or protested. In the event that a cassation appeal or cassation protest has been brought, the judgement, unless it is vacated, shall take legal effect upon the examination of the case by the higher court.

A judgement not subject to cassation appeal shall take legal effect from the moment of its pronouncement.

A judgement of conviction shall be executed upon taking legal effect.

A judgement of acquittal and a judgement releasing the prisoner from punishment shall be executed immediately upon the pronouncement of the judgement. Where the prisoner is in custody, the court shall release him from guard in the courtroom.

Supervision of the legality of the execution of judgement shall be exercised by the procurator.

ARTICLE 54. *The Binding Nature of Court Judgements, Rulings and Decrees*

The judgements, rulings and decrees of the court which have taken legal effect shall be binding on all government and non-government institutions, enterprises and organisations, officials and citizens, and shall be subject to execution throughout the territory of the USSR.

FUNDAMENTALS OF CRIMINAL LEGISLATION OF THE USSR AND THE UNION REPUBLICS*

SECTION I

GENERAL PROVISIONS

ARTICLE 1. *The Tasks of Soviet Criminal Legislation*

Criminal legislation of the USSR and the Union Republics shall have as its task the protection, against criminal infringements, of the Soviet social and state system, socialist property, the person and rights of citizens and the whole of the socialist legal order.

To carry out this task, criminal legislation of the USSR and the Union Republics shall determine which socially dangerous acts are criminal, and shall establish the punishments to be applied to persons who have committed crimes.

ARTICLE 2. *Criminal Legislation of the USSR and the Union Republics*

Criminal legislation of the USSR and the Union Republics shall consist of the present Fundamentals, which define the principles and lay down the general provisions of the criminal legislation of the USSR and the Union Republics; of all-Union laws which determine responsibility for individual crimes; and of the Criminal Codes of the Union Republics.

All-Union criminal laws shall determine the responsibility for crimes against the state and for military crimes and, whenever necessary, also for other crimes aimed against the interests of the USSR.

---

* The Law of the Union of Soviet Socialist Republics of December 25, 1958, on the approval of the Fundamentals of Criminal Legislation of the USSR and the Union Republics as decreed by the Supreme Soviet of the Union of Soviet Socialist Republics; *see* GAZETTE OF THE SUPREME SOVIET OF THE USSR No. 1, Items 6 and 15 (1959). For amendments of October 6, 1969 *see* GAZETTE OF THE SUPREME SOVIET OF THE USSR No. 41, Item 367 (1969).

ARTICLE 3. *The Basis of Criminal Responsibility*

Only a person guilty of committing a crime, that is, one who has, either intentionally or negligently, committed a socially dangerous act provided for by the criminal law, shall be subject to criminal responsibility and punishment.

Criminal punishment shall be applied only by a judgement of the court.

ARTICLE 4. *The Operation of the Criminal Laws of the USSR and the Union Republics with Respect to Acts Committed on the Territory of the USSR*

All persons who have committed crimes on the territory of the USSR shall be subject to responsibility under the criminal laws in force at the place of the crime.

The question of the criminal responsibility of diplomatic representatives of foreign states and of other citizens who, under the laws and international agreements in force, do not come within the jurisdiction of Soviet judicial institutions in criminal cases, shall, in the event of such persons committing a crime on the territory of the USSR, be decided by diplomatic means.

ARTICLE 5. *The Operation of the Criminal Laws of the USSR and the Union Republics with Respect to Acts Committed Outside the Boundaries of the USSR*

Citizens of the USSR who have committed crimes abroad shall be subject to criminal responsibility under the criminal laws in force in the Union Republic on whose territory criminal proceedings have been instituted against them or where they have been committed for trial.

Stateless persons staying in the USSR who have committed crimes outside the boundaries of the USSR shall incur responsibility on the same basis.

Where the said persons have undergone punishment abroad for the crimes they have committed, the court may make a corresponding mitigation of the punishment it has assigned, or completely relieve the guilty person from serving the punishment.

For crimes committed outside the boundaries of the USSR, aliens shall be subject to responsibility under the Soviet criminal laws in the instances provided for by international agreements.

ARTICLE 6. *The Operation of a Criminal Law in Time*

The criminality and punishability of an act shall be determined by the law in force at the time of the commission of the act.

A law eliminating the punishability of an act or mitigating a punishment shall have retroactive force, that is, it shall also apply to acts committed before its promulgation.

A law establishing the punishability of an act or increasing a punishment shall have no retroactive force.

SECTION II

CRIME

ARTICLE 7. *The Concept of Crime*

A socially dangerous act (commission or omission), provided for by the criminal law, which infringes the Soviet social or state system, the socialist economic system, socialist property, the person or the political, labour, property and other rights of citizens, or any other socially dangerous act provided for by the criminal law, which infringes the socialist legal order, shall be deemed to be a crime.

A commission or omission, even one formally containing the indicia of an act which is provided for by the criminal law but which, by reason of its insignificance, does not represent a social danger, shall not be deemed to be a crime.

ARTICLE 7¹. *The Concept of a Grave Crime*

Intentional acts enumerated in the second part of this Article, which are of heightened social danger, shall be deemed grave crimes.

These shall be: especially dangerous crimes against the state; banditry; actions disorganising the work of corrective labour institutions; smuggling; mass disorders; damage of communication lines and of the means of transport; the making and uttering of counterfeit money or securities; violation of the rules on currency operations and speculation in currency or securities under aggravating circumstances; stealing of state or social property on a large or an especially large scale; open stealing under aggravating circumstances; assault; intentional damage of state or social property or the personal property of citizens under aggravating circumstances; intentional homicide (with the exception of homicide involving excess of necessary defence or in a state of strong mental agitation); intentional grave bodily injury (with the exception of grave bodily injury involving excess of necessary defence or in a state of strong mental agitation); rape; speculation under aggravating circumstances; giving a bribe or intermediacy in bribery under aggravating circumstances; taking a bribe; bringing of a clearly innocent person to criminal responsibility under aggravating circumstances; passing of an obviously unjust sentence, ruling or interlocutory order which has entailed grave consequences; forcing to give evidence under aggravating circumstances; attempt on the life of a militiaman or a people's patrolman; malicious or especially malicious hooliganism; stealing of firearms, ammunition or explosives; stealing, making, acquiring or keeping narcotics for the purpose of sale, and also sale of such substances; disobedience under aggravating circumstances; resistance to the chief or forcing him to violate his official duties; violent action in respect of a chief; desertion; intentional destruction or damage of military property under aggravating circumstances; violation of the rules of military patrol duty under aggravating circumstances.

ARTICLE 8. *Intentional Commission of a Crime*

A crime shall be deemed committed intentionally where the person who has committed it was conscious of the socially dangerous nature of his act or omission, anticipated its socially dangerous consequences, and willed or consciously allowed such consequences to ensue.

ARTICLE 9. *Commission of a Crime by Negligence*

A crime shall be deemed committed by negligence where the

person who has committed it anticipated the possibility of socially dangerous consequences ensuing from his commission or omission, but thoughtlessly relied on their being prevented, or failed to anticipate the possibility of socially dangerous consequences ensuing, although he could and should have anticipated them.

ARTICLE 10. *The Responsibility of Minors*

Persons who, before the commission of a crime, have attained the age of sixteen years, shall be subject to criminal responsibility.

Persons who have committed crimes between the ages of fourteen and sixteen years shall be subject to criminal responsibility only for homicide, intentional infliction of bodily injury causing an impairment of health, rape, assault with intent to rob, theft, malicious hooliganism, intentional destruction or damage of state or social property, or the personal property of citizens, entailing grave consequences, and also for the intentional commission of actions which may cause a train wreck.

Where the court finds that a person who, while under the age of eighteen years, has committed a crime not representing a great social danger can be reformed without the application of criminal punishment, it may apply to such a person compulsory educational measures which are not criminal punishment.

The types of compulsory educational measures and the manner of their application shall be established by the legislation of the Union Republics.

SECTION III

PUNISHMENT

ARTICLE 20. *The Purposes of Punishment*

Punishment shall not only be chastisement for a committed crime but shall also have the aim of correcting and re-educating convicted persons in the spirit of an honest attitude to work, strict observance of the laws, and respect for the rules of socialist community life, and also of preventing the commission of new crimes by convicted and other persons.

Punishment shall not have the purpose of inflicting physical suffering or degrading human dignity.

ARTICLE 21. *Types of Punishment*

The following basic punishments may be applied to persons who have committed crimes:

1) deprivation of liberty;
2) exile;
3) restricted residence;
4) corrective labour without deprivation of liberty;
5) deprivation of the right to hold specified offices or engage in specified activity;
6) fine;
7) social censure.

Punishment in the form of assignment to a disciplinary battalion may also be applied to military personnel on active service.

Apart from these basic punishments, the following supplementary punishments may be applied to convicted persons:

confiscation of property;

deprivation of military or special rank.

Restricted residence, exile, deprivation of the right to hold specified offices or engage in specified activity and fine may be applied not only as basic but also as supplementary punishments.

Other types of punishment, apart from those indicated in the present Article, may be established by the legislation of the Union Republics, in conformity with the principles and general provisions of the present Fundamentals.

ARTICLE 22. *The Death Penalty—an Exceptional Measure of Punishment*

Application of the death penalty—by shooting—shall be allowed as an exceptional measure of punishment, pending its abolition for good, for crimes against the state, in the instances provided for by the Law of the USSR On Criminal Responsibility for Crimes Against the State, for intentional homicide under the aggravating circumstances indicated in the articles of the criminal laws of the USSR and the Union Republics which establish responsibility for intentional homicide, and, in the individual instances expressly provided for by the legislation of the USSR, also for certain other crimes of especial gravity.

Persons who, before the commission of a crime, have not attained the age of eighteen years, and women who are pregnant at the time of the commission of the crime or at the moment judgement is rendered may not be sentenced to death. The death penalty may not be applied to a woman who is pregnant by the moment judgement is executed.

ARTICLE 23. *Deprivation of Liberty*

Deprivation of liberty shall be prescribed for a term of not more than ten years; for crimes of especial gravity which have entailed especially grave consequences, and for especially dangerous recidivists, in the instances provided for by the legislation of the USSR and the Union Republics, for a term of not more than fifteen years.

In applying punishment to a person who had not attained the age of eighteen years before the commission of the crime, the term of deprivation of liberty may not exceed ten years.

The serving of punishment in the form of deprivation of liberty under a judgement of the court shall be assigned in corrective-labour colonies with ordinary, reinforced, strict and special regime or in prison, and also in educational-labour colonies with ordinary and reinforced regime.

The serving of punishment in corrective-labour colonies shall be assigned to men:

who are being sentenced for the first time to deprivation of liberty for crimes which are not grave or who are being sentenced for the first time to deprivation of liberty for grave crimes for a term of up to three years—in colonies with ordinary regime;

who are being sentenced for the first time to deprivation of liberty for grave crimes for a term of more than three years—in colonies with reinforced regime;

who are either being convicted of especially dangerous crimes against the state or who had earlier served punishment in the form of deprivation of liberty—in colonies with strict regime;

who have been deemed especially dangerous recidivists—in colonies with special regime.

The serving of punishment in corrective-labour colonies by women sentenced to deprivation of liberty shall be assigned: to women deemed especially dangerous recidivists, and also women sentenced for especially dangerous crimes against the state—in colonies with strict regime; and to other women sentenced to deprivation of liberty—in colonies with ordinary regime.

The serving of punishment in educational-labour colonies shall be assigned:

to male minors sentenced for the first time to deprivation of liberty for crimes which are not grave, or sentenced for the first time for grave crimes for a term of up to three years, and also to female minors—in colonies with ordinary regime;

to male minors who had earlier served punishment in the form of deprivation of liberty and also those being sentenced to deprivation of liberty for grave crimes for a term of more than three years—in colonies with reinforced regime.

Depending on the nature and degree of social danger of the crime committed, the character of the guilty person and other circumstances of the case, the court may, stating the motives for its decision, assign the serving of deprivation of liberty by convicted persons not deemed especially dangerous recidivists in corrective-labour colonies of any type, with the exception of colonies with special regime, and by convicted male minors—in educational-labour colonies with ordinary regime instead of colonies with reinforced regime.

Deprivation of liberty in the form of committal to prison for a full term of punishment or for a part thereof may be assigned to especially dangerous recidivists; persons who on attaining 18 years of age have committed especially dangerous crimes against the state; persons who on attaining 18 years of age have committed other grave crimes and who have been sentenced to deprivation of liberty for a term of more than five years.

Change of type of corrective-labour institution assigned to the convicted person shall be made by the court on the grounds and in the order established by the legislation of the USSR and the Union Republics.

ARTICLE 23¹. *Especially Dangerous Recidivist*

The following may, by a judgement of the court, be deemed especially dangerous recidivists:

1) a person previously sentenced to deprivation of liberty for an especially dangerous crime against the state; banditry; the making or uttering of counterfeit money or securities under aggravating circumstances; breach of the rules on currency operations under aggravating circumstances; stealing of state or social property on an especially large scale; assault with intent to seize state or social property or the personal property of citizens under aggravating circumstances; intentional homicide (with the exception of homicide involving excess of necessary defence or in a state of strong mental agitation, and also the killing by a mother of her newborn child); rape committed by a group of persons or resulting in especially grave consequences, or the rape of a minor; attempt on the life of a militiaman or a people's patrolman in connection with their official or social activity in maintaining public order; aircraft hijacking; who has thereafter again committed any one of the enumerated crimes for which he is being sentenced to deprivation of liberty for a term of not less than five years;

2) a person twice previously sentenced, in any sequence, to deprivation of liberty for an especially dangerous crime against the state; banditry; mass disorders; the making or uttering of counterfeit money or securities; breach of the rules on currency operations; stealing of state or social property under aggravating circumstances (with the exception of small-scale stealing); assault with intent to seize state or social property or the personal property of citizens; intentional homicide (with the exception of homicide involving excess of necessary defence or in a state of strong mental agitation, and also the killing by a mother of her newborn child); intentional grave bodily injury (with the exception of grave bodily injury involving excess of necessary defence or in a state of strong mental agitation); rape; theft,

open stealing or swindling committed under aggravating circumstances; speculation under aggravating circumstances; taking a bribe; attempt on the life of a militiaman or a people's patrolman in connection with their official or social activity in maintaining public order; especially malicious hooliganism; aircraft hijacking; stealing of firearms, ammunition or explosives under aggravating circumstances; making, acquiring or keeping narcotics for the purpose of sale, and also sale of such substances; who has thereafter again committed any one of the enumerated crimes for which he is being sentenced to deprivation of liberty for a term of more than three years;

3) a person three or more times previously sentenced, in any sequence, to deprivation of liberty for malicious hooliganism or for crimes enumerated in par. 2 of the first part of the present Article and who has thereafter again committed malicious hooliganism or any of the crimes enumerated in par. 2 of the first part of the present Article for which he is being convicted to deprivation of liberty;

4) a person serving punishment in the form of deprivation of liberty for any of the crimes enumerated in par. 2 and 3 of the first part of the present Article who has again committed an intentional crime for which he is being sentenced to deprivation of liberty for a term of not less than five years.

In considering the question of deeming a person an especially dangerous recidivist, the court shall take account of the character of the guilty person, the degree of the social danger of the crimes committed, their motives, the extent to which the criminal intent has been realized, the extent and nature of participation in the commission of the crimes, and other circumstances of the case. The decision of the court must be motivated in the judgement.

In deciding the question of deeming a person an especially dangerous recidivist no account shall be taken of the record of conviction for a crime committed by the person before the age of eighteen years, or of the record of conviction that was either written off or cancelled in the order provided for by law.

The deeming of a person an especially dangerous recidivist shall be cancelled when the record of his conviction is expunged.

Articles of the criminal laws of the USSR and the Union Republics prescribing responsibility for the commission of a crime by an especially dangerous recidivist shall be applied in the instances where the person was deemed an especially dangerous recidivist in the order provided for by law before the commission of the given crime.

ARTICLE 24. *Exile and Restricted Residence*

Exile shall consist in the removal of the convicted person from the place of his residence, with obligatory settlement in a specified locality.

Restricted residence shall consist in the removal of the convicted person from the place of his residence, with prohibition to live in specified localities.

Exile and restricted residence may be assigned, as a basic and as a supplementary punishment, for a term of not more than five years.

Exile and restricted residence may be applied, as a supplementary punishment, only in the instances expressly indicated in the law.

Exile and restricted residence shall not be applied to persons who, before the commission of a crime, have not attained the age of eighteen years. Exile shall also not be applied to pregnant women, and women with dependent children under the age of eight years.

The procedure, places and conditions for serving exile, as also the procedure and conditions for restricted residence, shall be established by the legislation of the USSR and the Union Republics.

ARTICLE 25. *Corrective Work Without Deprivation of Liberty*

Corrective work without deprivation of liberty shall be assigned for a term of up to one year and shall be served either at the convicted person's place of work or in any other place in the area of the convicted person's residence. Deductions for the benefit of the state shall be made from the earnings of the person sentenced to corrective work without deprivation of liberty in the amount fixed by the judgement of the court, but not in excess of twenty percent.

In the event a person who is sentenced to corrective work without deprivation of liberty maliciously evades the serving of punishment the court may replace the remaining part of the term of corrective work by a punishment in the form of deprivation of liberty for the same term.

The procedure for serving corrective work without deprivation of liberty shall be established by the legislation of the USSR and the Union Republics.

ARTICLE 26. *Deprivation of the Right to Hold Specified Offices or to Engage in Specified Activity*

Deprivation of the right to hold specified offices or to engage in a specified activity may be assigned by the court as a basic or a supplementary punishment for a term of up to five years.

This punishment may be assigned where, because of the nature of the crimes committed by the guilty person in his official capacity or when engaging in a specified activity, the court deems it impossible to allow him to retain his right to hold specified offices or to engage in a specified activity.

ARTICLE 27. *Fine*

Fine shall be a monetary exaction imposed by the court in the instances and within the limits established by the law.

The amount of fine shall be established depending on the gravity of the crime committed, taking account of the guilty person's material position.

There shall be no substitution of deprivation of liberty for fine or fine for deprivation of liberty.

ARTICLE 28. *Social Censure*

Social censure shall consist in a public expression by the court of censure of the guilty person, this being brought, where necessary, to the notice of the public through the press or by other means.

ARTICLE 29. *Assignment of Military Personnel Who Have Committed Crimes to a Disciplinary Battalion and Substitution of Detention in the Guardhouse for Corrective Work*

Assignment to a disciplinary battalion for a term of three months to two years may be applied to military personnel on active service in the instances provided for by the law, and also in instances where the court, taking into consideration the circumstances of the case and the character of the convicted person, finds it appropriate to apply, instead of deprivation of liberty for a term of up to two years, assignment to a disciplinary battalion for the same term.

For military personnel, detention in the guardhouse for a term of up to two months shall be substituted for corrective work without deprivation of liberty.

ARTICLE 30. *Confiscation of Property*

Confiscation of property shall consist in the compulsory seizure and transfer into the ownership of state, without compensation, of all or part of the property constituting the personal property of the convicted person.

Confiscation of property may be applied only in the cases provided for by the legislation of the USSR and in the cases of crimes of avarice where this is provided for by the legislation of the Union Republics as well.

The procedure governing application of confiscation of property, the list of articles not subject to confiscation which are necessary for the convicted person himself and for the persons dependent on him, and the conditions and manner of meeting any claims on the confiscated property under the convicted person's obligations shall be established by the legislation of the Union Republics.

ARTICLE 31. *Deprivation of Military and Other Ranks and Also of Orders, Medals and Honorary Titles*

Upon conviction for a grave crime, a person who has a military or special rank may be deprived of it by a judgement of the court.

In passing sentence upon a person convicted of a grave crime who has been awarded an order or medal or who has an honorary title conferred by the Presidium of the Supreme Soviet of the USSR, the Presidium of the Supreme Soviet of a Union or an Autonomous Republic, or who has a military or other rank conferred by the Presidium of the Supreme Soviet of the USSR or the Council of Ministers of the USSR, the court shall decide on the advisability of submitting a proposal to the body that has awarded the order or medal to, or conferred the rank upon, the convicted person, to deprive him of the order or medal, honorary title or military or other rank.

SECTION IV

ASSIGNMENT OF PUNISHMENT OR RELIEF FROM PUNISHMENT

ARTICLE 32. *General Principles for Assignment of Punishment*

The court shall assign punishment within the limits established by the articles of the law providing for responsibility for the committed crime in strict accordance with the provisions of the present Fundamentals and the Criminal Code of the Union Republic. In assigning punishment, the court, guided by the socialist concept of justice, shall take into consideration the nature and degree of social danger of the committed crime, the character of the guilty person, and the circumstances of the case mitigating or aggravating responsibility.

ARTICLE 33. *Circumstances Mitigating Responsibility*

In the assignment of punishment, the following shall be deemed to be circumstances mitigating responsibility:

1) prevention by the guilty person of any harmful consequences of the crime committed or voluntary compensation for loss inflicted or elimination of the damage caused;

2) commission of the crime in consequences of a concurrence of grave personal or family circumstances;

3) commission of the crime under the influence of threat or constraint or by reason of material or other dependence;

4) commission of the crime under the influence of strong mental agitation provoked by the unlawful acts of the victim;

5) commission of the crime in defence against a socially dangerous infringement, even where the limits of necessary defence have been exceeded;

6) commission of the crime by a minor;

7) commission of the crime by a woman who is pregnant;

8) sincere repentance or voluntary surrender to the authorities.

The Criminal Codes of the Union Republics may provide for other circumstances mitigating responsibility.

In assigning punishment, the court may also take into consideration mitigating circumstances not indicated in the law.

INDEX